MISCALCULATED RISKS

Attacked, Crippled, Paralyzed, Drowning,
Unconscious *and* Freezing *in* The Wild
(Just Not All at Once)

MICHAEL COOPER

LARREA PRESS

SISTERS, OREGON

LP

Published in the United States of America by Larrea Press, Sisters, Oregon.

First Edition – Published 2025

Library of Congress Control Number: 2025909830

Larrea Press trade paperback ISBN: 979-8-9989095-0-4

eBook ISBN: 979-8-9989095-1-1

https://michaelcooperadventurer.com/

Printed in the United States of America

Praise for *Miscalculated Risks*

"Harrowing and engaging."
—Jedediah S. Rogers,
author of *Roads in the Wilderness*

"An outdoors adventure memoir packed with hair-
raising encounters, gripping moments of life-or-death, and
confrontations with nature that will leave readers on the
edges of their seats. . . . Nothing short of remarkable."
—D. Donovan,
Senior Reviewer, *Midwest Book Review*

"A masterpiece. Not just a chronicle of close calls
but a glimpse into another age and insight into why we
humans challenge ourselves with hard tasks."
—Warren C. Easley,
author of *The Cal Claxton Mysteries*

"The wilderness comes alive on the page in this (literal)
trailblazer's memoir. . . . Cooper portrays his adventures in
immersive detail. His descriptions of his experiences in untouched
areas are lyrical. . . . Lovers of the outdoors and armchair
travelers alike will enjoy adventuring along with him."
—*Kirkus Reviews*

"Outstanding and inspiring. A beautiful story told remarkably well."
—Courtney Purcell,
author of *Zion National Park: Summit Routes*

In memory of my beloved mother Harriet Roslyn Cooper, to whom I owe everything

-1-

WRONG FORECAST

It was supposed to be a leisurely vacation, a meditative six-day solo back-pack on easy trails in Oregon's luxuriant Cascade Range. Nothing like the alpine mountaineering and hardcore cross-country desert expeditions I usually did. No, this trip was meant to coddle and relax me after four months of enduring grueling ninety-five-hour workweeks at my business, a commercial recording studio in Eugene. Add my work writing regularly for four music-industry magazines, and I was itching to jettison the viselike pressure, escape into quiet forests and deflate.

I should've stayed home.

The National Weather Service and two local TV broadcasts had prom-ised in convincing terms I'd be hiking under mostly sunny skies and in T-shirt-loving 65 to 70°F temperatures—goldilocks weather. The first inkling I had that their forecasts were dangerously off was when I woke up on the third morning of my trip to a snowstorm and two and a half inches of the white stuff already blanketing the ground outside my tent. My first reaction: oh shit.

But I thought about it some more, this time applying reason (not nec-essarily *sound* reason). Stray storms in early June usually don't last long. And camped as I was at a relatively low 4,400 feet altitude, the snow would likely mostly melt off by sometime the next day, especially if the weather also were to rebound to meet the sunshiny 70°F forecast. Man, I would be bummed if I cut my vacation short and fled in a panic all the way back to my truck only to arrive in shorts, staring at bare ground. No, I would stay here, camped alone in this snow-carpeted forest at the headwaters of French Pete Creek, and ride out the weather on a layover.

I was truly alone. I hadn't run into anyone else while hiking in this little-visited corner of the 281,190-acre Three Sisters Wilderness. A couple days earlier I had driven my small pickup truck fourteen miles from Cougar Reservoir and around 3,000 feet in elevation up narrow gravel Forest Service Road 1993, to the French Pete Creek trailhead at Pat Saddle. There were no vehicles parked in the trailhead's primitive parking area—just the way I liked it. Peace and quiet. But now, with this snowstorm, that solitude was making me feel a little edgy, a little more vulnerable. I managed, barely, to get a small campfire going in the storm shadow of a large Douglas fir tree, partly for warmth, partly for cheering me and partly out of boredom from just standing around waiting out a storm with nothing better to do. But with only cold and wet wood at my disposal, it was a constant struggle all day long to keep the fire from expiring.

That afternoon, the snow began falling more heavily, continuously now, larger flakes forming a polka-dotted sky and dressing the trees in worrisome winter armament. My tiny thermometer remained disconcertingly stuck in the low-30s Fahrenheit all afternoon, barely inching above freezing for just one hour. As dusk began to smother what little diffuse light was struggling to break through the ominously thick gray clouds bulging overhead, the snowfall accelerated and I realized I'd made a terrible mistake staying in the wilderness. This was no ordinary late-spring storm. Nor was it looking like a one-day event.

I finally gave up on keeping my sputtering campfire going, as the negligible warmth it provided, surrounded by refrigerating snow banks in the cold of twilight, wasn't worth the effort. It was 8 P.M., time to turn in. My clothes felt damp on my cold skin as I crawled into my small three-season nylon tent for the comfort of my dry sleeping bag. Except it wasn't dry. Melting snow had apparently leaked water all day through tiny stitch holes along the floor seams of the tent while I obliviously manned my pitiful fire. The entire floor inside the tent—and my synthetic sleeping bag and down vest I'd left on it all day—was soaking wet. My shelter was fucked, my sleeping bag's insulation severely compromised, my vest a soggy dishrag, all my few remaining clothes—which I was wearing—cold and damp, and I was facing a long, wintry night completely alone in the middle of nowhere.

I mopped up the floor of my tent as best I could with my soggy vest and crawled into my wet sleeping bag wearing my rain pants and jacket, the jacket's hood cinched tightly around my head. Doing isometric exercises inside the bag to keep myself from shivering, I was soon barely holding off panic in the dark, worried I'd become helplessly hypothermic by morning and too enervated to hike back to my truck. I eventually warmed up and calmed down enough to doze off.

I slept fitfully for around five hours as the wind alternately shushed and howled through the night, occasionally dumping a fresh load of snow onto my tent from heavily laden, swaying overhead branches. Awakening in the dark at 4:30 A.M., I unzipped my tent's door to nervously shine my flashlight on the scene outside.

My heart sank. An additional ten inches of snow had fallen overnight, and it was still snowing hard. Now there was no question I was in a fight for my life. Waiting out a storm this strong inside a dry three-season tent would be nutty enough. Doing it in a wet tent, sitting on a water-soaked floor in wet clothing, would be slow suicide. I bolted out of the tent, did some jumping jacks to warm up, fired up my camp stove and considered my options over a cup of hot soup: hiking the most direct route back to my truck would require gaining 800 feet in altitude and traversing the east side of Olallie Mountain, doubtlessly post-holing—for 6.7 miles—through potentially much deeper snow. (Mountains attract weather.) If I made it to my small pickup, parked at virtually the same altitude as my current camp, it would unquestionably be snowbound. I had brought no traction tires or devices, and the narrow gravel road down from Pat Saddle traversed steep mountainsides in places. I would be stuck at the trailhead, for God only knew how many days.

The only other option—the only sensible one—was to turn my back on my truck and hike away from it. That way was the quickest down to lower altitude and a road likely free of snow. But that road, Forest Service

Road 19—commonly known as Aufderheide Drive—was far from the perfect escape. A two-lane asphalt byway winding sixty miles through the Willamette National Forest, there were no towns or homes along its entire route save for at each far end. It was a very secluded road through wild country, and I would be exiting the Three Sisters Wilderness near the road's far-flung midpoint.

My hope was there would be someone parked at a trailhead there, at rustic Frissell Crossing Campground. I would backpack the more than six miles from my snowbound position to the campground and, if there was no one there, then walk another twenty-four miles along Aufderheide Drive to the nearest two-lane highway, Hwy 126. But to get to any of that, I would first have to cross the unbridged French Pete Creek, along whose north bank I was camped. This became my desperate plan.

Now I needed to keep a level head and maintain laser focus. I could not afford to be swayed by fear, doubt or hesitancy. Still, my mind rebelled as I broke down my sopping wet tent—my only shelter from the storm, however terribly compromised. But I knew I couldn't stay. As heavy snow continued to fall and dress my hooded head and shoulders, I hurriedly packed my backpack and threw it on.

Scouting up and down French Pete Creek in the snow, I found a decayed, mossy log suspended across its banks to my escape. Covered on top with snow, it looked very slippery. Falling from it into the creek, relatively shallow though it was here, would be really bad, at the very least drenching my legs and feet that were already numb with cold. A badly sprained ankle would be a death sentence. Rather than risk walking the log, I scooted across it on my butt.

Gaining the creek's opposite bank, I slogged through the snow back up to the trail. I took the trail 400 feet higher in altitude over the next hour before it crested, thankfully without encountering significantly deeper snow. Continuing a mile farther south, the trail took me to the rim of a very steep mountain slope soaring above the South Fork McKenzie River, churning out of sight 2,000 vertical feet below at Frissell Crossing. I headed down. As I dropped 800 vertical feet down the mountainside, the falling snow gradually turned into freezing rain and I eventually celebrated my return to hiking on bare earth. An hour later I lurched into Frissell Crossing Campground, drenched through and through and shivering.

The rainy campground was completely deserted, dashing my hopes for quick rescue. I went to the trailhead register and wrote a note in pencil on a blank permit: "Michael Cooper stranded, 35 miles from truck. Heavy snow in high country forced alternate emergency escape route. Making my way on foot north on 19 to 126. Need help! 10:30 am, 6/6/95 (Tuesday)."

I stuck the note inside the trailhead's register, hoping a ranger would check the wooden box for permits later that day or the next, although I knew that in this weather that was a long shot. It was 40°F and still raining steadily as I abandoned the campground and stepped out onto Aufderheide Drive, turning north. I was fighting off fears I wouldn't make it to Hwy 126, still twenty-four miles away, as I was becoming increasingly hypothermic. I needed my luck to change, and fast.

I was walking along the road just ten minutes later when I heard the unmistakable hum of a motor vehicle. A National Forest Service truck, with two men inside, suddenly came around a bend in the road behind me. The driver rolled down his window as the vehicle approached and came to a stop.

"What are you doing out here in this weather?" he asked, staring wide-eyed.

I told him through chattering teeth of my bail out of the mountains.

"Really nasty storm up there," he acknowledged. "I'm glad you got out okay. Ten minutes later you would've missed us, as we're headed back to the station. We're not supposed to pick anyone up, but we can't exactly leave you out here in these conditions."

They drove me to Blue River, a rural town on Highway 126. From there I hitchhiked to Eugene and home. During the ride to Eugene, I thought about other times I almost died in the wild. Half-drowned in rapids on a remote Oregon river (during another winter snowstorm). The rockfall while climbing Mount Shasta. The bear in Northern California. All very close calls. But they paled in comparison to what happened to me, seventeen years ago, in the jungle in Mexico.

-2-

YELAPA

In late February 1978, as I prepared with Richard Watson and Rick Stuman to leave for Mexico, our globetrotting friends who had previously toured the country warned, fairly or not, that Mexican drivers were the most dangerous in the world. They had apparently never seen Richard drive. As we hurtled down Mexico's narrow and bumpy Federal Highway 15, my hands were locked on the dashboard like Vise-Grips.

This was before I first stepped foot in wilderness, but my life was already pretty wild. Having graduated valedictorian from high school in 1971 with a full college scholarship toward a double major in math and science, I quickly decided I didn't want to pursue academia after all—too much work and responsibility. I spent the next several years playing guitar in rock, pop and disco bands in Long Island nightclubs, fueled by a steady diet of drugs and junk food. My health suffered for it.

Realizing I needed to clean up my act, I swapped LSD and Twinkies for Transcendental Meditation and vegan raw foodism,[1] on an obsessive mis-

---

1   Raw foodism is a cleansing dietary regimen in which virtually only uncooked fruits, vegetables, nuts, seeds, and sprouted legumes are consumed. While today you can find scads of videos on YouTube extolling the health benefits of raw foodism, in New York culture in the mid-1970s it was virtually unheard of. Even in progressive Southern California during that period, raw foodism was practiced mainly by an extremely small subset of the countercultural community.

sion to detoxify. Performing for boozers in smoky nightclubs had become a drag, my prison. Reading a book extolling the back-to-the-land movement embraced by rural communes in California, I felt inspired and hatched my escape. I quit my band, sold all my worldly possessions, and hitched a nonstop ride across the US to the outskirts of sunny Los Angeles.

I spent the next couple years thumbing my way around San Diego County, enjoying my newfound freedom, bouncing from one hippie commune to another, never content to stay very long in one place. It was at those communes that I first met Rick and Richard, fellow vagabond raw foodists in their mid-twenties who were, like me, steadfastly dedicated to bodily purification and unemployment. We knew few other people who were such extreme outliers as us. Our mutual recognition quickly bonded us and reinforced our magical thinking. We cooked up a lunatic plan to abscond civilization and live in a tropical jungle, subsisting only on native fruits—the quixotic fruitarian lifestyle glorified by Viktoras Kulvinskas in his fringe manual *Survival into the 21st Century*. Our escapist pipe dream drove us to Mexico. Had I foreseen the horrifying struggle for survival that lay in store for me there, I would have never left the US.

Now we were careening in Richard's red VW Bug across a sun-scorched desert plain, headed for the tropics a thousand miles south of the border. Just before nightfall we made Guaymas, a fishing town of 70,000 on the razor edge of the Sonoran Desert and the Gulf of California. On the opposite side of the large C-shaped bay that harbors the small city, we rolled out our sleeping bags on the parched gravel shoreline and fell asleep to the sound of the wind gently coaxing tumbleweed into a scratchy chorus with waves lapping the stony beach.

The next couple days driving south, through Ciudad Obregón and Culiacan, brought us to tiny rustic Elota, where we parked the car to stretch our legs. Walking through a quiet neighborhood of spartan single-story adobe houses spaced apart on dirt streets, we came upon a group of skinny, threadbare children playing inside a dirt yard crudely fenced four feet high; thick, roughly cut branches had been secured upright along the lot's periphery by burying their butt ends in the ground, possibly to pen in chickens unseen. The lot, though not particularly large, was significantly more generous in dimension than the house it loosely hosted. A lone tree, fifteen feet high, shaded the dusty yard, its branches laden with golden *naranjitas*, or small oranges.

The children immediately noticed us. With our long hair, light complexions and foreign clothing, we must've looked to them like we were from another planet. Rick and Richard each sported a thick blond beard and mustache and hair falling to mid-back, Rick's mane tied in a ponytail and Richard's in twin French braids. My curly hair, falling in Shirley Temple-like ringlets below my shoulders, framed a cropped goatee and light mustache. Oblivious to the country's deeply conservative cultural norms at the time, Rick and Richard both wore white T-shirts and shorts; the leg-baring pants were regarded as effeminate to Mexicans and therefore highly inappropriate for men to wear. I had on a flimsy long-sleeved shirt and pants that both looked like pajamas.

The children were unfazed by our appearance. They energetically waved to us, and we waved back.

"¡*Esperen*!" one of the boys, maybe nine years old, shouted to us, urging us to wait. He turned, ran to the citrus tree and disappeared into its dense foliage. Moments later, he reappeared at the top of the tree, waving jubilantly before throwing around a dozen oranges to us. That this indigent child would share what very little he had so willingly—make that joyfully—with peculiar aliens like us touched me to my core.[2]

We would experience the wholehearted generosity of the rural Mexican people again the following day. We made it almost to Guadalajara, a sprawling city of 1.4 million people at the time, as dusk began to fall. Four miles north of the city, we came upon a late-thirty-something man and woman

2   My observations of widespread poverty in rural Mexico in 1978 are echoed by Viviane Brachet Márquez's paper "*Poverty and Social Programs in Mexico 1970-1980: The Legacy of a Decade*," which distills five years of research sponsored by the Mexican government. Márquez concludes in her work that "Even using the lowest possible standard . . . [i]n 1978, 70 percent of the total [Mexican] population was . . . undernourished," and those failing to meet the minimum nutritional requirement included "practically the entire rural population." She further observes that, during the mid-1970s, "in some regions, the crisis acquired famine proportions, and emergency food distribution programs were required."

standing outside their meager adobe home on a small dirt lot. Rolling down the car's passenger-side window, I asked the couple in Spanish—I was quite fluent in the language, having studied it for four years in school—where we could find a place to camp for the night. Without hesitation, they invited us to stay on their modest property.

The couple's eight children—six boys and two girls ranging in age from two to fifteen—already filled their tiny single-story house to the gills, so they offered a ramshackle wood shed, where they long ago kept pigs, as our sleeping quarters. Flecks of matter on the shed's dirt floor looked suspiciously like dried manure. We would've preferred to sleep outside the shed but didn't want to offend by declining the shelter offered.

The next morning our hosts offered us breakfast, a gesture I found deeply moving considering how manifestly poor they were. Not once did they or their children look askance at our strange clothes and long hair. They all treated us like family.

As we loaded our sleeping bags and tarps into the car, I suggested Richard take a photo of me with the family, subject to their approval. The parents and kids all became extremely excited; it quickly became clear to me they did not own a camera and had no family photos. I promised I would mail them the photo after I returned to the States—a promise kept—which elicited outbursts of joy.

"Wait, please!" the woman entreated me in Spanish, as she and her husband and kids quickly ran into the house. A few minutes later, they all came tumbling out to gather side-by-side in front of the sole tree on their tiny lot, motioning cheerfully for me to join them. They had all put on their best clothing, indistinguishable from what they'd had on previously save for its lesser state of disrepair. The mother held a triangular piece of broken mirror, measuring no more than three inches to the side, up to her face as she fastidiously combed her long, straight hair, jet-black save for a few premature gray streaks. Passing the shard among them, each person in the family primped until they were satisfied they were looking their very best. Seeing that some of the kids had no shoes, I deliberately removed my sandals for the photo. As we assembled shoulder to shoulder for the camera, the way everyone was beaming you would've thought we were at a wedding or *quinceañera*. With the exception of the distracted youngest of the children, we all waved at Richard as he snapped the photo. I jotted down the family's address, we all said our genial goodbyes, and then off to Guadalajara my buds and I went.

Our sole reason for visiting Guadalajara was to indulge in its sprawling fruit markets, legendary among our world-traveling peers who'd come before us. Any hardcore touristic foodie would understand our fixation. Tales of exotic fruits trucked in from all over Mexico and Central America promised black sapote with flesh of chocolaty custard, and creamy cherimoya with combination strawberry- and pineapple-flavored juice, rivaling any confection or nectar.

We rented a small room at the modest El Hotel Americana and then walked to a massive indoor fruit market we'd heard about. As we approached the market's substantial open-sided building, four elementary school-age boys ran gleefully over to us, fascinated by our long hair and odd clothes, shouting "¡*Hippies* americanos! ¡*Hippies* americanos!" Their two mothers walked over and briefly engaged us in friendly conversation before whisking their chattering children away.

Inside the market, down many narrow aisles, woven baskets brimming over with thousands of ripe tropical fruits rested on sturdy wooden tables. Red mamey, cream guava, knobby cherimoya, orange papaya, "chocolate" and green sapotes, peculiar bananas and bizarre fruits whose names were totally unfamiliar to me lay spread out before us like in a fruitarian Mecca, posed underneath scores of piñatas and colorful woven handbags hanging from the building's rafters. While Rick and Richard reverently pored over the tables, cherry-picking the choicest fruits, I walked over to a carrot-juice bar strategically planted at the center of the market's layout. It was just one of many natural refreshment stands in the Guadalajara fruit markets where you could order a tall glass of raw carrot juice, made on the spot.

I requested a glass of the sweet juice, a temporary exception to the ascetic fruitarian diet my friends and I had adopted since leaving the States. As the young woman manning the bar ran each carrot in turn through an industrial-size centrifugal juicer, she flashed a stiffly protracted smile at me, her white teeth bared inches wide. She was evidently trying to look seductive but looked instead like she was cooperating in getting her teeth cleaned. She playfully bobbed her head. Then came the pitch.

"How big is your ranch in America?" she gushed, eagerly awaiting my response.

"Oh, not that big," I replied, not wanting to burst her bubble. I should've just leveled with her. Her eyes were focused like lasers on me as I quickly drank the sweet juice, eager to retreat. I couldn't help but reflect on how back in the States I was just an impoverished and directionless hippie, while simply being an American in Guadalajara meant instant promotion to desired trophy husband. If you were an American, you must be rich. I humbly realized that in some very real ways, by local standards, just the benefits of my US citizenship made me so.

The young men in Guadalajara gave my friends and me a completely different reception. Longhair hippies were antithetical—and apparently considered a threat—to their conservative, macho culture. Our appearance immediately provoked aggressive responses. On three occasions, loud jeers and insults were hurled our way by a scrum of late teens, attempting to goad us into a street fight. The groups were always larger than ours, and you could tell these guys had been in fights before. The most common provocations were explicit remarks about their having sex with our wives—which, even given the seriousness of the situation, was mildly humorous to us because we neither had wives nor believed in the institution of marriage. Sometimes our mothers were substituted for wives in their taunts. We didn't take the bait. Luckily, we managed to walk away.

The next morning, Guadalajara offered its better side again. We splurged at another gargantuan fruit market and took our sweet pickings outside into an adjoining paved courtyard to enjoy. Devouring our juicy bounty at tables shaded by large white and yellow umbrellas, we were unintentionally serenaded by a five-piece mariachi band, directing their talents toward a neighboring table of more respectable patrons. If this was so great, we thought, the fruit markets of the much larger Mexico City must be amazing. We left Guadalajara that day around noon, eastbound for Mexico's namesake metropolis.

We made an early camp that afternoon—the last day in February—in the hills an hour east of Zacapu, in a broad clearing surrounded by pine and oak trees. Driving east the next day to the broad, open highland valley surrounding Toluca, we caught our first views of the massive volcano Nevado de Toluca, towering on the horizon around twenty miles to the south.

The dominant—virtually exclusive— feature of its namesake national park, the long-extinct Nevado de Toluca pierces the sky to a dizzying elevation of 15,354 feet, making it Mexico's fourth tallest peak. We'd heard there were two lakes, Lago Del Sol (Lake of the Sun) and Laguna de la Luna (Lake of the Moon), inside the snow-capped mountain's huge crater, and hazarded a guess the dry month of March might be a good time to visit if the road up to there was open. As the afternoon sun dipped below the horizon, we drove a long and winding road up the volcano's forested flanks—passing no other vehicles en route—hoping to make camp inside the caldera for the night. (Never mind the crater's floor was at over 13,000 feet altitude, it was still late winter and we were dressed in thin cotton summer clothes.) The air grew thinner and cooler as we slowly ascended in the dusky light, fir trees gradually giving way to lanky pines, until our way forward was blocked by a large isolated snow bank about half a mile below timberline.

This was not the cozy clime of Guadalajara; it felt like it was going to freeze overnight. We had not brought a tent. Rick and Richard rolled out their sleeping bags on the flattest patch of earth they could find while I elected to shelter in the back of the car. I quickly fell into a deep sleep, but didn't snooze for long. I awoke suddenly in the middle of the night, gasping for breath in the oxygen-starved air—my first-ever experience with altitude sickness. Recovering enough to doze off again, my sleep was punctuated by startled awakenings to anxious, involuntary hyperventilation.

The next morning, we left the car and laboriously hiked up the now dirt road. The green pine forest quickly gave way to open alpine meadows of bleached-blond grasses and gray boulders, Toluca Valley sprawling into the distance thousands of feet below us. It was windy and cold, an unsuitable 40°F for our thin cotton clothes, but brilliantly sunny. The rarefied air made each step higher exhausting, but the protracted effort warmed us until we reached the crater rim's blown-out east side, where the dirt road descended gently from a rocky lip into the caldera—and a scene of ineffable beauty.

Lago Del Sol lay stretched out before us on the floor of the mile-wide crater, the surface of its blue-gray water dappled with thousands of tiny ripples by the raw, bone-chilling wind. On the far side and flanks of the magnificent lake, the desolate and nearly perpendicular walls of the volcano towered well over 1,000 feet by conservative estimation above us, its stern gray couloirs still dressed in the virgin-white snows of winter. An ancient stone building—its walls roughly assembled in times long past from large blocks of unpolished rock, the roof either never finished or long gone—stood broken on the lake's barren rocky shore as if to say, Nothing remains for long.

We were totally alone. I was cold, but strangely ecstatic. This was my first up-close taste of wild alpine scenery, and its austere majesty and emptiness, dead quiet save for the forlorn wind, was a vacuum into which my busy list-checking mind dissolved into soft focus. In that moment, I felt a kind of peace I had never before known. I wanted more. Years later, my alpine yearnings would impel me to climb the ten highest peaks in the Oregon Cascades mountain range—several multiple times—and backpack by map and compass for a week above timberline in the most remote area of California's Sierra Nevada range.

But it was too cold now for us to linger for long. Besides, the mythic fruit markets of Mexico City awaited us. By early afternoon that same day, we had driven off the mountain and into the capital city—and wished we hadn't. The city's air was so polluted by diesel exhaust—so thick, we couldn't see farther than a few city blocks—we felt poisoned after just ten minutes of breathing outdoors. We quickly booked a small hotel room, inside which we sheltered until we made our escape out of the city early the next morning.

We drove the next three days west to the Pacific Coast, arriving at the palm-tree-lined cobblestone streets of Puerto Vallarta, where we booked a small room at the rustic Posada de Roger Hotel. We spent the remainder of the day eating ripe mangoes, sipping with a straw the refreshing liquid from green immature coconuts—"Jellies" in the local lingo—and leisurely strolling along the city's placid oceanfront.

We'd had fun touristing Mexico the past couple weeks, and seductive Puerto Vallarta could have tenably served as our last port of call if sightseeing was all we'd had in mind. But idyllic a journey's end though Puerto Vallarta may have been to the well-heeled tourists there, to us it was only a gateway to our ultimate destination: the fruitarian tropical paradise Yelapa.

Since leaving the States, Yelapa had always been forefront in our minds. All our preceding travels in Mexico had merely been requisite mileage or temporary detours, saving the best for last. While Puerto Vallarta and Yelapa both nestle in the same immense bay—Bahía de Banderas, or Bay of Banderas—less than twenty miles apart as the bird flies, they might as well have been on different planets. Puerto Vallarta ("P.V.," in tourist patois) was a booming vacationland, a city of roughly 50,000 people that boasted an international airport, luxury hotels and world-renowned beach resorts. Yelapa was a tiny, virtually roadless seaside fishing village with no dock, sewer system, water infrastructure, phones or electricity (the latter save for that produced by gasoline-powered generators the lucky few could afford). Puerto Vallarta's population was perennially bloated with tourists arriving from all over Mexico and abroad. Yelapa's cohort was comprised of Indigenous people and a smattering of adventurous expats, cut off from the rest of the world by the sea on one side and roadless jungle mountains on the other. The only means of travel between the two places was by small motorboat—one round trip scheduled every twenty-four hours—ferrying the more adventurous tourists to Yelapa's pristine golden beach to soak in a slice of timeless rural Mexico before returning the same day to their pampered accommodations in Puerto Vallarta.

Yelapa itself was also of two worlds. The quaint bayside village that lay at the mouth of the El Tuito River counted perhaps two-dozen brick buildings, unaffectedly roofed with sheet metal or half-round tiles. Modest though it was, the village supported a tiny one-room post office, which sent and received mail to and from P.V. once every Tuesday, and a primary school for the local children.[3] Upriver, Indigenous people lived in widely spaced *palapas*[4]—small primitive homes with thatched-palm roofs, dirt floors and external walls of slatted native wood, the walls only half-height on one or two sides for ventilation against the sweltering tropical heat and humidity of summer.

Rick, Richard and I had previously heard from our vagabond friends in SoCal that you could rent a palapa for a full month for less than a cheap meal would cost back in the States, and live off the locally grown mangoes, papayas, pineapples and coconuts for even less. Our plan was to rent a palapa for Yelapa's remaining dry season, leaving before drenching summer monsoons arrived and turned the valley into an intolerable wet sauna; the wider area receives on average around four feet of rain for the four months of June through September,[5] when daily high temperatures typically reach into the stifling 90s Fahrenheit. In contrast, from February through April only a paltry third of an inch of rain damps the dense broadleaf forest and high temperatures average a pleasant 85ºF.

Perfect early-spring weather, a pristine environment, fresh tropical fruits, inexpensive living and a self-directed immersion into Indigenous culture—all these Yelapa promised us. The only detractor—little more than abstract in our minds—was that Yelapa, and its local state of Jalisco, was

---

3   Yelapa in the 2020s bears little resemblance to the area in 1978 when I lived there, the tourism industry having long since thoroughly co-opted the quaint village. Modern buildings now carve in tiers Yelapa's sloped west shoreline. Scores of mani-cured thatched-palm buildings and lounge chairs choke its fine-grained sand beach. Dozens of yachts and other small boats dot its once paradisiacal bay. Google "Yelapa," and you'll quickly find an assortment of luxuriously appointed hotels, condos and vacation homes to rent there, some offering free WiFi, and over a dozen restaurants at which to enjoy pizza, fish, ribs, chicken and beer. According to an article written by Samantha Schoech for *www.sunset.com* in 2008, movie stars now flock to the village for yoga retreats.

4   According to the website *www.palapainyelapa.com*, Yelapa is a legal land grant or reservation—protected in the Mexican Constitution of 1910—for the Indigenous people who have always lived there, a status shared by only a few other areas in Mexico. No one owns the land, but Indigenous residents (only) may claim it by cultivating or otherwise using it.

5   World Meteorological Organization, *Climatological Information for Puerto Vallarta*

also home to several of the most lethal species of scorpions in Mexico.[6] Some people we'd met in P.V. warned that March and April were very active months for scorpions, and they counseled we should carry with us the antivenin; derived from horse serum, the antivenin was the only prescribed antidote for scorpion sting. Others warned that 50 percent of people who took the antivenin ended up having a severe reaction to the medicine itself, sending them to hospital or their death; they advised carrying instead dexamethasone, an injectable corticosteroid, to treat scorpion sting. Opposed to the idea of polluting our bodies with an unnatural pharmaceutical, and thoroughly confident in the ability of our stash of carried medicinal herbs to treat any condition, we declined procuring either medicine. Besides, we chose not to live in fear, but to fully embrace paradise; positive thinking and pure intentions would protect us. The night before leaving P.V. for Yelapa, we reluctantly killed a large tan scorpion that had trespassed our hotel room.

The following morning, March 7, we boarded a small motorboat, helmed by an operator and accompanied by several well-heeled tourists, for the ride south across the Bay of Banderas to Yelapa. The hour-long ride hugged the jungly shoreline, taking us past fantastic partially submerged rock arches just offshore. Where the coastline began curving toward the west, the intriguing rock buildings at Mismaloya Beach, where American director John Huston famously filmed his 1964 movie *The Night of the Iguana*, captivated our attention. Farther west, the jungle-choked headlands became steeper, spawning dramatic breaks in the surf crashing on their wild, rocky shore—and warning of no practical return by land.

---

6   In January 2009, *Guadalajara Reporter* (Guadalajara's largest English-language newspaper) would report that Jalisco had more victims of scorpion stings—53,319 the prior year—than in any other state in Mexico. Most stings occurred in Jalisco's coastal areas, of which Yelapa was one. The newspaper urged rapid medical attention as the most important action to survive a sting and discouraged self-medication. Scientists at the Universidad Autonoma de Guadalajara similarly cited coastal Jalisco and Nayarit—the state whose southern border lies just a few miles north of Puerto Vallarta—as the epicenter of stings. According to the College of Agriculture & Life Sciences at the University of Arizona, up to 800 people died of scorpion stings in Mexico during the 1980s, a peak period.

The tempestuous surf would not batter the shoreline along its entire western excursion. Rounding a verdant headland, a large horseshoe-shaped cove came slowly into view. Breathtakingly beautiful, its crystal-clear turquoise water calmly lapped a wide golden beach rimmed with tiny palapas and coconut palm trees. The El Tuito River—barely wider than a short jump across in this, its thirsty season—languidly emptied into the cove on the west side of the beach. Through the tall coconut palms and leafy mango trees to the right of the river's mouth, several modest single-story brick buildings, all painted vivid white, peeked brightly at us on a short rise. It was Yelapa. My heart was singing.

There was no pier at which to dock. A weathered, dark-skinned man paddled out to meet us in a dugout canoe. As he ferried us to shore, my gaze fixed on the exotic river valley before us. Gracefully carving land to the southeast, its broad and sandy channel slowly narrowed upstream into a tangle of wild primeval country into the distance. It was picture-postcard perfect.

The bow of the canoe beached, and we stepped barefoot into the cool shallow water and walked the few remaining paces to shore. Our motorboat companions headed straight for the beachside palapas, in front of which the locals were setting up lounge chairs and alcoholic refreshments.

Rick, Richard and I made a beeline for the village. Interspersed among the modest brick buildings were a few traditional palapas, much larger than the touristic centerpieces on the beach. We stopped at a tiny brick-built cantina. The cantina had an outdoor area with small tables, set up under a sheet-metal roof held up by unfinished tree trunks, likely cut from mango trees. A hand-painted sign hung from the eave, announcing the availability of "Pedro y Eva's cold beer."

Speaking in Spanish, I asked a man in the cantina where we might be able to rent a palapa, preferably one away from the village. He passed us off to Epifanio, a wiry, matter-of-fact man roughly forty years old who offered to rent us a palapa a mile and a half up-river from the bay—precisely our fantasy!

Like kids entering Disneyland, we excitedly followed Epifanio on a dirt trail along the north side of the El Tuito River, walking in and out of the shade of exotic trees I could not name. To break the ice along the way, I attempted—mostly unsuccessfully—to engage in small talk with our guarded prospective landlord. As we walked up the valley, the sandy riverbed gradually narrowed and became progressively strewn with large boulders. We passed several palapas along the way, each home to an Indigenous family and all increasingly set apart from the closest neighbor's hut the farther from the village we went. A forty-minute walk along the foot-worn path brought us to Epifanio's rental, a palapa more perfect than my imagination could render, in a clearing at the top of a gentle slope and roughly a hundred yards from the river.

Measuring roughly thirteen by eighteen feet, the long front side of the palapa faced south into the hot mid-day sun but the A-frame roof, densely thatched with dried palm fronds layered over a framework of cross-braced poles, deeply overhung the half-height front wall to fully shade the palapa's interior. The walls, full-height elsewhere save for in the palapa's southwest corner, were constructed of vertically oriented, contiguous slats of unfinished local native wood, cross-braced at two heights with long poles and rope across their rough spans.

Walking through the front (and only) door, the palapa instantly felt to me like home. A rudimentary ladder led up to a small loft around seven feet off the dirt floor. A small cot, constructed of natural local materials, was secured underneath the raised platform to the palapa's rear wall. The only other furniture was a short stool and a chair, both made of native woods and so tiny they were more suited to a child than an adult. There was no plumbing, no electrical service, no toilet; the nearby El Tuito, waist-deep but languid, would be our running water for drinking and bathing. We would live like the native people, the closest whom lived a couple hundred yards away, far out of earshot and blocked by tropical trees from our line of sight. It was perfect.

We paid Epifanio rent for two months. He casually counted the pesos, thanked us and then abruptly went on his way. And just like that, we were alone, pinching ourselves in disbelief inside our newfound home, the silence broken only by the sound of yakking parrots and the drone and chirps of unfamiliar insects outside.

With my blessing, Rick and Richard respectively claimed the loft and cot for sleeping; I was happy to sleep on a large blanket I laid out on the dirt floor. We leisurely unpacked our few belongings and settled comfortably into our utopian digs. The day was still young, so we walked back toward the village to buy some local melons, pineapple and papaya. On the outskirts of the pueblo, we met Pablo, an affable and stocky man roughly twenty years of age, who would quickly become our go-to person for mangoes and coconuts.

A highlight of my days in Yelapa would be watching Pablo quickly and effortlessly scurry barefoot up palm trees to harvest green Jelly coconuts for us. Taking our haul home, we'd place a Jelly on top of an old tree stump outside our palapa and hack off its top with a machete Epifanio had loaned us, so we could drink the sweet water and scoop out the creamy flesh inside the shell. *Manzanas*, the spongy and sweet sprouts inside mature coconuts, were another favorite delicacy.

Life was slow and mellow, and refreshingly foreign. We bathed in the river a minute walk down-slope from our palapa, assured in our privacy. Our neighbors' cattle freely roamed the lower valley, and a few would occasionally graze the sparse clumps of grass outside our palapa. The favorite part of my day was having long conversations with our Indigenous neighbors, learning about their lives and views of the outside world; I loved that none had any desire to leave the valley to partake in the comforts of civilization, and any question to that predisposition was met with quizzical looks. Everyone was unhurried and interested in talking with me, often for more than an hour at a time, and they appreciated that I was quite fluent in their language; I often received compliments on how well I spoke Spanish, my excellent pronunciation and inflection.

I hungrily asked questions about the local customs, and sometimes got surprising answers. For one, all my neighbors let their many chickens roam freely inside their palapas for practical reason: chickens eat scorpions. A frequently consumed vegetable, eaten raw, was the endemic prickly pear cactus; my Indigenous neighbors would prepare the flat, broad green leaves by first knocking off the needle-sharp spines with a stick. One of the local kids would sometimes stop by our palapa carrying a large green iguana nearly half his size, trying to interest us in buying the creature; when we politely declined, he would explain in earnest that it was a female pregnant with many delicious eggs.

We spent our days meditating, doing yoga, reading the few books we had packed for our trip and occasionally walking a well-worn dirt trail upriver deeper into the jungle. We'd been advised by the locals to watch out for wild pigs in the untamed forest, as the ill-tempered animals were known to sometimes attack people, but we brushed off the warnings; the hike through the jungle was too beautiful for such concerns to dissuade us. A few miles upriver from our palapa, the canyon narrowed dramatically. There the river lazily coursed through a jumble of car-size boulders before plunging twenty-five feet off a bare-rock cliff face into a large placid pool below. We always had the pool to ourselves and would spend hot afternoons skinny-dipping its refreshingly cool water.

But if our first three weeks in Yelapa seemed idyllic, they did not pass without recurring red flags. We'd fairly often find scorpions inside our palapa, typically hiding under a blanket or misplaced shirt during the day and scurrying about at night; the ones that were yellow to tan in color and two to three inches long were reportedly the most serious threat to life. The locals emphasized how important it was to wear shoes after dark, when the nocturnal arachnids would come out of hiding. We had only open sandals, and dismissed wearing even those when at home or walking the three miles round-trip to the village and back. Reflexology tomes we'd studied back in the States advocated walking barefoot to stimulate energy meridians and promote good health;[7] to wear shoes was to rob yourself of that benefit and disconnect your electromagnetic body from the Earth's grand circuit. Besides, the soles of our feet were so leathery from a couple years walking barefoot in the States that only stepping on a sharp rock or stick would hurt. So, barefoot we went, almost everywhere, day and night.

---

7   According to reflexology, acupuncture and traditional Chinese medicine, chi is a life force that flows along a set of twelve pathways, or meridians, in the body. Stimulating those pathways by applying pressure or inserting acupuncture needles at specific points, including on the soles of the feet, is believed to enhance the flow of that energy and maintain good health.

But nighttime was not the only dangerous time to go barefoot in Yelapa. During a visit to Pablo's small coconut grove one afternoon, the usually relaxed fruit-monger suddenly became very alarmed. Swiftly yanking a hatchet from a holster on his hip, he threw it narrowly past me, killing with incredible precision a colorful snake slithering just two feet from where I was standing.

"It was beautiful!" I complained loudly, in Spanish. "Why'd you kill it?"

"Red and yellow," Pablo replied darkly, pointing at the snake's adjacent colored bands—wide red flanked on both sides by narrow yellow. "Very venomous."

It was a coral snake—a snake whose venom is second only to the black mamba's in toxicity.[8] Like Yelapa's yellow-tan scorpions' venom, the coral snake's neurotoxin paralyzes the victim's breathing muscles, causing respiratory failure within hours of the bite. I'd never had any of that explained to me, but Pablo's unusually anxious demeanor was all it took to make a big impression. Just not long enough to discourage me from continuing to walk barefoot.

For all my naiveté and insouciance, I must've had an angel watching over me during my first three weeks in Yelapa. But it was only a matter of time before my luck ran out.

I was already sleepy by nine o'clock in the evening on March 29, 1978. The sun was down, the moon had not yet risen, and the night was ink-black. The tropical air felt warm and thick, bereft of the slightest breeze and broken only by the mesmerizing music of hundreds of unseen frogs and insects singing down by the river.

I had to pee. Grabbing my small flashlight, I went outside into the darkness and headed for some bushes behind our palapa to relieve myself. Walking barefoot through a large pile of discarded coconut shells that we'd accumulated, I suddenly felt a powerful electrical jolt—immediately scorching hot and dealing a hammer-like blow—in my left big toe that

---

8   Tara A. Spears, "Silent Danger – Nayarit Coral Snake," *Sol Mexico News,* 2015

brought me nearly to my knees and produced a strangely jagged shriek from my lips I didn't know I could make. Whipping the weak beam of light from my flashlight toward the ground below me, I spied a scorpion, light in color and about three inches long, scurrying off into the rubble.

Hobbling pitifully back to the palapa, I breathlessly cried out to Rick and Richard, "I've been . . . stung . . . scorpion . . . bad . . . bad."

"Are you sure?" Richard asked anxiously, as I collapsed, moaning loudly, onto my blanket on the palapa's dirt floor, clutching my foot with both hands and rocking uncontrollably in excruciating pain. The searing burn and to-the-bone throbbing was unlike any hurt I'd ever experienced before—exponentially worse by degree.

"What should we do?" the usually taciturn Rick asked, his voice calm but his wide eyes betraying alarm.

The more pertinent question, I realized, was what *could* we do. We had no antivenin. No dexamethasone either. Yelapa had no medical facility, no pharmacy. The next boat to P.V. would not arrive at Yelapa's shore until around noon the next day. There was no path to P.V. through the jungle on foot and, even if there were, I'd be dead before I got there; staying completely still was key to limiting the venom's circulation to my vital organs. Then there was the issue of body weight: the odds of surviving the most lethal scorpions' sting drops progressively the less the victim weighs. On my calorie-starved fruitarian diet, my six-foot frame had been whittled down to roughly 115 pounds, dangerously close to the dire line of certainty.

The full weight of my predicament, and its likely mortal consequence, now came crashing down on me and I began to panic, then quickly realized I had to calm down to prevent my racing heart from pumping the neurotoxin more efficiently throughout my body. There was no question as to the advance the venom was already making. I could precisely trace the horrible river of fire creeping up my great saphenous vein: over the top of my left ankle, up the inside of my lower leg and then up the inside of my thigh, almost reaching my groin—all in just two minutes time.

I had Richard pack wet clay on the site of the sting, hoping it would draw out the poison. Then I made a critical error: hoping to impede the flow of blood to the site of the sting and circulation of the venom back to critical organs, I propped my injured foot up on a stool, elevating it about two feet above my heart; I would later learn medical protocol directs the scorpion's victim to position the site of the sting *below* the level of the heart. I was stupidly aiding in my demise.

Over the next hour, frequent self-medication with herbs—folk remedies I'd used successfully for far less serious maladies—proved utterly ineffectual: large doses of blood-purifying myrrh and sarsaparilla extracts, and nerve-calming valerian root and skull cap, had no discernible effect on the venom's inexorable course, my agonizing pain or my growing terror. I began to develop a fever. I slowly started losing feeling in all my limbs—at first below my knees to my feet, and then below my elbows to my hands—but they were oddly only becoming numb to external stimuli. As my nervous system began to revolt, I began feeling at once fiery hot and freezing cold pins and needles over my entire body. The slightest movement instantly produced the sensation of being superficially electrocuted—a stream of current flowing through the skin on the moving body part, accompanied sometimes by stronger jolts. Then came the "ants."

"Get them off me!" I cried, brushing my face frantically.

"What?" Rick and Richard asked in virtual unison, confused by my erratic behavior and alarmed by my panicky tone.

"Ants!" I cried. "They're all over me!"

My buddies quickly inspected me, reporting back, "There's nothing, Michael. No ants, nothing."

And yet I could feel them, at first dozens, then hundreds scurrying all over my body at an increasing tempo—not just on my arms, legs, buttocks, genitals, chest, back, neck, throat, face and scalp, but also eventually inside my ear canals, under my eyelids and across my eyeballs. My nerves were going haywire. My muscles began to twitch and jerk uncontrollably, then convulse violently and lock up in terrible spasms, alternately bending me at the waist and arching my back. Through it all, I knew there would be no help coming. I just had to ride it out. But the worst was yet to come.

Around 11 P.M., two hours into my ordeal, came the onset of "spines," an apt term the locals who had survived scorpion stings used to succinctly describe the illusory sensation of cactus spines stuck in the inside throat, scraping and tearing with each swallow. A thermometer check confirmed I was now running a fever of 105°F, adding to my multiple miseries of fiery pins and needles, ants (also the locals' term) and unrelenting convulsions. I was drenched in sweat and shivering uncontrollably, my teeth chattering like a typewriter. I had two sleeping bags and a blanket placed over me, yet I felt as if I was lying naked in snow.

Despite my agony, I managed to pee into a jar. My urine was brown, as dark as milk chocolate. The room, and my companions, began looking increasingly distorted and surreal in the light cast by our gas lantern, as my visual perception began to corrupt and devolve into full-blown double vision and, eventually, hallucinations. My eyes, as if the maddening "ants" crawling over them were not enough to endure, felt like they were on fire.

I could now no longer move my legs and was beginning to have difficulty swallowing, as a slowly creeping paralysis began to eclipse the growing numbness throughout my body. By midnight my throat was clamped shut. I was unable to swallow and, worse, having trouble breathing, as copious mucus rapidly filled my nose, throat and lungs. This is how the scorpion kills, filling the lungs with fluid, paralyzing the breathing muscles and suffocating the victim in their own slimy scum. I was soon completely paralyzed from the throat down and would have choked to death if it were not for faithful Richard, who once or twice every minute lifted my head and turned it sideways so I could spit out the thick fluids into a cup. (Rick, at first relatively unconcerned, had fallen asleep in the loft.) When the advancing paralysis eventually robbed me of the ability to spit, Richard rolled me onto my side so the fluid would drain on its own out of my mouth. Every time he turned me, and despite the numbness now afflicting most of my body, I felt I was being simultaneously electrocuted and fried in oil, every nerve on fire. I would drain the slimy fluid, and then Richard would roll me onto my back—burning electrocution again—so he could elevate my foot once more.

By 2 A.M., five hours into my unremitting ordeal, I was having trouble moving my eyelids and my lower jaw. The few times I spoke, I sounded like I had advanced muscular dystrophy: I was having increasing difficulty voicing consonants. My voice continually cracked as it lost control midsentence, and it was strangely higher in pitch than usual. My stomach muscles were now in unrelenting iron knots, seemingly anchoring my dia-phragm down so it would not rise to grant me any but the shallowest of breaths—so shallow, I imagined a candle's flame close to my lips would not have flickered. The sensation, or lack thereof, was that my diaphragm was not moving at all and I was *thinking* my breath, willing air to seep in and leak out, in order to survive. That was my laser focus for the next three hours. Breathe and stay alive. Breathe and stay alive. Breathe and stay alive. All while the swarming ants, intense muscle spasms, spines in my throat, shivering, and electrical pins and needles continued unmercifully, compet-ing for my critical attention. Death was beginning to seem appealing.

It would have been so easy to just let go, ending my suffering. Just one split-second lapse of resolve and concentration, breaking the slender thread, would be all it would take. But then there would be no more sun. No birds or ocean or mountains. No music. I would never make love to another woman. My mother would be crushed.

Now there was no question that finding scorpion antivenin was my only shot at survival, if it wasn't already too late. Richard, exhausted and lying down for a moment to rest, had succumbed to sleep along with Rick, leaving me on my right side to drain. Risking a fatal choking fit, I weakly croaked one word: "help." It may not have even been intelligible, but it was enough to awaken Rick, who hurried to my side. Taking one look at me, he instantly understood the gravity and tenuousness of the situation and woke up Richard.

"Antidote," I rasped, my voice skidding into a pitiful falsetto on the last syllable.

"You want the scorpion antivenin?" Rick asked, peering intently into my eyes.

I slowly blinked twice. He understood. Turning to Richard, he didn't mince words for my sake.

"He's going to die if we don't get it, and quick. I remember there's an expat nurse living in the village. She might have some." Grabbing a flash-light, he urged Richard, "Keep him alive until I get back." Then he hurried out the door and was gone. It was 5:20 am. I had been stung over eight hours earlier.

. . .

Sunrise was still an hour and a half away when Rick Stuman left our palapa for the village, a mile and a half down-river. Twenty minutes into his walk, the batteries in his flashlight died. Fortunately, the gibbous moon had risen shortly after midnight, and it was now high in the sky and softly kindling the pathway into the village in silver light.

Upon entering the sleeping village, Rick went directly to where he remembered the expat nurse lived and pounded on her front door. An old man came to the door and delivered bad news: the nurse had moved out of Yelapa, and he had no antivenin. Determined not to return to our palapa empty-handed, Rick hurried to a small clothing store on the beach and woke up the owner, another expat who could speak English. Rick quickly explained to the man the scorpion's size and color, when I was stung and my symptoms.

"It's a very bad scorpion sting," the man assessed gravely. "Your friend is lucky to have made it through the night."

He had both dexamethasone and the antihistamine Benadryl. He hurriedly gave Rick instructions on how to inject the medicines, using a medical syringe he also supplied. Rick thanked him graciously and turned to leave. The man gave Rick some parting advice.

"You should prepare yourself emotionally," he said solemnly. "Don't be surprised if your friend is dead by the time you get back."

It was 7 A.M. when Rick returned to our palapa. Richard was kneeling over me, praying. I was completely paralyzed from my lower jaw down to my feet, had lost all sense of touch throughout my body and was feeling very far away. I felt like a spent battery draining its very last reserve, everything decelerating and quieting prior to total and final collapse. I was barely aware of Rick's return, focusing resolutely as I was on each shallow breath and on a simple mantra I'd been repeating silently to myself for the past couple hours: "Live."

"I've got medicine, Michael," Rick encouraged. "Hang on, brother." The sound of his voice had a strange, short echo to it and was difficult to understand.

Rick quickly drew the dexamethasone from its vial into the syringe, pointed the needle skyward, and then carefully pumped out a tiny spurt of liquid. He turned and looked intently at me. Even despite my double vision, I could tell his countenance was very serious.

"I've never done this before," he said. "If I haven't got all the air out of the needle, you could have a heart attack or stroke. You have to promise you won't hold me responsible." As if I'd be around to blame him.

"Do . . . it," I wheezed.

He pulled my pants down and, with Richard's help, rolled me onto my right side. I was surprised, and extremely relieved, I didn't feel the burning electrocution anymore. I felt nothing. In fact, I only knew I had been turned because my view of the palapa had changed: now I was looking at a wall and not the ceiling. Rick gave me two shots of medicine in my buttocks, first the dexamethasone and then the Benadryl. I didn't feel either injection; I only knew when they'd been given because I smelled a medicinal odor, not in the air but in my circulating blood. My view of the palapa rotated again, back to the ceiling, with Rick and Richard kneeling over me. Their faces, and the ceiling, slowly drew closer.

"I'm . . . floating," I croaked.

"We're lifting you up, Michael," I thought I heard Rick say.

Past their heads I slowly rose, facing the ceiling of the palapa. The ceiling grew ever closer, until it was just a few inches from my face. My field of vision slowly rotated to my right, 180 degrees, and I was startled to see Rick and Richard ten or more feet below me, kneeling over my seemingly lifeless body.

My vision quickly faded to pitch black, all sound quieted to profound silence. No smell, no taste, no touch. All my physical struggles quickly faded like a volume knob being whipped down. No more struggling to breathe; I no longer had any lungs, any body at all. Every shred of stimulus, of external awareness, dimmed to zero. For how long, I don't know; there was no time. The only thing I was aware of was a deceleration more fathomless than the deepest sleep, and an equally profound and growing sense of peace.

The blackness had no dimension, no depth, at first. Then, almost imperceptibly, the center point of my perspective began to grow lighter; it was a diffuse white circle, very small at first but slowly growing in diameter. I began to feel strangely euphoric. As the circle of light grew larger, it began to take on depth, like a tunnel, and with its gradual transformation my euphoria grew by leaps and bounds. The edges of the light were fuzzy, the very center indistinct, yet I had the distinct impression I was being slowly drawn into it as the edges extended progressively outward toward the limits of my peripheral "vision." The nearer I got to the threshold of the tunnel's opening, the more ecstatic I became—a high exponentially greater than any I'd ever experienced with recreational drug use or meditation. The accompanying sense of peace became fused with understanding: There was no right or wrong. All actions between people, and animals—murderers and saints, predators and prey—were like weather on the land, a give and take between opposing forces in a dancing equilibrium maintaining balance throughout the universe. And observing it all, with a profound love and empathy and understanding of all the suffering and struggle and striving and nobility and depravity, was an omniscient immaterial being whose invisible presence I was slowly, astonishingly, becoming aware of, as I drew closer to the center of the light. Who, or what, was this supremely divine and knowing presence? It had no discernible form or gender, but yet a palpable nature and consciousness, as real as any person or thing in my life. All I knew was it loved me—and all else—unconditionally, and with overwhelming effect: I fervently and single-mindedly yearned to be closer to it.

To do that, I had to go into the tunnel of light. I wanted nothing more. These overpowering feelings of euphoria, peace, understanding and love, I never wanted to surrender them. I wanted to bathe in them, forever. But as I was drawn to the very threshold of the tunnel, its perimeter at the very limits of my peripheral vision—whatever that sense actually was—I realized there would be no going back if I went any farther. In that instant, for the first time, I realized I was dying. Not just in the process, but on the razor's edge of the binary state. As ecstatic as I felt, I didn't want to go there. Not yet. It was too soon.

In that moment I made a promise to God—the energy, the being or whatever it was in my mortal arrogance I presumed to label then with a name, as if I could possibly hope to ever understand it. It was my plea to strike a bargain: let me live, and I promise to dedicate my life to helping others, to be a force for good. To my later deep regret and shame, I would never fully live up to that fervent promise. But I completely believed my commitment at the time. I began to pull away from the tunnel of light, or it began to pull away from me, I don't know which.

And then there was nothing, and I lost myself.

Where does a soul go when it is not conscious? How long is it gone, when time ceases to exist? And how does it manage to return to consciousness, when any effort to do so implies its unbroken continuation in the first place?

However it worked for me, I vividly remember it began with the realization "I am." All was pitch black, and there was no sound. I had no body, and I could not sense the physical dimension, touch, smell or taste.

The question that logically came next was "Who am I?" I drew a blank at first, but then remembered my name, eliciting a flood of memories: I'm from Long Island. Hold on, I now live in Southern California. I traveled to Mexico and was stung by a scorpion. Was I still in Mexico? I had to find my body. I struggled to find my eyes in the black empty void, so I could open them. But I was unable to.

I slowly began to sense dimension and my place in it, and then direction: up and down. Suddenly, I heard the most beautiful celestial sound, faintly at first and then growing louder: a sequence of exquisitely lovely musical notes, playing in some foreign microtonal scale and cascading in an echoing trail as it circled overhead. It was a noisy flock of parrots, flying in a circle over our palapa. Now I could feel my eyes. I opened them, and saw with double vision the bespectacled Rick kneeling over me with a mile-wide smile on his face, no more than twelve inches from my nose.

"Welcome back, Michael!" he said, emphasizing the first syllable of each word as if he were announcing over loudspeaker a grand public event. It was a bright and warm and sunny morning. Richard rushed over to my side.

"You were out for two or three hours," Rick chattered. "It was amazing. You were delirious, just babbling nonsense. I've never witnessed anything like it. How are you feeling?"

The truth was I felt terrific. No pain; in fact, no feeling at all in my body. My only symptoms were seeing double vision, hearing all sounds echo, and I was still completely paralyzed except for being able to blink my eyes. I was overjoyed to be alive. On the heels of the completely black and empty void, it felt like I had been reborn. The sweetly singing parrots seemed to celebrate all would now be well.

If only it were true. As my nervous system began to rebound and come alive again, I would go through all of the horrific effects of the scorpion's neurotoxic venom once more, this time in reverse. But at least I had my two dear friends to help me through it. The blanket I had laid on all night had become very rumpled and dirty, so they moved me off it to clean and smooth it, to make me more comfortable (not that I could yet feel anything). Lifting the blanket off the ground to shake it out, they discovered a dead yellow scorpion underneath. It had apparently crawled under the blanket and gotten squashed to death when Richard rolled me over during the night.

Around 10 A.M., one of the locals, the mysterious Santiago, stopped by our palapa to visit. He had heard from someone in the village that one of the hippies living in Epifanio's rental had suffered a serious scorpion sting, and he was stopping by to offer his help. Santiago was regarded by the Indigenous locals a *brujo*, or sorcerer, although I never heard him claim this of himself. A lean, dark and handsome man of few words, he was fifty-four years old but looked no older than thirty. People in the valley held him in very high esteem, in part because he had survived fifty-eight scorpion stings. (Santiago would later tell me he typically survived by applying a tight tourniquet above the wound, if on a finger or toe, and either cutting open the wound and milking out the venom or burning it badly in a fire to inactivate the toxins—the latter method being the only recourse for a sting to a more central body part.)

Entering our palapa, Santiago wasted no words after "*hola*." He immediately asked me about my symptoms and how many hours ago I'd been stung. I told him I could now swallow, cough and turn my head, but I was still completely paralyzed below my neck. He nodded matter-of-factly and told me that, now that I could swallow, the worst was over and I would definitely live. Key to my survival, he said, was that I had been able to urinate after being stung. He made a small fire outside the palapa, and boiled a couple of fresh shrimp in a quart of water in a pot. Bringing the hot broth over to me, he insisted I drink it all, one half-teaspoon at a time, no matter how difficult it was for me to swallow, until there was none left.

"The shrimp is like the scorpion," he said, noting their similar appearance, quietly explaining the broth's value like he would to a student, as Richard spoon-fed me. "This is the best remedy for the throat symptoms, which are the most serious. Once the spines in the throat are gone, the ants, paralysis, fire, muscle knots and visions will disappear." And then he abruptly left.

My recovery was, to put it mildly, rough. It took until late afternoon the following day for my paralysis to wear off sufficiently to where I could, with Rick's help, sit up in a chair and eat some watermelon. Two days after the sting, my tongue and gums were still numb, and I still suffered constant double vision, fiery pins and needles, ants and numbness from my neck to my feet. On the third day of my recovery, I was able to crawl on all fours to a chair and pull myself into it unaided, an important milestone; my urine was still disturbingly orange to tan in color, but I had my first bowel movement since the sting, another promising sign. Later that afternoon I began doing short, frequent walks using two long sticks for support—Santiago had urged I do this as soon as I was able—despite my arms below the elbows and my feet below the knees remaining completely numb. It would take me a week to retire the sticks. Santiago predicted it would take up to a month for my numbness to disappear, which proved accurate save for the inside of my left leg below the knee, which remained dead to touch for six more months.

I was severely emaciated, having lost around 20 percent of my body weight during my ordeal, my six-foot frame now eroded to around ninety-five pounds. Beginning three days after the sting, I had started showing signs of B-vitamin and calcium deficiencies; the scorpion's venom had drained me of all reserves of nutrients that maintain a healthy nervous system. I developed a rash over my entire body and tetany: I could not abduct my outstretched arms more than forty-five degrees from my midline. Extremely weak and sick, I was trapped in a cruel catch-22: I desperately needed therapy and resources I could not get in Yelapa, but I had to recover sufficiently enough to endure the rigors of travel before I could leave. Paradise had become my prison.

It took another five weeks for me to get strong enough to make my escape. On May 8 I bid farewell to Rick and Richard, who were staying on until the end of the month, and took the boat ride to Puerto Vallarta. The following day I caught the ferry from P.V. to the tip of Baja California. Three days later I crossed the US border into San Diego County on a bus. Gazing out the bus's window at a huge cloverleaf interchange on the expressway, one I had previously despised as a gross example of overdevelopment, I was never so happy and relieved.

Michael Cooper in the palapa on the El Tuito
River, Jalisco, Mexico (March 1978)

Michael Cooper bathing in the El Tuito River, one
week after the scorpion sting (April 1978)

-3-

MADRE GRANDE

I returned to the States from Mexico in May 1978 a different person. The scorpion that had very nearly killed me had also blessed me with a sacred gift. I had peered over the brink and seen what lay beyond, and I was no longer afraid of dying. Not that my instinct for self-preservation and pain avoidance had diminished in the slightest; on the contrary. But I had experienced the ecstasy of the final process. The previously terrifying unknown had become known, and it was nothing to fear.

When I'd left for Mexico a few months earlier, I was an agnostic. Now I could not deny the existence of a higher being or energy, however inscrutable. But to attempt to describe my ineffable experience—and especially my brush with the divine—to others would, I felt, only serve to trivialize it. I imagined the politely skeptical responses to my telling of the too-fantastic story, and how it would afterwards feel to me cheapened and betrayed. No, it was a precious seed, not to be dug up and displayed under bright lights for consideration of its merit by those who could not possibly understand. And so I largely kept it to myself, telling only a few family members and the closest of friends over the following decades. But private and revelatory though the experience was to me, I would quickly learn it was not unique.

Immediately upon my return to the States, I traveled to my childhood home in Brentwood, Long Island, where I would stay with my parents for a couple months to heal, put on much needed weight and regain my strength. One night while channel-surfing alone, I landed on a documentary special about death and dying. In the TV show, one interviewee after another recounted having an out-of-body experience after a serious accident or during touch-and-go surgery. My jaw dropped as they each described having felt intense euphoria while approaching a tunnel of white light and sensing a divine presence. Now my experience in Yelapa had a name: near-death experience. I felt a mystical connection to the strangers who shared their experiences on the show, all conventional people who would normally have been invisible to me. I realized we were all headed to the same destination, just on different paths.

By late June I felt I had fully recovered my health save for one vexing problem: I still had no feeling on the inside of my left leg below the knee to my big toe, where I'd been stung three months earlier by the Yelapa scorpion. Like the roots of a tree in poisoned soil, the nerve endings closest to the venous blood supply at my toe had apparently died while bathing in the scorpion's neurotoxins. Even pricking my leg with a pin, I felt no sensation.

Returning to Southern California in July, I was yearning for sanctuary and knew just the place. A couple years earlier, I had renounced performing in Long Island nightclubs and fled the East Coast in search of a healthier lifestyle. On the day I arrived in Southern California, a serendipitous tip led me to a nascent commune called Madre Grande Monastery, twenty-eight miles east of San Diego. The monastery in the Laguna Mountains would end up being the first of four rural communes I would briefly live in over the following two years, before my ill-fated trip to Yelapa.

Ensconced in a beautiful secluded valley, Madre Grande was back then a refuge for a couple dozen nudists—hippies, gypsies and other free-spirited eccentrics—who lived part-time on the recently purchased 264-acre parcel. The official backstory for the place was far more pedestrian. Founded in 1975 by John Drais, president of the Theosophical Society's San Diego branch, the monastery was formally run under the auspices of the ad hoc Paracelsian Order of the Johannine Catholic Church. But despite the affiliation's intimated Catholic leanings, the monastery's residents apparently didn't adhere at all to the beliefs or practices of any organized religion. Instead, what I found was a group of people pursuing peaceful communal living, spiritual awakening and alternative healing practices in harmony with their natural surroundings—on the face of it, a melding of Paracelsianism and theosophy. Although socially disorganized and poor in infrastructure—hosting only a modest ranch house and run-down barn—Madre Grande was the aspirational commune I had fantasized about finding when I left Long Island in 1976.

Three months after the scorpion sting in Yelapa, my thoughts turned again to the monastery. I hitched a ride from San Diego east on the two-lane State Route 94 to the outskirts of bucolic Dulzura, and walked the steep miles up the long dirt road to Madre Grande's hidden valley. There were only two people living on the sprawling property now: an affable and industrious carpenter named Tom Schwartz and an ostensible groundskeeper named Star. The thickly bearded Star was a very private man, forty-something, who lived with his cat in a small shed about twice the size of a tollbooth at the entrance to the property. Tom was a tall lean blond fellow in his twenties who lived out of an old refurbished USPS van. A couple dozen other commune members lived in San Diego, captives of day jobs there, and came up to the land typically only on weekends; several recognized me from my brief time on the commune two years earlier and invited me to stay on the land again. I would end up spending the next three years, some of my happiest and most carefree, calling it home.

The ranks of the commune quickly swelled. Not long after I arrived, Jim Cannon and Jan Muller-Cannon joined with their preschool kids from previous marriages—son Jairus and daughter Moon Blossom[9]—in tow. Jim, Jan, Tom and I quickly transformed a disused half-acre horse corral into a thriving organic vegetable garden, one that famed Findhorn Garden founder Peter Caddy would later esteem as second only to Findhorn. Longtime members Lee and Sequoia Zook moved up to the land from the city with their infant son to renovate, along with Tom, the property's old brick barn, transforming it into a well-appointed kitchen and dining hall we all dubbed the Sun Center. De jure chef Peter Girard whipped

---

9   Jairus Cannon would grow up to become an accomplished professional surfer two decades later and appear in the short surfer flick *The Ombak* in 2002.

up scrumptious vegetarian meals for the community in the Sun Center at the start and end of each workday. Asha Deliverance, a midwife, used her Singer sewing machine to fashion a geodesic dome from waterproof sailboat canvass, pulled over a hemispheric frame of interconnected electrical metal tubing Jim constructed; the design would become the prototype for the homes they would teach the rest of us to build for ourselves. (Several years later, Asha would move to Ashland, Oregon, and found Pacific Domes, whose clientele now includes Fortune 500 companies.) The entire community would rally to build a solar-heated shower house and adjoining hot tub—in just one day. A greenhouse, fruit orchard and composting toilet quickly followed. As the amenities multiplied, more and more people moved permanently onto the land and overall membership in the commune swelled to almost sixty. Although we were all nudists, we designated the community as "clothing optional" so as not to dissuade the self-conscious urban public from visiting.

Our garden quickly began to produce much more food than we needed, enabling us to sell the surplus to natural food stores in San Diego on a regular basis. Protecting our bounty was a constant battle, as ground squirrels and wild rabbits repeatedly attempted to breach the chain-link fence around the garden's perimeter to feast on our luxuriant crops. They did so at their peril: Star's monster cat, Who Two—the successor to his first cat, named Who—regularly patrolled the garden's outside perimeter. Who Two was built like a cougar in miniature, the largest American Shorthair I'd ever or since seen, his outsize frame rippling with muscle. I would often see him proudly carrying a rabbit nearly twice his size in his jaws, his brawny neck arched backward and chin pointed skyward to keep his kill from dragging along the ground as he trotted off to somewhere private to dine.

Madre Grande—situated roughly five miles north of the Mexican border as the crow flies and in the mountainous transition zone between the Pacific Coast and Colorado Desert—was home to many rattlesnakes; I would encounter them on average once or twice a week. But they were usually easy enough to detect from a safe distance and avoid; clapping my hands loudly when approaching the many bouldery areas on the land, in which they might be sheltering out of sight and sun, reliably made them shake their rattles and betray their location. Nobody ever got bit in the three years I lived on the land.

I initially lived in a large canvas tent at the north end of the property, on a rise overlooking the head of Pringle Canyon and a small lake in which I loved to skinny-dip. But I quickly built on-site one of Asha and Jim's inspired six-sided geodesic domes, atop a wooden platform. For insulation, I lined the lower half of the canvas shell with colorful blankets I'd bought in Tijuana. A sleeved opening in the curved ceiling held in place a flanged metal collar through which passed a pipe from my tiny wood stove, which I used for heat on brisk winter nights. As my home lacked plumbing—and electricity—I once a week hauled in a wheelbarrow a ten-gallon container filled with water out to it from the Sun Center, a distance one-fifth of a mile.

Every night, I fell asleep in my primitive home to the alternately pitch-bending and punctuated sounds of coyotes calling to each other, their mournful howls and excited yips echoing off the hundreds of huge boulders crowding the nearby ridges surrounding the valley. I learned to expertly mimic the coyote's song and, during the day, would often answer their calls, eliciting a minute-long repartee that would amuse my friends to no end. The primal call and response would last until my voice involuntarily cracked—producing the hoarse, high-pitched calls was hard on my throat—betraying the deception to my wild interlocutor. No reply from the beast after that.

Life at Madre Grande was unhurried, stress-free and supremely sweet. Living in a tight-knit community with shared beliefs and working together toward common goals—with community service foremost in mind—was uplifting and nurturing. We became a single organism, an ingrown family of outliers and rebels living in harmony on the land, each of us developing day by day a deeper appreciation of the others who were helping make the dream possible. I had no goals planned beyond twenty-four hours, didn't care to muse about my future. It seemed impertinent. Living for the moment was liberating and serene.

It was partly my immersion in community and Peter's fabulous meals that led me to abandon raw foodism and start eating cooked food again, for the first time in three and a half years. But I was also grasping at straws, hoping a change in diet would coax feeling back to the inside of my lower left leg, which was still completely numb several months after the scorpion sting. No other regimes or therapies had helped in the slightest. Not juice fasting, not massage, not acupuncture or chiropractic treatments—nothing.

Six months after the sting, I was beginning to despair I would never regain feeling in my lower leg. I began studying all I could about the nervous system, searching for answers. After reading all the books about natural healing modalities in Madre Grande's substantial library, none of which proposed remedies I hadn't already tried, I started studying American Medical Association journals. Over the course of 150 hours, I read in detail every report on research and clinical trials I could find regarding the nervous system, but always came away from my studies bereft of new ideas. And then I saw it.

It was just one paragraph long, easy to overlook. Two researchers had discovered that garlic and, to a lesser degree, onions contained what they dubbed a mysterious "X factor" that raised the respiration rate of cells throughout the body—remarkably, even in extremities where there was little to no blood flow. My pulse quickened as I remembered research I'd read years earlier that maintained that oxygen fostered renewed growth in nerve endings.[10] An increase in the respiration rate of my cells would raise their oxygen level. The increase in oxygen level in turn should, theoretically, repair the nerve endings in my numb lower leg. It was worth a try.

Each and every day for the next two weeks, I ate an entire bulb of raw garlic; I did not want to risk that cooking the garlic might destroy the so-called X factor and thwart its hoped-for therapeutic effect. Chewing the first few cloves was deceivingly easy. Halfway through each bulb, my mouth on fire, I did anything I could to munch and choke down the next clove. After a few days of this routine, uric acid was streaming out of every pore in my skin; my friends told me I smelled—even from a distance—like I had

---

10   Decades later, the Oxford Recovery Center would cite several studies documenting the successful use of hyperbaric oxygen to improve peripheral nerve regeneration, including in cases of ischemic neuropathy.

urinated all over myself. By the end of the fourth day eating garlic, I began to sense—for the first time in six months—pins and needles when rubbing the inside of my leg. By the tenth day, feeling had completely returned to my leg. To ensure the numbness wouldn't return, I continued my mouth-blistering regime for another four days. But the scorpion's last hold on me had been vanquished.

In early December 1978, famed herbalist William LeSassier visited Madre Grande and proposed to the community that he teach on the land a series of fee-based courses in botanic medicine, starting the following month. As part of his suggested arrangement, members of our commune would be allowed to attend free of charge all the classes, which would run ten hours daily for twenty-one consecutive days inside the Sun Center. The thirty-year-old LeSassier had gained prominence nationwide particularly for developing his Triune System of Formulation, a unique approach to concocting a proportioned herb formula based on the specific strengths and weaknesses of each patient, a system that would remain in use by many of the most eminent herbalists into the 2020s. I jumped at the chance to attend the courses.

Far from being instruction solely in herbalism, LeSassier's intensive courses were a deep dive into numerous modalities in alternative medicine and diagnostics. Students were taught how to use physiognomy, iridology, the smell of a patient's breath and the appearance of their tongue and fingernails for diagnosis of constitutional imbalances. Discussed at length were using specific foods, herbs, traditional Chinese medicine and reflexology to treat specific ailments, including those that were asymptomatic, and strengthen weak organs. I listened with rapt attention and took copious notes.

LeSassier's classes inspired me to learn more about herbs. I began studying ethnobotany in my spare time, cataloging the numerous plants on Madre Grande's land and investigating, including through careful self-dosing, their medicinal uses; I only got sick once, due to my following atypically incorrect dosing information in one of my reference books.

I made my acquaintance with a professor of botany at San Diego State University, to whom I regularly brought plant specimens for his coaching on their identification. I pored over Philip A. Munz's authoritative botanical taxonomy reference *A California Flora and Supplement* and his less formal *California Mountain Wildflowers*; Alma R. Hutchens's *Indian Herbalogy [sic]of North America*; Jeff Callegari and Keith Durand's *Wild Edible and Medicinal Plants of California*; and Lowell John Bean and Katherine Silva Saubel's *Temalpakh – Cahuilla Indian knowledge and usage of plants*, to name but a few of dozens of tomes. Using Munz's milestone treatise and a compound microscope at SDSU's botany department, and upon the professor's confirmation, I identified over 200 wild plants on Madre Grande's land. I subsequently gave weekly herb walks and ethnobotany discourses in the spring at Madre Grande for visitors from the city. Madre Grande dedicated a pantry off the kitchen to dozens of jars filled with herbs, including many I'd wildcrafted, and I eventually became the community's de facto (pro bono) practicing herbalist.

The more I explored the land, the deeper and more precious grew my connection to it. The highest crest on the ridges delimiting the valley was the eponymous Madre Grande Peak, atop whose summit sat an improbably level slab of smooth rock the size of a house—a perfect perch from which to survey the serene valley 900 vertical feet below, if you knew how to navigate the maze of car-size boulders on the mountain's steep slopes to get up there. The summit was, and remains today, named Mother Grundy Peak on USGS (US Geological Survey) topographic maps—an Anglo bastardization of Madre Grande, which literally means Big Mother. Indeed, the peak was like a grand mother to commune members; with our animistic leanings, it seemed to embody a nurturing spirit. Visible from nearly every place on the land, the mountain watched over us like a protective parent keeping track of its children.

I occasionally ate magic mushrooms and wandered alone the wild area at the foot of the sacred peak, communing with its native children: the plants and animals that had been born in the valley. I tried to understand what hidden qualities the plants were expressing in their form, their fragrance, their pigments, the volatile oils in their flowers, and the resins in their leaves and roots. I would call out to coyotes and, if I were lucky, they would answer from afar. The land had a living pulse, the sun-bleached white boulders a light and vibration, the wind a voice, and the sky and earth and water a delicate balance with which all the animals and plants in the valley and on its surrounding ridges were in flux and harmony at once. I loved the land. Loved it like I loved a brother.

I had had this feeling before, but only briefly, in other wild places: standing on the windswept shore of Lago Del Sol on the crater floor of Nevado de Toluca, and skinny-dipping in the jungle pond on the El Tuito River miles upstream from Yelapa. I yearned to know more wild places, but immersing myself for days instead of minutes.

I had seen spectacular photos of wilderness areas in California's Sierra Nevada, the craggy mountain range that skewers most of the state from north to south, and was particularly wowed by scenes of the high back-country in Kings Canyon National Park, northeast of Fresno. I ordered by mail USGS topographic maps covering the nearly half million acres inside the park—most of which was rugged wilderness accessible only to the hardy—and set about learning how to interpret the maps' extended squiggles, so-called "contour lines" that noted the land's elevation above sea level contiguously from point to point. Studying the trail system inside the park for hours on end, I slowly began to formulate a backpack trip that seemed feasible for a novice like me to pull off: one that would take me, over the course of five days, forty miles through deep canyons, along rushing creeks, up into high cirque basins at timberline and over a sky-high mountain pass where trees could not grow. I excitedly showed the map to Tom Schwartz, tracing an index finger along my proposed route and extolling the imagined scenery, and asked if he was interested in joining me in the wild venture. He flashed me a thumbs up, and we set a date.

On an early morning in July, Tom Schwartz and I drove north to Kings Canyon National Park in his renovated USPS van, our backpacks chockablock with supplies and stashed in the back of the vehicle. Arriving at the park in the late afternoon, we drove slowly east into its interior on the Kings

Canyon Scenic Byway, a narrow blacktop that took us through stunning ancient groves of towering sequoia and cedar trees growing alongside the free-running South Fork Kings River, until we came to the road's end.

Parking the van and donning our backpacks, we stepped onto the Paradise Valley Trail and began hiking east toward the Pacific Crest, brimming with excitement over what lay ahead. After a couple miles, the canyon swung north and became progressively narrower, its sheer granite walls towering up to 5,000 feet above us and gleaming stark white in the late afternoon sun as we made our way alongside the South Fork's riotous white-water cascades. Around four miles from the trailhead, as shadows cloaked the tops of the canyon's ramparts, we made camp at the base of a house-size glacial erratic just below Mist Falls, the lee of the huge boulder shielding us from the 100-foot-high cataract's direct spray carried hundreds of yards down the canyon. The sound of the torrential falls drowned out all else, and the sweet-smelling, cool air was supercharged with endorphin-spawning negative ions carried on the mist, as dusk first grayed the canyon walls above us and then plunged the chasm into darkness.

This was wildness. Just like I had imagined, only better: more raw, pure and primal. I had backpacked, technically speaking, two years earlier to the site of the sixth annual Rainbow Gathering in New Mexico's Gila National Forest,[11] but that was with thousands of other people carrying literally tons of supplies in an almost circus-like parade. This was astonishingly and magnificently different. We were profoundly alone, in much wilder country. Yet to my surprise, I felt strangely at home.

We headed deeper into wilderness the following day, backpacking several miles farther north up the South Fork's canyon before heading east along the Woods Creek Trail, beside which we made our second camp.

---

11 The Rainbow Gathering was, and remains today, an informal festival held during the first week of July that draws tens of thousands of hippies, gypsies, nudists and other bohemians to a different remote forest selected each year by the organizers. The idealistic goal of the festival in the 1970s was the promotion of a more equitable and harmonious society free from capitalism, consumerism and the identically purposed influence of mainstream media. True to its principles, the Gatherings charged no admission fee, food was distributed freely and generously, and people camped—some, in a co-option of Native American tradition, in teepees—wherever they cared to.

On the third day we joined the Pacific Crest Trail and took it south along South Fork Woods Creek, steadily gaining elevation. Now the trees, mostly whitebark and foxtail pine and mountain hemlock, were much shorter and growing in progressively sparser stands the higher we hiked. The subalpine forest was gradually being replaced by spongy, open meadows of red and green mountain heather and purple Sierra shooting stars, bathing in countless rivulets of fresh snowmelt.

As we approached timberline at about 10,500 feet, the incomparably beautiful Rae Lakes, a string of crystal-clear pearls at the base of magnificently craggy, sheer-faced peaks, came splendidly into view. We made camp on a short rise above one of the pristine lakes. The sun was vivid but the alpine air cool and thin. Tom, an excellent swimmer, announced he was going for a dip. From my high vantage point, I watched him make strong, confident strokes out toward the middle of the windswept lake, its snow-fed waters still frigid from winter's thaw. His pace began to slow when he got about a third of the way toward the center of the lake. To my surprise, he abruptly turned and began swimming back toward the shore, but now he appeared to be quickly running out of steam. I watched with growing concern as his pace braked to a crawl, the lake's shore still worrisomely out of reach, his mouth wide open and gasping for air, the cold evidently sucking the last few calories from his numb arms and legs. When he finally dragged himself onto dry land, he was totally spent and shivering. He stumbled back to camp, humbled and with a newfound respect for high-altitude lakes.

We broke camp in the morning and continued south on the Pacific Crest Trail, continuously gaining elevation and soon leaving the last cold-stunted trees behind and below us. Plodding up a broken and seemingly endless staircase of unstable boulders, we finally arrived at barren and oxygen-starved Glen Pass. At 11,926 feet, winter had barely relinquished its icy grip on the rocky gap, where only mountain sorrel grew in isolated clusters among the chaotic piles of boulders. Desolate though it was, it was supremely inviting in its windswept cleanliness. Unrestricted views in every direction revealed jagged mountain peaks for as far as the eye could see. I thought of Nevado de Toluca's caldera and its similarly austere alpine splendor, but Glen Pass was a strikingly different universe, with no manmade structures visible out to any horizon and two days from the nearest road. Here, we had only ourselves to rely on for safety, shelter and survival. No one was going to drive up here to give us a ride out. Somehow that made the pass seem more fantastic. In that moment, the remoteness and emptiness of the place cleansed me like a giant but silent vacuum cleaner, sucking out my last vestige of stress and leaving me gazing off into the far, untamed distance completely free of thought. This is what I had come for, wilderness's greatest gift.

I hated to leave that barren pass, even though staying would've been totally irrational. It was downhill all the way from there, both literally and figuratively, as we descended into the forested watershed of Bubbs Creek, where we camped our last night out. A long slog west along the creek the next day brought us full-circle back to the South Fork Kings River. As we approached the parking lot at the trailhead, I couldn't help but feel it was way too soon. It was then and there I decided I would return the next summer for a month-long wilderness trip.

-4-

HIGH SIERRA

An astrologer who lived at Madre Grande once told me my Virgo sun and Pisces moon signs were "in opposition" in my birth chart. She said the resulting tug of war between my rational and emotional sides predisposed me to extreme behavior. That might on some level explain why, after years regularly fasting and eating raw fruits and vegetables to purify my body, I suddenly became obsessed with eating protein, albeit lacto-vegetarian, and exercising like mad to pack on muscle. But this about-face was far more deliberate and down-to-earth than some purported impulse driven by celestial bodies. After returning to Madre Grande from a magical five-day backpack trip in Kings Canyon National Park with Tom Schwartz in July 1979, I was determined to get as strong and fit as possible so I could pull off a month-long backpack in the Sierra Nevada the following summer.

It wasn't Tom but Tony Morel, another Madre Grande chum, who quickly signed on to my Sierra dream. Tony was a charismatic, easy-going guy whose company I thoroughly enjoyed, and he had valuable prior experience backpacking. Beneath his soft-spoken and understated demeanor, he was hilariously and irreverently ironic. Roughly my age, his shoulder-length black hair and trimmed beard and mustache framed a handsome visage that could've almost won him an early-'70s Paul McCartney-lookalike contest if only his hippie hairdo had been coifed.

To train for our joint Sierra expedition, Tony and I became exercise buddies. Every morning for eleven months, we worked out together, beginning with a run from the Sun Center to the north end of Madre Grande's 264-acre property and back, followed by doing dozens of pull-ups on an out-of-service windmill and several sets of pushups and sit-ups. After several months of that routine, our trim bodies were positively ripped.

Women began looking at me differently. With my curly hair falling in ringlets to my shoulders and my newly muscular physique, I looked like a combination rock star and rock climber. While shopping in stores in San Diego, beautiful women would walk right past the stocker to ask me where they could find this or that item. As I walked down a city street one afternoon, a gaggle of teenage girls whistled and catcalled at me from their speeding convertible. Young women were asking me out to dinner left and right. The skinny vegan hippie had become a chick magnet.

My motivation for getting in tip-top shape, however, was never about attracting women's attention and always driven by the upcoming Sierra expedition. And so it was a crushing disappointment when, in early July 1980, after nearly a year of planning, training and anticipation, Tony suddenly quit the expedition with little more than a month to go before launch. Nobody else I knew was interested in joining me on the trip and, considering my inexperience in wilderness travel, I deemed it too dangerous to go alone. Besides, the weight of gear required to pull off such a long trip—the advent of commercially available ultra-light equipment was still decades away—necessitated I bring a partner along to help shoulder the load. My fantasy trip was dead in the water.

A dark cloud hung over me as I shuffled off to work in Madre Grande's vegetable garden. As I toiled half-heartedly in the soil, lamenting the expedition's cancellation, a gorgeous woman approached me. Kim Howell was a lithe, fit Canadian blonde in her twenties who was visiting the commune for the day, fresh off a trip to Mexico. After exchanging polite introductions, she sensed I was despondent and asked why. I told her of the canceled expedition, obsessively detailing my quashed plans to visit towering ancient sequoias and lush wildflower meadows and sky-high mountain passes, living free as a bird for a full month in paradise.

Kim listened intently without speaking; I was impressed by how empathetic and understanding she was. When I finished my lament, she told me about a multi-month canoeing expedition she had been on the year before—led by a mentor—in Northern Canada's Yukon Territory. I was stunned. This beautiful woman had far more experience in wilderness travel and self-sufficiency than I. I asked her on the spot if she would like to go on the Sierra expedition with me. Her eyes brightened and she immediately said yes. I was absolutely thrilled.

Over the following three weeks, Kim and I exhaustively organized the expedition, from itinerary to supplies, referring often to Harvey Manning's seminal book *Backpacking: One Step At A Time* as a guide. She and I had the same sort of trip in mind: although we wanted to see lots of beautiful backcountry, making miles was not our primary goal. We wanted to immerse ourselves in wilderness, to live in it, study the native flora and use our travels through complex terrain to practice reading topographic maps ("topos") and learn compass skills. Although we planned to hike entirely on trails, we would take frequent "map and field" compass bearings to track our exact position on the land and identify all the surrounding peaks, ridges, passes, canyons and streams. To that end, we would follow routes that offered the most sweeping views, crossing the Great Western Divide several times.

We packed Bjorn Kjellstrom's definitive navigation treatise *Be Expert With Map and Compass* and Norman F. Weeden's *A Survival Handbook to Sierra Flora*—the latter a decision that would prove prescient. I made up a batch of homemade bug dope—combining oils of white thyme, citronella, pennyroyal and eucalyptus—to ward off the Sierra's infamous summertime hordes of mosquitoes and gnats. We would sleep in Kim's North Face dome tent on buggy or cool nights, but the lightweight sleeping bag I would bring was chosen for expected warm summer temperatures (a decision I would come to regret). Eschewing commercially available dehydrated meals, we packed eighty-seven pounds of whole grains, nuts, seeds, lentils, beans, dried fruit, sea vegetables, garlic, salt and vegetable broth powder. We brought thin nylon parachute cord for counterbalance-hanging our food away from thieving black bears.[12] During our preparations, we enthusiastically discussed wilderness survival; I learned from Kim to always carry a compass and matches—survival essentials—on my person, not in a backpack that could accidentally be dropped over a canyon rim or into a raging river and be lost.

A couple weeks before our trip's start, fellow Madre Grande resident Jon Cedar (given name Jon Pope) expressed interest in joining Kim and me for the latter half of the expedition; we planned to rendezvous with him out in the wild on the trip's sixteenth day. At one minute past midnight on August 2, 1980, Kim and I left San Diego on a Greyhound bus bound for Visalia, California, the city nearest to Sequoia National Park's west boundary. I didn't sleep a wink on the cramped and smoky bus—cigarette smoking was still allowed on public transit in those days—during the entire eight-and-a-half-hour ride. From Visalia, we hitchhiked east to road's end at rustic blink-and-you'll-miss-it Mineral King, basically a small group of cabins at a trailhead inside the park. There we convinced a charitable park ranger to store thirty-eight pounds of our food—we didn't need all we brought immediately—in his cabin for safekeeping while we spent a week and a half exploring the park's backcountry.

We set out north that afternoon on a 1,900-foot climb by trail up to Timber Gap, a mid-elevation mountain pass three miles from the trailhead, where we would camp for the night. The moment the cabins disappeared from our sight—leaving us immersed in quiet, sweet-scented forest—my mind effortlessly slipped into the same carefree space it had been in a year ago in the backcountry of Kings Canyon National Park; it was as if all wilderness was one connected, timeless place and I had returned to its gentle fold. We stopped many times along the way up to the pass to study the local

---

12   To secure their food away from marauding bears overnight, savvy backpackers use a thin rope or parachute cord to hang the food—divided equally by weight between two nylon bags—from a relatively slim tree branch, using a technique called counterbalancing. There are several variations and fine adjustments to the technique, but the goal is always the same: each bag hanging ten feet off the ground, suspended ten feet below the tree branch and hanging ten feet away from the tree trunk. In forty years of backpacking, I've never had my "10-10-10" hangs get robbed by bears.

flora, identifying around two dozen species of wild plants; by the end of the expedition, I would come to know over fifty. That night as we bedded down under the whitebark pines and red and white fir trees at the pass, Kim and I were elated; that this was the start of a month-long trip made it even more precious.

Over the next couple days, we backpacked along the willow- and fern-clad banks of Cliff Creek and visited subalpine wildflower gardens of purple lupine, yellow wallflower and pink and white swamp onion. Gaining 3,000 feet in elevation, we arrived at barren Black Rock Pass far above timberline on the Great Western Divide. Kim and I both got altitude sickness at the 11,600-foot pass, suffering nearly overpowering fatigue, nausea and shortness of breath. We quickly recovered after descending over a thousand vertical feet down the mountain ridge's snowbound east side—in a slippery skid Kim called "cross-country skiing without the skis"—to relatively thicker atmosphere beside a beautiful, windswept alpine lake. From our makeshift camp there, the spectacular fluted cliffs of Kaweah Peaks towered on the northern horizon.

The next day we dropped another 1,000 vertical feet into deeply forested Big Arroyo Canyon. We made the mistake of drinking from the deceptively clear Big Arroyo Creek without first filtering the water and, as a result, spent that evening doubled over in camp with intestinal cramps and diarrhea. Fishing a lump of jet-black charcoal out of our campfire, I crushed it in my Sierra cup with a spoon. Kim and I each stirred a level teaspoon of the gritty stuff in a cup of filtered water and quickly guzzled it down before the heavy sediment could settle. It was like drinking sand, difficult to swallow without gagging, but it did the trick: a few hours later our cramps had calmed, and by the next morning we were both completely cured of our intestinal ailment.

We camped the following two nights in the wildflower-painted Nine Lakes Basin. From the subalpine basin, we backpacked the High Sierra Trail over snowy Kaweah Gap and 3,000 vertical feet down the other side to Bearpaw Meadow, where we camped exhausted but content. The resinous leaves of Mountain Misery (*Chamaebatia foliolosa*) made excellent tinder for starting a warming campfire.

Breakfast the following morning included a side dish of wild goose-berries mixed with the cooked flowers, leaves and inflorescence stems of fireweed. A couple more days of backpacking, under giant sequoia trees and over swollen streams on wobbly logs, returned us to Mineral King, where we retrieved our remaining food from our ranger-friend's cabin. We had originally planned to backpack another forty miles over the next five days to a rendezvous with Jon Cedar at Rowell Meadow, just outside Kings Canyon National Park's west boundary. But Kim's heels were blistered and toes ground into pink hamburger from wearing poorly fitted hiking boots, and she needed time off her feet to heal. So we hitchhiked instead to a trailhead a couple miles west of our rendezvous point and did the much shorter hike in.

Unfortunately, Rowell Meadow was a breeding ground for thousands of hungry mosquitoes—brushing my shoulder would kill at least twenty of the pesky bloodsuckers with one stroke. When Jon met up with us five days later, we shot out of that hellhole like a lightning bolt for Kings Canyon National Park. As her blistered feet still couldn't tolerate wearing her torture boots, Kim hoofed it barefooted, carrying a backpack weighing at least fifty pounds. She would continue to backpack with bare feet over the next three days, through almost twenty miles of wilderness, never complaining and as fully—and happily—committed to the expedition as Jon and I. I was in awe of her steadfast resolve, strength and wild spirit. I tried hard not to fall in love with her.

Kim was not the only one with bum boots. Only a day after leaving Rowell Meadow, now backpacking through Sugarloaf Valley into the heart of Kings Canyon National Park, I discovered one of my boots was literally falling apart: the upper was separating from the sole at the toe, and the gap was already an inch long. At the rate it was deteriorating, I reckoned the boot would be hanging off my foot after another twenty miles, if not sooner. Weeks of backpacking still lay ahead, including two climbs over the rock-and-snow Great Western Divide that even Amazon Kim would have to lace up for. That evening in our camp beside the Roaring River, I wondered how I could avoid aborting the trip.

The solution came to me the next morning: placing the end of our parachute cord in our campfire until it burst into flame, I let the molten nylon drip into the breach in my removed boot. The nylon quickly bonded with the boot leather as it cooled, forming a rough plug. To strengthen the repair, I harvested pitch oozing from a pine tree and slathered it on and around the nylon plug, sealing the kludge.

The repair would hold up for only ten miles of hiking before the dirtied pitch dried and the nylon plug fell out. But by repeating the mend every evening—when above timberline, using pine pitch stored in my pack and burning the parachute cord with matches—that bogus boot made it through the remainder of the expedition in no worse condition than after the initial repair.

It was on the Roaring River that I abandoned my longstanding vegetarian diet. Jon had caught four trout in an eddy. We gutted the fish, speared them with willow branches and cooked them over our campfire. It was my first flesh food in five and a half years, and the flaky texture and delicate taste were unlike that of any fish I'd ever had before. Fresh-caught trout is the cotton candy of the Sierra.

Nearing the Roaring River's headwaters the next day, views south to the Great Western Divide began to open up as the forest became sparser. Stopping for lunch, my gaze wandered across the water, off-trail and upslope to a necklace of barren peaks towering 3,000 vertical feet above us. To my amazement, I spied a lone figure coming down from a rocky pass on the divide. His backpack was large—not a day pack like you would wear on a short jaunt from camp—yet his stride was nimble and confident as he dropped quickly down the precipitous talus slope, hopping from boulder to rock slab to boulder.

"Holy crap, there's someone up there!" I exclaimed, my jaws and eyes wide open, pointing in disbelief. "What the hell is he doing way up there?"

I took out my compass and topo map and quickly took some field bearings to triangulate our position. On the map, I could see there were some unnamed lakes out of sight just beyond the mysterious backpacker. It suddenly hit me like a thunderbolt: he'd been up there camping.

"Check it out!" I said excitedly, showing the map to Kim and Jon. "That guy must've navigated his way off-trail up to these lakes. That is so fucking cool." I fell silent, the impact of my revelation sinking in, then heard words automatically spill from my lips, as if spoken by someone else: "*That's* what I want to do."

And I would. That moment was a seed, the inspiration for my becoming an expert cross-country navigator, planning and executing over the following decades scores of remote wilderness routes far from paint-by-number trails. But for now, an expedition wholly on trails was plenty adventurous to me, especially in this remote area; we'd seen only two other people, men on horseback, over the prior couple days.

We began eating more plants growing wild on the land, striving to meld with the primal essence of the place as deeply as possible. That evening for dinner, we steamed flowering fireweed, succulent stonecrop, sweet red paintbrush and spicy swamp onion, adding it to the buckwheat and toasted sunflower seeds we'd packed in. Jon and I each caught four trout up at subalpine Colby Lake the next day and ate them with barley soup Kim cooked with swamp onion, stone crop, fireweed, wild aster leaves and lemony sorrel. We stayed an extra day and night at the lake, catching three more trout and eating them with toasted millet, wild dock, fireweed and Jeffrey's shooting star leaves. The fishing at Colby Lake was stupid easy, even using my primitive ad hoc tackle: my reel was fishing line wrapped multiple times around a stick about seven inches long. Attaching a treble hook and lightweight sinker on the end of the line, I used Velveeta cheese for bait.

It got very cold and windy both nights we were at Colby Lake. Our layover there was on August 22, but hints of autumn were already in the air in the high mountains. I began to worry my lightweight summer sleeping bag, comfortable down to only about 40°F, would not be sufficient to keep me warm for the remainder of the trip.

My concern proved prescient. Two days later, camped now in Kern Canyon on the other side of the Great Western Divide, I woke up at 4 A.M. shivering in my thin sleeping bag. Stumbling from the tent half-awake, I stoked our campfire's dying embers with fresh wood, nursing the coals into a blaze once more. I rolled some large rocks with a stick into the fire and waited until they were glowing red-hot. Removing my clothes beside the relative warmth of the fire and placing them on the ground, I rolled the hot rocks out of the blazing hearth and onto my T-shirt and pants. Carefully tying the lot into secure bundles, I stuck them in my sleeping bag and crawled in. The heated rocks kept me warm for a little over an hour, allowing me to sleep until the first light of dawn. I would have to repeat this improvisation every night thereafter until we got out of the wilderness.

The next morning, we took stock of our remaining food. We had hoped to extend our stay in the wilderness eleven more days, but we now reckoned our dwindling food stores would only last us six (an overestimate, it turned out). We were about thirty-five miles away from Mineral King, with the Great Western Divide between our camp and the trailhead. We decided to backpack to wilderness hot springs five miles away, take a layover day there, and then head for Mineral King.

Three days later we had already finished the bulk of our food, leaving only a few cups of grains, sea veggies and a bulb of garlic left to eat for the remaining seventeen miles to Mineral King; we would need to rely more on harvesting wild foods to sustain us until we got out of the wilderness. The temperature dropped that night below freezing well before daybreak, stirring me to take more campfire-heated rocks to bed.

Another day of backpacking brought us to sparsely timbered Little Claire Lake (altitude 10,450 feet). That's where we met Buzzard. A back-country ranger based in Kern Canyon, Buzzard was a friendly and fit young man sporting a black beard and mustache under a wide-brimmed white hat. Ambling into our camp on a dark horse, a white pack horse trailing behind on rope, he informed us that a hurricane off the coast of Baja was due to blow in to the Sierra the next day, bringing sleet and snow to the high country. His voice sober but calm, he advised we hightail it over the Great Western Divide to Mineral King early the next morning before the storm hit.

"We had the same type of weather pattern blow in to the park last summer," Buzzard said. "It forced the evacuation of backpackers by navy helicopter, but not before four people froze to death. It's going to get really cold and windy tonight up here. Better for you guys to move your camp to Forester Lake, which has more forest cover and protection from the wind."

We sincerely thanked Buzzard for his weather forecast and advice, and he rode off in search of other backpackers to warn of the impending storm. We made the one-mile hike south to Forester Lake in a jiffy and quickly set up camp, guying our tent in anticipation of the tempest. That night, we watched ominous cloud formations stream in from the south, veer east of our camp and break up over the rugged Sierra Crest in spectacular fashion. The hurricane had passed us by. But the night would nevertheless be bitterly cold, and I would awaken again before dawn to heat rocks in a campfire.

Hurricane or no, we still felt an urgency to get out of the wilderness the next morning. The cold front had marked an end to summer in the high country, and the temperature was below freezing as we set out for Forester Pass on the Great Western Divide, well over a thousand vertical feet above us. A biting 50mph wind assailed us as we neared the top of the barren pass, plunging the wind chill to around 12°F. From the wind-scoured top, the panoramic mountain views were stupendous. But timberline—offering relative shelter from the bone-chilling gale—was fully three miles away in the distance and over 1,500 vertical feet below us on the west side, urging our prompt descent. A dash down from the magnificent but inhospitable pass brought us quickly to Franklin Lakes and, beyond, into the aptly named Farewell Canyon.

As we dropped into Farewell Canyon, the view to the north revealed Mineral King Valley in the distance and, just beyond it, Timber Gap, where Kim and I had started the expedition four weeks earlier. I was a different person back then. Stronger now. Four weeks in the wilderness had made me more resilient, mentally bulwarked against anything civilization could throw at me. I had lived far away from the safety net of modern life, fording ice-cold streams and crossing the Great Western Divide over rock and snow four times. Survived sickness in the wilds. Foraged wild plants when our packed food ran low. Slept with hot rocks to keep from freezing at night. Kludged parachute cord and pine pitch to repair a disintegrating boot. Lived amongst the bears, securing our food reliably beyond their reach. I felt comfortable in my bones in wilderness. It felt like home.

A few miles shy of Mineral King, we came upon a group of day hikers taking a lunch break. The men and women all had on freshly laundered sweaters and jeans. One wore street shoes. All the women had on makeup, and one was wearing strong perfume. One of the men smiled politely, briefly, as we approached, then looked away. Nobody engaged us in conversation. I understood why. My grubby T-shirt was held together with bobby pins and pockmarked with burn scars from hot rocks, one pant leg ripped almost up to the knee, hair and moustache and newly sprouted beard filthy and unkempt, and fingernails and eyebrows black with dirt. Jon and Kim arguably looked no more presentable. We were wild animals to these people. Maybe they were right.

We would hitchhike out of Mineral King for Madre Grande the next morning, 131 miles of wilderness travel behind us. More significant, twenty-nine days of intensively studying topo maps and taking hundreds of map and field bearings had grown my incipient navigation skills by leaps and bounds. But I realized I was still a baby taking first steps. I was eager for the next challenge. An image of the cross-country backpacker I'd spied a week and a half earlier, dropping off a remote mountain pass into the Roaring River's canyon, was burned into my memory. It was a fire I could not put out. I yearned to travel my own routes through wilderness, far from pedestrian trails, to explore where virtually nobody else had gone before. Four months later, in the winter of 1981, I would take that leap.

Michael Cooper at Madre Grande Monastery, circa February 1980

-5-

ANZA-BORREGO

As the setting sun bumped the San Ysidro Mountains far off on the western horizon, my Madre Grande buddy Tony Morel and I rolled out our sleeping bags a few yards from the stony lip of a sheer cliff. It had taken us a day and a half to backpack to this breathtaking overlook of Southern California's Colorado Desert, navigating cross-country by map and compass. Now, several thousand acres of the Borrego Badlands lay sprawled 300 feet below us, a wrinkled mishmash of deeply eroded brown, gray and pink ravines. We watched in silence as the setting sun cast ever-lengthening shadows, like stripes on a zebra, over the shattered moonscape, the profound stillness of the place unbroken for want of even a breeze. To the east, approaching clouds blushed a rosy glow, forming a red-over-blue sky sandwich atop milk-chocolate badlands slowly fading to silhouette.

Relatively few people venture far into desert backcountry on foot. The deterrent, of course, is finding enough water to stay alive. Knowing there'd be none along the first part of our route, Tony and I had carried water in lightweight plastic gallon jugs inside our backpacks. Our insurance policy: empties lashed onto the outside of our packs. We would transfer water into them if a filled jug sprang a leak.

The problem was we could only carry so much of our liquid lifeline. A gallon of water weighs 8.33 pounds, not counting the container that holds it, and a person generally needs to drink a gallon a day out in the desert. Carrying two gallons each—enough for only a couple days—our pack weights were pushing 60 pounds each. But this was no overnighter. We were hoping to backpack in the desert for a week and a half.

The site of our expedition was Anza-Borrego Desert State Park, two hours northeast of San Diego by car. The second-largest state park in the US' contiguous states, Anza-Borrego is a massive reserve spanning approximately 600,000 acres, or roughly three-quarters the size of Rhode Island. Tony and I planned to backpack over fifty miles, 90 percent of it off-trail, through the primitive north end of the park. It was an ambitious plan, and the first critical test of my incipient navigation skills—in an area where heat and lack of shade and water could turn a mistaken deviation off-course very costly. More serious still would be a disabling injury, for when you can no longer walk in the desert, the clock starts quickly counting down to death from heat stroke after your carried water runs out.

Launching the backpack as we did in late January, typically the wettest and second-coolest month of the year for the area, made our quest a lot safer. Still, historical meteorological data for Anza-Borrego informed winter daytime temperatures could potentially soar as high as 90°F on the desert floor during a rogue heat wave, and lows plunge potentially below 20°F at night up in the San Ysidro Mountains we planned to explore during the last half of our trip. We packed clothes for every type of weather.

The morning of January 22, 1981, dawned hat-and-jacket cold in our clifftop camp above the Borrego Badlands, with thin cloud cover overhead—a good omen, considering our route over the next couple days would take us across large stretches of open, flat terrain offering zero shade. But even with overcast skies, the day would warm to 76°F by early afternoon, when we stepped out onto a large desolate plain in short sleeves. Three miles distant lay a water cache we'd previously hidden at the foot of parched-brown Coyote Mountain, a short carry from the two-lane asphalt County Highway S22 that traverses the park.

Hiking out onto the sandy plain, we quickly learned to keep our knees slightly bent, as the ground was scattershot with innumerable hidden burrows; the shallow tunnels immediately collapsed under the weight of our heavy packs and hyper-extended our knees before we got the memo.

Scattered creosote bush, spiny cactus and thorny ocotillo cast little more than pencil-thin shadows on the sun-bleached ground but provided camouflaged cover for the flat's small inhabitants. Time and again as we made our way across the arid plain, panicky roadrunners and jackrabbits made sudden mad dashes away from our heading. I was amazed by how many animals lived on this waterless flat.

We had very little water left in our packs when we finally reached the far end of the plain, crossed S22 and arrived at our water cache at the base of Coyote Mountain. Three days earlier, we had gingerly buried four plastic gallon jugs of water under a pile of large rocks to keep coyotes from disturbing them. Mindful that a hard freeze could split the jugs open before our return, we had also drained a couple ounces of water from each, creating enough room for ice to expand.

With fresh stores of water now secured in our packs—rebounding the weight of each to over 60 pounds—we left the cache site behind and lumbered into desolate Clark Valley in the primitive Santa Rosa Mountains State Wilderness. We made camp late that afternoon in scattered creosote bush near the east base of Coyote Mountain, enjoying unhindered views five miles across the parched valley to the towering Santa Rosa Mountains.

The weather gods were with us again the next morning, dawning very pleasantly cool and cloudy. A light wind blew as we approached Clark Dry Lake, an impossibly stark and inhospitable flat granting not even a shred of vegetation a foothold across its two-mile-wide expanse. Large asymmetrical plates of sunbaked, cracked earth spread out across the playa into the distance like a giant ceramic jigsaw puzzle. On the near edge of the playa inexplicably sat an evidently decades-old rusted cab for a truck, riddled with more bullet holes than Bonnie and Clyde. Completely gone was the rest of the vehicle, including the cab's doors, leaving only the metal chassis to hint at the reason for its mysterious demise. There were no roads or tire tracks leading to this, its unlikely grave. Setting the timer on my Minolta camera for a delayed shot, Tony and I jumped inside the cab to pose as motorized tourists sightseeing the area, our faces affecting an exaggerated air of first-class leisure.

Hoisting our packs again, we continued across the monochromic playa and up the austere valley for several more miles in deteriorating but still dry weather. The wind blew hard as we approached the upper terminus of the valley, wending our way around isolated patches of cholla cactus, ocotillo and creosote bush clawing the stony ground. As I paused to look back and gauge our progress, the view was absolutely breathtaking, the rose and blue-gray and chocolate Santa Rosa Mountains soaring 5,000 feet over Clark Valley's mélange of beige and gray-green and gold like a mosaic tapestry. It was everything I had longed to see in desert backcountry: wild and empty and desolate, terribly magnificent in both its promise and threat.

Against this satisfaction, our dwindling water supply was now a growing concern; it occurred to us we might've underestimated what we needed to carry. On the other side of a high ridge demarcating the south side of the valley reportedly lay a desert oasis where we could drink water to our heart's content. But with the oasis still around six stiff miles away and the afternoon sun sinking fast in the sky, we'd have to make camp that night on the north side of the divide and cross over the next day. The gusting wind was buffeting us terribly as the sun dove below the horizon.

"We gotta get off this open ground," I shouted to Tony over the wind. He nodded assent as I whipped out our topo map and pinned it to the hard ground.

Quickly orienting the map to true north, I weighted its corners down with rocks so it wouldn't blow away and took hurried field bearings to triangulate our position. After marking the converging bearings with penciled lines on the map, I established a compass heading to Alcoholic Wash, a ravine in which I presumed we would have some protection from the wind. Sure enough, we found a sheltered spot in the wash just before dark and made a cushy camp on its sandy bottom.

We each had less than two quarts of water left when the next morning dawned under clear and warming skies. The oasis was still around five miles off, with the lion's share of the ridge's elevation still standing in our way. But we weren't too concerned, for the way over the ridge looked very quick and straightforward on our map: Alcoholic Wash formed a direct mile-and-a-half sand expressway up to Alcoholic Pass, a gap from which the descent off the south side of the ridge looked like a slam dunk.

But that morning, the hike up the wash took longer than we'd anticipated, and for the worst of reasons. After about two miles of slow uphill slogging in increasing heat, we finally reached the crest of the ridge at noon. The precipitous view south that greeted us, of Borrego Valley over 1,000 vertical feet below our perch, looked absolutely gorgeous but absolutely wrong. Field bearings confirmed the terrible truth: we were around two and a half miles off course, east of Alcoholic Pass. We realized then that we had not camped in and hiked up Alcoholic Wash but in the wash immediately east of it—a mistake we could ill afford, as we now each had only one quart of water remaining. It was a hot and sunny day, and there was no shade to be found anywhere on the ridge.

A more experienced navigator likely wouldn't have made the same grave error, and if they had, they surely would've corrected it before it led them so far astray. My undoing was a lack of experience hiking in deep desert washes; you can't see out of them to take compass bearings and update your position. As we hiked earlier that morning, I should've regularly climbed out of the wash to shoot bearings and confirm we were still on course. Instead we blindly trusted our original presumption of our camp's position and carelessly followed the wrong wash, compounding our mistake and angling farther and farther away from Alcoholic Pass and the oasis beyond. Worse still, we topped out at a higher point on the ridge and above a much steeper slope than where we'd been aiming for at Alcoholic Pass; the scarp plunged here around 800 vertical feet in just the first half mile. We were literally left high and (nearly) dry.

Studying our topo map, Tony and I grimly assessed our options. A descent from Alcoholic Pass still looked to be the safest by far, so we decided to hike west along the ridge top to the gap. But the ridge was hardly a straight shot, meandering this way and that over rough ground, and our progress turned out to be worrisomely slow. After about a mile of laboriously wending along the undulating ridge in the hot sun, Tony abruptly stopped and whirled around to face me.

"To hell with Alcoholic Pass," he said impatiently. "Let's go down here."

He had barely glanced at the steep, unstable slope below us before making up his mind. But he was right. At the rate we were going, by the time we got to Alcoholic Pass we might be completely out of water. The quickest way to the oasis was across the easily hiked desert floor far below us. We needed to get off that damn ridge.

So, off the ridge we dropped, plunge-stepping steeply down loose rubble,[13] grabbing hold of large boulders en route to avoid sliding into needle-sharp cactus and thorny ocotillo. In the hot afternoon sun, the bright slope's nearly vertical southern exposure baked us like an oven on the way down. By the time we reached the bottom—concluding a 1,100-foot drop—we each had only a cup of water left to quench our thirst. The oasis was still three miles away across the shadeless desert floor. We crouched in the shadow of a car-size boulder, waiting for the hot sun to drop lower in the sky before attempting the exposed traverse.

Two hours later we got the break we needed when the sky turned thinly overcast with high clouds. We started briskly out across the open ground for the mouth of Coyote Canyon, where the oasis reportedly lay. As we hiked, the barren flat's deep blond sand slowly became compact and moist under our feet, then turned into a wide band of brown mud. A trickle of water appeared in the mud, grew into multiple broader rivulets, and eventually became a unified shallow stream.

We had reached the oasis at Coyote Creek, a beautiful destination made ever sweeter by our parched condition. There were willows, cottonwoods and sycamore trees here. And a riot of birds: wrens, blackbirds, sparrows and finches. Most important, there was an abundance of flowing water. We had survived the desert's uncaring privation and now, relaxing in the shade of a large cottonwood tree and slaking our thirst by a burbling brook, we were reveling in its nurturing refuge. We ate wild watercress with dinner that evening, and fell asleep to the sound of the tinkling stream.

The next morning, we hiked west along the swelling creek—soon seven feet wide—through tangled brush and willows growing on its shaded banks. The day was pleasantly warm and sunny when we finally left the creek behind and entered the Anza-Borrego Desert State Wilderness. Eating red

---

13 The plunge step is a mountaineering technique in which the climber descends a steep slope by forcefully planting each heel in turn, anchoring their feet with each step.

chuparosa blossoms as we hiked, we headed south across stony Collins Valley to the mouth of Indian Canyon, gateway to the San Ysidro Mountains. We made camp late that afternoon a mile up the rocky and shrubby canyon, beside a delightfully murmuring creek. A few short California fan palms graced the canyon near our otherwise treeless camp.[14] As had been the case all along our route, it was apparent we were alone in the canyon.

The most challenging part of our trip lay ahead: a cross-country climb 2,000 vertical feet up to Palm Mesa, followed by thread-the-needle route-finding down its precipitous south side into the San Ysidro Mountain's narrow twisting canyons—extremely rugged and potentially confusing terrain that would again test my navigation skills. I was stoked for the adventure but also a little concerned we might not execute the route correctly. We had to. On our map, only one canyon off the mesa's south side looked likely to be a go.

We took a layover day at the foot of our climb, foraging wild rose hips and an edible species of nightshade berries. (Most are poisonous.) The next morning started auspiciously, with an overcast sky promising a cool climb up to Palm Mesa. Anticipating we would find water in the narrow canyons in the mountains, we each packed only two quarts of water from the creek beside our camp, cutting our pack weights to just fifty pounds each for lighter and faster travel.

The climb went easier than we expected, and in two and a half hours we made the 2,000-foot ascent and were atop Palm Mesa. On its stony ground, desert and mountain flora were locked in an undecided contest for dominance: yucca, agave and various cacti versus juniper, manzanita and yerba santa. The sky was still cloudy on our arrival, and at 4,400 feet altitude on a winter day it was quite cool on the mesa. Tony and I each donned a hat and jacket and surveyed our top-of-the-world view. To the north, we could see Collins Valley thousands of feet below us, the top of Coyote Mountain off to the right and the Santa Rosa Mountains soaring between the two in the distance. Beautiful.

---

14 The California fan palm (*Washingtonia filifera*) is the only palm native to the Western US.

I took a map bearing to establish the correct compass heading to take us across the mesa's puzzle of rolling hills and twisting ravines to the north branch of Borrego Palm Canyon, one of several defiles dropping south off the mesa. We threw our backpacks on again and hiked the relatively easy terrain across the mesa to the head of the canyon, which our map indicated fed the North Fork Borrego Palm River—yes, an actual river in desertic mountains—down below.

The head of the canyon was bone-dry. The subsequent easy and relaxing descent along its sandy canyon bottom—adorned occasionally with a shady sycamore tree, a fragrant ceanothus shrub or scratchy desert cat's claw—belied what was soon to come and lulled us into a false sense of security. A mile and a half down from the mesa top, our progress came to an abrupt halt where the canyon narrowed into a slot before plunging thirty feet down sheer, polished rock—a dry waterfall.

There was no way we could safely downclimb the pour-off without a climbing rope, which we had not brought; the few potential handholds and footholds on the dry fall's 90-degree face had been beveled and burnished slippery-smooth by flash floods, affording no purchase. At the bottom of the thirty-foot plunge lay huge blocks of rock in a body-breaking jumble. The only potential way forward was up the slot's wall and then around the falls. It looked iffy.

Removing our packs, we free climbed one person at a time in short pitches up the east wall of the slot, the person below lifting the packs up to the person in the lead above. Where the wall's pitch finally began to moderate, we began traversing in a stooped crawl down-canyon along its steeply sloped face to bypass the dry waterfall, dragging our unwieldy packs behind us on the ground to avoid carrying them and throwing off our center of gravity. Once we cleared the dry falls, we descended carefully to the canyon floor. Safely down, we hoped there were no more dry waterfalls ahead of us in the canyon.

In fact there were, but none nearly as bad as the first. Some we went around, others we were able to downclimb after first lowering our packs with a short length of parachute cord we had packed. After a long series of drops over polished rock, we started hearing water ahead of us—the headwaters of the North Fork Borrego Palm River—apparently entering from a side canyon.

We joined the boulder-filled stream and hiked it down-canyon a mile, scrambling from one bank to another across the water's snaking and swelling course. The canyon became very narrow again, and the funneled stream picked up speed. As the sun sank over the canyon's west wall and dusk fell, we made camp about a mile shy of the North Fork's confluence with the Middle Fork Borrego Palm River. Crawling into our tent, I was very tired but feeling a newfound, deep satisfaction from the serial thrill-and-relief of cross-country travel through rugged and remote wilderness.

We were awakened at six o'clock the next morning by the pitter-patter of rain on our tent. Well aware we were in a narrow, steep-walled canyon marked with clear evidence of past flash floods, we bolted out of our sleeping bags and made a hurried climb to higher ground, dragging our packs and the still-assembled tent upslope with us. After surveying scant bivouac options for about an hour in accelerating rain, we settled on shoehorning the tent onto a narrow ledge above the apparent flood zone of the river and crawled inside to wait out the weather.

The sky was darkly overcast, the rain unrelenting. We worried that if it didn't let up soon, the river might swell enough to flood the canyon from wall to wall in swift current and block our exit down to the Middle Fork. If that happened, we would run out of food; we had not brought along extra rations to allow for a potential delay in getting out. I made a mental note to pack emergency rations for the next trip.

Thankfully, the rain diminished to scant sprinkles around noon. We waited for another half hour to see if a delayed wall of water would come crashing down the canyon from the watershed above us. None came. Assessing that our escape route out of the canyon was still open, we hastily broke camp and made our way through knee-deep river and over slippery boulders to finally arrive at the Middle Fork. There, to our relief, the canyon was much broader.

We came upon a crude, narrow trail—a veritable highway to us after the touch-and-go cross-country travel we'd pulled off higher up in the San Ysidro Mountains. Under intermittently dripping skies, we sauntered down-canyon on the easy trail alongside the Middle Fork Borrego Palm River, the wild stream quickly increasing in volume but no threat to us now in the relatively wide canyon. The river was aptly named, for where its banks spread to ten feet apart, we passed successive spectacular groves of towering California fan palms, some over fifty feet tall and laden with black pea-size dates.

We camped that evening around a mile and a half from the mouth of the canyon. Our trip was essentially over. But its conclusion would also mark a beginning, a sea change in the way I would approach backpacking from that point on. Wilderness trips were no longer just about seeing spectacular scenery and learning new outdoor skills. Now I wanted to dramatically raise the adventure quotient. I was hooked on the adrenaline rush of cross-country exploration.

Over the next several years, I would do serial backpacks—each up to two weeks long—in remote mountain wildernesses in California, Oregon and Washington, incorporating increasingly difficult routes off-trail. I won all my backcountry gambles at first. Then, in the winter of 1985, I rolled snake eyes. My luck wouldn't run out on land, however, but on water.

-6-

OWYHEE

A couple years before my horrible survival test in Yelapa, I spent a summer hitchhiking with a girlfriend 8,000 miles around the US and Canada, just for fun. Starting out with only $50 and some modest camping equipment, we thumbed our way up the California Coastline, through the Pacific Northwest and BC, across the Mountain States and Midwest to New York, down the Atlantic Seaboard, through the rural South and across the Desert Southwest. A particularly memorable spot on our bargain-basement sightseeing tour was the rustic Illinois Valley in Southwest Oregon. Little did I know I would return five years later to that beautiful mountain-rimmed valley, this time to stay.

Two things would lead me back. First, by the summer of 1981 Madre Grande's consensus model of governance had begun to wear thin; hours-long community meetings that debated everything and decided nothing left me wishing for greater autonomy. Second, after fabulous backpack trips in the Sierra Nevada and Anza-Borrego Desert State Park, my priorities had changed and I was now yearning to spend a lot more time in wilderness. My thoughts returned to the magnificent Illinois Valley, surrounded by expansive national forests and mountainous wilderness areas. I bought a 1968 Chevy Impala on the cheap, and turned my wheels north.

The Illinois Valley was exactly as I'd left it half a decade earlier, an odd blend of 1950s Americana and psychedelic Woodstock frozen in time. The rednecks in the small city of Cave Junction and nearby hamlet of O'Brien worked in the local timber industry. The hippies in the satellite outpost of Takilma—several miles south-southeast of Cave Junction—had established a thriving, illicit cottage industry growing weed and magic mushrooms. An outdoor drive-in movie theater offered entertainment every weekend for the motley community, a jarring sea of baseball caps and love beads. Somehow it all worked.

For the next five and a half years, I lived in one place or another in the valley, making just enough money to support my growing backpacking addiction. Mine was a pauper's existence, far below the poverty line, but I didn't mind. Five years residing on rural communes had taught me to live extremely frugally, and I didn't need or want any material possessions besides my backpacking gear, a car to get me to trailheads, and an electric guitar and amplifier I'd bought in 1979.

I rediscovered a passion for songwriting, a pastime I had pursued on and off since learning to play guitar at age twelve. I made friends with an aspiring impresario named Lu Judd who lived in the valley. Lu and I formed a music-production partnership: I was the talent, the one who wrote and performed the songs. Lu was the moneybags; he bought some low-end recording equipment on which I would create rough pre-production demos. He subsequently paid for a few sessions, with backing musicians and singers, at Bear Creek Recording Studio, a tiny eight-track recording facility in the mountains outside of Santa Cruz where we created fully realized productions. The most memorable recording session was with future Grammy Award-winning singer-songwriter Ashley Cleveland, then unsigned and, if memory serves me correctly, working as a bank teller somewhere north of San Francisco. Even then, you could tell she was a rising star on the cusp of a breakout.

When I wasn't producing music or working the odd job, I spent as much time as possible backpacking, often alone, in the two mountainous wilderness areas—the Siskiyou and the Kalmiopsis—that border the Illinois Valley. Every year, I'd also plan a climactic one- or two-week backpacking adventure in a national park in Washington or California.

I was living my bliss—and getting harsh reminders of the urgency to do so. In November 1983, my older brother Mark died from leukemia at age thirty-three. Barely two months later, my fifty-seven-year-old father died unexpectedly of a heart attack. Glaring signposts. I had received the first cue in 1971, five days before I was to graduate from high school, when my close friend Bobby Brown drowned at the beach. Seven years later I was nearly killed in Yelapa. And now, after only five years respite, my brother and father were dead. I was hearing the message loud and clear: live life now.

I wanted to try whitewater rafting. In February 1985 I learned of an upcoming guided rafting trip on Southeast Oregon's remote Owyhee River, a high-desert outing to be sponsored by the Sierra Club's Portland chapter. Scheduled to occur in mid-March, the trip would be a five-day whitewater adventure running sixty-nine miles of the lower section of the recently designated Wild and Scenic River.

Few people rafted the Owyhee in the 1980s, partly because it is so remote but also because of the area's unpredictable Great Basin weather: in April and early May, the time of year most conducive to tackling the river, you could have oven-hot days and clear skies, or freezing temperatures and stormy weather. Even fewer dared raft the Owyhee in mid-March, when winter storms are still a distinct possibility and water temperatures typically hover around a bone-chilling 43°F.

I knew firsthand how cold Southeast Oregon could get in the off-season. Just a few months earlier I had joined a volunteer party, also sponsored by the Sierra Club, to do a field survey of two Wilderness Study Areas in the southeast corner of the state over the Thanksgiving holiday. The goal of the survey was to record any remarkable flora, fauna, historical assets or unique topography and present the data to support a case for the WSAs' inclusion in the national system of designated wilderness areas, which would afford them greater environmental protections.

The field survey, crewed by about ten people, was planned to last four days. We made our base camp just off Oregon Route 205, a two-lane blacktop in the high desert just north of Pueblo Mountain. During our first night out, camped at 4,700 feet altitude, the temperature plunged to 7°F. I slept in two sleeping bags, one inside the other, inside a tiny nylon tent. Vapor from my breath instantly crystallized into delicate rime ice on the tent's ceiling, prompting me to restrict my movements; the slightest jostling of the tent's walls would cause an ephemeral blizzard of frozen white flakes to fall on my face and outer sleeping bag.

The next morning over breakfast, I learned not to place my wet metal spoon in my metal Sierra cup for more than thirty seconds or it would freeze to it—so hard, I could lift up the cup by the spoon's handle. After two nights and mornings at punishing temperatures, everyone had suffered enough that they decided to terminate the survey early and flee back to Portland. Everyone, that is, except for me and a guy named Larry.

As the rest of our party drove away, a light morning snow began to fall on our camp. It was well below freezing and a 25mph wind was blowing, plunging the windchill factor to around 0°F. Undeterred, Larry and I decided to attempt climbing nearby 8,632-foot Pueblo Mountain to its summit. Considering the brutal weather, we had little doubt we'd have the mountain all to ourselves. Maybe the entire zip code.

As we climbed the barren volcanic peak, its snowpack quickly grew to a depth of about twelve inches, but it did not slow our pace. It was so cold on the mountain, the snow was as light as dandruff and dry as ash. Every time I lifted my foot out of the powder to take a step higher, my boot came completely clean.

The wind intensified as Larry and I climbed higher. There were no trees to break the force of the gale, only sagebrush and scattered short rock outcroppings barely three feet high, if that. Even with the exertion of climbing, we were nearly shivering in the unrelenting wind. We literally sprinted uphill from one rock outcropping to the next higher, where we crouched in the wind shadow for several seconds before repeating the process again and again.

After climbing about 1,000 vertical feet in deteriorating weather conditions, it became apparent it would be foolish for us to continue higher. Due to lowering clouds, we couldn't see that much by that point anyway. We made a hasty retreat off the mountain to base camp, and packed up just as nature's claws came out. A full-throated blizzard battered us as we drove back across the high desert and over the Cascade Mountains to Eugene, where my car was parked.

I remembered that bitterly cold trip a few months later when I called to register for the Owyhee River run. I asked the woman who answered the phone if floatation devices and wetsuits would be provided.

"Life vests, yes," she answered, "but not wetsuits. You won't need one. Nobody's going to fall into the water."

I was surprised by her response, in light of the fact we'd be running Class III and IV rapids on the Owyhee.[15] But she sounded like an expert, whereas I had no prior experience rafting. I deferred to her judgment.

A few weeks later, just a couple days before the trip was scheduled to launch, I got a call back from the Sierra Club. A weeklong snowstorm was forecast to blow in to Southeast Oregon exactly at the start of our outing. The trip was still on, but I was being informed of the heightened risk and afforded a chance to cancel my participation. I decided to stay on.

At dawn on the morning of the trip's launch, I and eight other intrepid individuals gathered in a parking lot at a community college in Portland for a briefing with the trip's two river guides, capable-looking men who appeared to be in their thirties. Their outlook for the expedition was sobering.

"Make no mistake," one of the guides said, "this will be a hardcore winter-rafting trip. The area is extremely remote, and we'll be on our own. It is forecast to snow every day we're on the river. It will probably be below freezing. You will get wet. Nobody will be looked down on for bailing out now."

The group was silent. Nobody budged.

"Okay then," the guide said. "Let's do it. Everyone has a floatation vest and wetsuit?"

His question was met with blank stares.

"We were told we didn't need wetsuits," I volunteered.

---

15 Rapids are classified in ascending order, from Class I to Class VI, according to the difficulty and risk inherent in running them. Class I indicates small waves and few or no obstacles in the water. Class IV and especially V are assigned to rapids that present dangerous obstacles such as boulders that require more skill and complicated maneuvering to navigate around safely. Class VI rapids are regarded as extremely dangerous and impossible to run, with a high probability of serious injury or death from attempting to do so.

The guides' jaws dropped in unison. A grim discussion ensued about the risks of whitewater rafting in winter conditions without wetsuits, but it was too late to requisition them now. Still, the trip would go on as planned, and everyone was left of his or her own accord whether or not to join it. Nobody bailed. Forms were handed out for everyone to sign, indemnifying the guides and Sierra Club from claims of loss of life or limb. That task finished, we all piled into a single large van, to the roof of which two deflated five-person paddle rafts and an oar boat were lashed, and drove off under brooding skies for Southeast Oregon.

If the decision to raft in snowy conditions was an abstraction in Portland, the full weight of its practical consequence came crashing down on us when we arrived many hours later at the "put in" outside Rome, a tiny outpost beside the Owyhee River and US Route 95 in Oregon's remote southeast corner. Another party's raft was parked at the boat launch. It was draped in a light blanket of snow and had small icicles hanging off it. The temperature was below freezing. A very light snow was falling.

As one of our guides inflated our three rafts, the other had us all gather in a circle for instruction on how to use paddles as a synchronized crew to steer a raft forward, backward, to the left and to the right. The captain sits at the rear of the raft, he explained, and shouts directional commands to the four paddlers in front of him while using his paddle as a rudder to help effect turns.

"If you fall out of your boat into the rapids, ride them on your back, feet pointing downriver," our guide advised. "Better to hit boulders in the river with your feet and legs than with your chest or head. Don't try to catch up to the boat. You will have no control, and the river will take you where it wants to go."

And with that sobering advice, we were off. One guide took command of the oar boat, laden with tents, sleeping bags, food and cooking and medical supplies. The rest of us crewed the two paddle rafts.

It was cold but everyone was dry—dressed in wool or synthetic shirts, wool hats and Gore-Tex jackets and pants—and the first stretch of river was on tame, flat water. The scenery was breathtaking. Sheer gray and brown cliffs dropped from flat-topped mesas on either side of the river, the slopes at their feet littered with piles of large slate-gray boulders down to the water's edge. Farther downriver, grand plateaus and domes topped fluted walls white, rose, beige and dark brown. Columnar basalt formations and deeply eroded volcanic spires and pillars periodically decorated the sagebrush-clad canyon, replaced intermittently by orange, red and beige peaks. But the most impressive scenery would come a few days into the trip, where the river gets squeezed between cliffs over 1,000 feet high into narrow, boulder-filled whitewater runs.

It was an adventurer's paradise—until the heavy snow showers began. Each squall didn't last more than a couple hours at a time, but that was long enough to cover everything—landscapes, rafts, supplies and people—in an inch or two of the white stuff before gradually melting off. A couple times each day, we'd pull our rafts over to a riverbank and do calisthenics in the snow for twenty minutes to keep hypothermia at bay. To prevent frostbite, we waved our arms while alternately kicking our legs, throwing blood circulation out to our fingertips and toes. Then it was back into the boats again, regularly running Class II and III rapids. We never saw other people, or wildlife; all sane creatures were sheltering from the storm.

After three days of running Class II and III rapids without incident in nearly constant sub-freezing temperatures, everyone had grown a bit more confident and somewhat acclimated to the brutal weather. No calamities had befallen us, and it seemed increasingly likely we were going to come through this wild and crazy adventure unscathed. In the late afternoon of our fourth day on the river, we all looked forward with nervous anticipation to the capstone of the trip: running the Class IV Montgomery Rapid.

The highest-class rapid on the lower Owyhee River, Montgomery was in a narrow section of the canyon hemmed in by sheer cliffs. The universal strategy employed by river rats running that stretch was to enter the rapids on the left to avoid scores of rocks, then pull right at the last moment to avoid a short waterfall dropping off between two large boulders. But rivers can change, especially with varying water levels. It's always good practice, we were told, to scout dangerous rapids by getting off the river above them and walking the bank to see what they actually look like, so you can plan your maneuvers through them.

That's what we did, and to us neophytes, chaotic and raucous Montgomery looked highly intimidating viewed from the east bank of the river. The waterfall between the two large boulders looked to be around four to six feet high. From our vantage point, it also appeared as if there might be a large submerged rock in the hole at the bottom of the fall, and a whirlpool immediately beyond. Just upstream from the fall were two big standing waves we would need to go over before pulling hard to the right to avoid hitting the boulders or, worse, going over the falls and possibly flipping.

"I wouldn't want to be the one to fall into *that*," I joked nervously, as we walked back to our rafts parked a couple hundred yards upriver.

I volunteered to captain a paddle raft through the whitewater. Piling into our raft, my boat mates and I pushed off from the riverbank and paddled nervously out to the far side of the river channel. Sitting on the boat's stern as we approached the white-capped rapids, I firmly shoved my feet under the rearmost thwart to anchor my body to the boat. Leaning back, I thrust my paddle into the water behind the raft's stern to steer us through the roiling rapids dead ahead. As we approached the crux, I worried the river's rapids would be too loud for my companions to hear my command to pull hard to the right just before the waterfall.

I never got my chance. As the raft launched over the first standing wave, the stern of the boat bucked violently upwards and threw me into the air like a cork popping out of a champagne bottle. When I came down, the raft was already three feet ahead of me in the rapids. I was stunned that I was in the river—it happened so quickly—and the water was so cold it initially felt hot, stinging my skin for a second before the cold shock against my chest and face knocked me breathless.

The river was so turbulent, I could not keep my head above water for more than a split second at a time to grab a breath of air as I was swept downstream. But that was not my main problem. I knew all too well what the river was swiftly carrying me toward—the waterfall with the submerged rock at its bottom. I panicked, forgot everything the river guides had instructed us to do, and began desperately trying to swim to the boat, in which my fellow paddlers were also now freaking out as they realized they were hurtling, rudderless, to the brink of the falls. After a few futile strokes, I realized I would not catch up to the boat. I tried to throw my feet ahead of me to brace for impact, but the river's current was too strong to correct my attitude. I was speeding toward the waterfall headfirst.

The second standing wave submerged me for a few seconds. When I came up for air, the paddle raft was already beyond the waterfall and lurching in disarray down the choppy river. A split second later, I plunged over the falls headfirst, with just enough lift to allow me to take a deep breath. It seemed like I was underwater forever at the bottom of the pour, the river spinning me violently around and head over heels like a massive washing machine off-kilter. When I finally popped up on the far side of the whirlpool, I was coughing up water and nearly completely spent.

Miraculously, I had not hit any rocks. But the ice-cold river's swift current had sucked so much heat out of my body, my limbs were totally numb and virtually useless. Tossed about in the rapids below the waterfall, it was all I could do to keep my head raised and out of the water. My boat mates—now beyond the rapids—furiously back-paddled in flat water until the current brought me to them. I could not lift my arms more than a couple inches to assist them as they reached into the water, grabbed me and hauled me up into the raft.

"Get him to the riverbank immediately!" one of the guides shouted loudly from the oar boat, his tone of voice betraying unabated concern. My life was still in the balance. I was soaking wet and shivering uncontrollably in sub-freezing temperature.

As soon as I was on the riverbank—a narrow slice of dirt between a rock wall and the water—one of the guides ran to my side.

"We need to get you out of your wet clothes fast, okay?" he asked for permission. I nodded and tried to unbutton my shirt, but my hands and arms were shaking so violently I could not grasp any buttons. The muscles in the back of my neck were in such terrible spasm, it felt like I'd had a rock surgically implanted there. A couple men quickly stripped me naked while others in the party brought over their extra clothes for me to wear. They dressed me in two of everything—shirts, jackets, pants and hats—while others followed the river guides' instructions to quickly set up gas stoves and begin heating water.

A tarp was spread out on the frozen ground, and I was laid on top of it in a body sandwich with three other men: me on top of one of the guides, and two other guys on my respective right and left, all hugging me to provide warmth. Sleeping bags and another tarp were placed on top of us. I drank two quarts of piping hot water while lying there. An hour and half after beginning these warming therapies, I was still shivering uncontrollably in the body sandwich and my temperature read only 94.6°F. God only knows how cold I got at the worst.

Around a half hour later, dusk was falling. I'd stopped shivering at that point, so we all tumbled into the rafts—I riding in the oar boat with one of the guides—and floated to a better place downriver to camp for the night. That evening in camp, someone brought me a celebratory glass of brandy.

"Watching you in those rapids was amazing," he said. "You didn't even look human. It was like watching a dog or a wild animal fight for survival."

I thanked him for the brandy and excused myself. Walking downriver along the west bank until I was alone, I stopped to stare at the rushing water lit softly by starlight. It was a supremely peaceful scene, and the brandy felt wonderfully warm in my belly.

"Two down, seven to go," I said aloud to myself, reflecting on my second of nine lives lost, following the first in Yelapa.

I felt incredibly alive, and incredibly thankful to be alive. I did not rue the river, or fear it. It had granted me safe passage swimming the Montgomery Rapid in winter. In some weird way, that made me feel closer to the river, in harmony with it.

I would have more whitewater adventures in the years to come, just none in winter; I liked the survival odds for summer rafting better. Most of my rafting trips would go without a major hitch. It wasn't until the summer of 1994, in the Grand Canyon, that things would go FUBAR again on the water. That trip would give the Owyhee a run for its money.

Michael Cooper (fourth from left) and other members
of the Owyhee River run do warming calisthenics to
keep hypothermia at bay (mid-March, 1985).

Michael Cooper "swimming" the Class IV
Montgomery Rapid on the Owyhee River

-7-

WHITAKER

About a week after I returned to the Illinois Valley from the Owyhee River run in 1985, I snowshoed with four acquaintances into the Sky Lakes Wilderness for an overnight camping trip on the west slope of Mount McLoughlin. This was in late March, and McLoughlin, the highest peak in Southern Oregon's share of the Cascade Range, often creates its own weather in early spring. In fact, storm clouds had already capped the mountain by the time my companions and I began setting up camp at 6,800 feet altitude in the fading light of dusk. The mountain air felt like cold steel in my lungs, portending imminent snow. But my three-season Moss tent had easily withstood winter squalls on the Owyhee, so I wasn't at all concerned.

It was a hassle setting up the tent. Over the preceding several months, the rainfly's nylon fabric had become increasingly tacky. Eventually the flysheet became stuck to itself so stubbornly that it became difficult to unfurl. Not realizing the progressive adhesion was due to a manufacturing defect in the fly's waterproofing treatment, I continued to use the tent without a second thought—Tent Mistake #1.

It was already starting to snow on our Mount McLoughlin camp by the time I had the tent body erected and the rainfly removed from its stuff sack. Grabbing the fly's fabric in both hands, I gave it a forceful yank to separate its sticky folds—creating, in a split second, a six-foot-long tear along the midline length of the fly. The sun was down, I was miles into wilderness, it was starting to snow and the rainfly was kaput.

Fortunately, I had packed a roll of ripstop-nylon tape in my improvised equipment-repair kit—just enough of it to seal the fly's breach along its entire length. The makeshift repair held against the storm, and I stayed warm and dry through the night.

Moss would make good on my tent's lifetime warranty. Because the tent had been recently discontinued, the company offered to send me a different model of equal value at no cost. The only qualifying model that met my needs, however, would not be in production until the next fall. Rather than shop elsewhere, I decided to wait for it—Tent Mistake #2.

Over the next several months, I did a few short backpacks in wilderness without a tent or any other shelter, in between forecast storms. In deference to the old saw that only fools and newcomers try to predict the weather in Oregon, I limited each trip's duration to three days max, kept a watchful eye to the sky for approaching storm clouds while I was out and never ventured farther than ten miles from the trailhead to allow relatively quick exit.

By mid-August I was determined to pull off a more protracted adventure, though I still had no tent. I proposed my younger brother Mitch and his wife Eileen—then living in Redmond, Washington—join me in backpacking the northern half of the Bailey Range Traverse, a fabled cross-country route in the state's Olympic National Park. Mitch's tent was only big enough to accommodate him and Eileen, but a friend of theirs kindly offered to loan me a tent for the trip. Olympic National Park is infamous for the prodigious amount of precipitation it receives—about 150 inches annually—so I pressed Mitch to inquire about the unseen tent's defenses against the elements. His friend told Mitch it had not leaked during a previous car-camping trip that saw light rain showers. I was jonesing so much to backpack the Bailey Range, I was willing to accept even this mildest assurance—Tent Mistake #3.

After a long drive north from my home in Southern Oregon on August 24, my thirty-second birthday, I arrived at Mitch and Eileen's house in Washington and eyed the loaner tent for the first time—with alarm. Bargain-store issue, it looked one step up from a playhouse for little kids. To think this would be my shelter on a weeklong, fifty-five-mile trek through storm-prone wilderness—including off-trail in the high-elevation Bailey Range—was unsettling. But the die was cast. I couldn't bear to pass up hiking the Bailey Range, not at the very last moment.

Over the next couple days, Mitch, Eileen and I backpacked by trail through breathtakingly beautiful ancient forest along the Soleduck River and up to a subalpine basin cradling tiny Heart Lake. The following morning, we hiked slack-jawed along the top of the spectacular High Divide, a dizzying canyon rim that looks 4,000 vertical feet down into the forested Hoh River Valley and, across the valley, 7,000 feet back up to the summit of glacier-blanketed Mount Olympus. The divide took us four miles east to the far side of Cat Peak, where the trail came abruptly to a dead end.

Before us lay the sprawling Bailey Range, a series of magnificent high-elevation peaks arcing south through trail-less wilderness. There was just one problem: to get onto the range's open subalpine slopes from where we stood, we first had to cross the notorious Catwalk.

Only about a third of a mile long, the Catwalk is a fearsome rib of rock that makes up for what it lacks in length with its sphincter-puckering vertical drop-offs—"exposure," in mountaineering argot—along its narrow, jagged ridgeline. A fall from the Catwalk would at the very least result in crippling, life-threatening injury, in a place difficult for a rescue team to access. Crossing it wearing a heavy and tippy backpack steepened both the physical and mental challenge. Still, from where we stood it looked like there were plenty of hand and foot holds, and some small trees to hang onto, across the intimidating span.

Eileen wasn't buying any of it. A year earlier, she had held her own as she and I crossed the Emmons Glacier—the largest glacier in the continental United States—without ice axes or crampons, during a nine-day backpack halfway around Mount Rainier. But the Catwalk's exposure had her spooked. She would not consider stepping foot on it.

The alternative was to turn back and hike manicured paint-by-number trails for the next five days, but I knew the lost opportunity to traverse the legendary Bailey Range—the planned cross-country climax of the trip—would eat at me the entire time. After much handwringing it was decided, with Mitch and Eileen's blessing, I would tackle the Bailey Range alone and they would backpack out. We said our regretful goodbyes, and I left their company to confront the Catwalk.

Happily, the Catwalk turned out to be a cakewalk, much easier than it looked from a distance. The main challenge was mental, staying calm and centered as I methodically worked my way across, focused like a laser on my center of gravity. Once I'd made it to the other side of the span, I looked back and decided I liked it. The popular trail to Heart Lake had been relatively crowded. The Catwalk, I knew, would thin the crowd dramatically, maybe to zero. In fact, there were no footprints at my feet now beside my own. Scanning the open slopes of the Bailey Range for miles ahead of me, I could see no one. I felt that odd synchronicity of quiet calm for being totally alone and buzzing excitement for the adventure ahead.

The backpack that day was sublime, like walking along the top of the world; the Bailey Range rises almost 5,000 vertical feet above the Hoh River Valley in only a mile and a half of slope. Most of my traverse of the range was through open subalpine wildflower meadows, punctuated only occasionally by a cluster of trees. The continuously unobstructed "airplane" views down to the river valley and across to glaciated Mount Olympus, and south at grade along the pristine mountain range, were stupendous and the route-finding straightforward, allowing me to take in the staggering scenery in a meditative reverie undistracted by technical calculation. My heart sang as I hiked for hours alone in nature's finest art gallery. This was the simple and real world, free from all of narrow-minded civilization's brainwashing lifestyle prescriptions and shackling career obligations—what I dismissively referred to with friends as the Mind Belt.

After several miles of blissful travel, I rounded a steeply inclined spur to see a theretofore hidden basin nestled in a clockwise bend in the mountain range. Fourteen hundred vertical feet below me in the basin lay tiny Cream Lake, where I hoped to camp for the night. But the 0.8-mile straight-line descent was frightfully steep, more like a mountaineering pitch than a backpacking route. I dropped about 400 feet while angling east over to a small bulge in the slope. There the gradient briefly moderated, and I dropped my pack on stable ground to reconnoiter the last 1,000-foot pitch down to the lake.

The precipitous slope below me had widely spaced trees clinging to it, but the duff underneath had been baked by its nearly vertical southern exposure to the sun into a hard crust on which it would be difficult to maintain traction. A slip here, I knew, would not result in just bruises and scrapes, but likely broken ribs or a sprained back, as the steep incline would propel me ass-over-teakettle several hundred feet down the mountainside before inertia—or, abruptly, a tree trunk—halted my fall. I spent the next hour traversing back and forth along the slope with my pack off, peering nervously below and assessing my options. None of it looked good—all of it much worse than the Catwalk—but where I had parked my backpack appeared to be the least bad place from which to descend. I donned my pack.

"God," I prayed aloud, "give me a sign if I should not go down this now."

No sooner had the last word escaped my lips than I heard a voice call out from far above me.

"Hello-o-o-o," the voice sounded in a long, descending glissando, and then, "Do you know the best way down?"

Looking up and to my right, I saw a man standing a couple hundred feet above me.

"Looks best from here," I yelled up to him, "but it's iffy. Come down to me, and we'll do it together."

That's how I met Bruce Schumm, a backpacker on vacation from Chicago. A bespectacled, sturdy-looking fellow five years younger than I, he sported a trimmed beard and moustache. He had a quiet yet confident persona, and I liked him immediately. Anyone who was traversing the Bailey Range alone, I thought to myself, has to be a quality person. After making our succinct introductions, I assured him I had "recced" the slope for a full hour and was confident in my conclusion the risky pitch below us was nevertheless our best way down.

Without further ado, we began our 1,000-foot descent—more like a barely controlled, braking slide—grabbing onto tree branches to arrest our skate down the mountainside, letting go at each branch's full extension, glissading in a sideways stoop down to the next tree branch, and repeating until we arrived safely at the bottom of the slope and the north shore of Cream Lake.

We had entered the Bailey Range's protective womb. Placid Cream Lake was surrounded on all sides by shady Douglas fir trees and flat, soft ground. Relaxed now, we leisurely set up our tents relatively close together at the edge of a small grassy clearing. But as we cooked our respective dinners, dark clouds quickly began to gather, crowding the sky above us and blotting out the sun. The weather turned surprisingly quickly, and by dusk a quickly accelerating rain chased us into our respective tents as the temperature plummeted.

Immediately, and to my dismay, I noted every seam in my borrowed dome tent was leaking badly, raindrops falling in quick succession from virtually every stitch in the ceiling and water seeping inside along the floor's periphery. I bolted out of the tent, yanked the waterproof groundsheet quickly out from under it and threw the sheet over the top of the tent.

My expletive-laced rustlings roused Bruce from his shelter. He helped me loosely tie the groundsheet's grommets to my planted tent stakes with parachute cord to keep it from flying away in the stiff wind. The kludge provided incomplete coverage but enough to reduce the amount of water coming into the tent that, along with regularly mopping up the floor with a shirt, everything was kept reasonably dry inside. It rained heavily throughout the night.

The next morning was unusually cold, like autumn. We took advantage of parting clouds and a temporary letup in the rain to assess our escape route to the southeast out of the storm-tossed basin. Nearly 2,000 vertical feet above us, an alpine mountain pass would be our ticket out of the Bailey Range to the safety of the lower-elevation Elwha River beyond, but its rocky approach now looked blanketed in fresh snow. The view lasted less than a minute before clouds slammed it shut and heavy rains returned with a vengeance.

"We can't go over that fucking pass until the weather lets up," I said to Bruce. "It's winter up there. Likely white-out conditions."

"Let's get out of this fucking rain," Bruce replied.

We retreated to my leaking tent—his was too small to fit two people—for conversation out of the downpour. Once inside, idle talk quickly focused on my bogus shelter's wet floor.

"This tent is completely fucked up," I said.

Bruce laughed. We noted with amusement how male backpackers' vocabularies quickly devolve into continuous obscenities, in good and bad circumstance alike, as soon as the trailhead is left behind. Beautiful scenery, we observed, is succinctly described as "fucking awesome," frigid weather complained about as "fucking cold," and exhaustion prompts "I'm fuckin' beat to shit" or similar.

Bruce shared with me some "fucking tasty" Almond Joy candy bars. Each wrapper for the candy cheerfully promised in bold font "With Real Almonds!" We wondered aloud what fake almonds would look and taste like. I suggested the candy maker should offer a limited production run of Almond Joy for male backpackers, with the sales pitch "With Real Fucking Almonds!" blazoned across the wrappers. Such boosterish catering, Bruce enthusiastically agreed, would surely increase sales among the testosterone-marinated outdoors crowd. This is how guys pass the time while stuck in a tent during a storm.

Bruce had a great sense of humor. A brilliant grad student in theoretical particle physics, he could've been an English professor. His deep vocabulary and quick wit often prompted him to spontaneously engage in hilarious wordplay and comically inane observations of the mundane, all dryly delivered with a poker face as if proposing some serious thesis. English had been my best subject, and my irreverent rejoinders would elicit in Bruce sputtering laughter: short and quiet monotone exhalations, as if to avoid waking somebody sleeping nearby. We hit it off like lifelong friends.

The unrelenting storm kept us hunkered down at Cream Lake all of that day and through the night. When the clouds finally lifted the following morning, we quickly gobbled a granola breakfast while simultaneously breaking camp, our eyes frequently scanning the upper basin and our route out of the Bailey Range.

The fresh snow in the upper basin would be melted by the time we got up there, but it was still a starkly different world from Cream Lake.

As we climbed, blond meadows and stunted trees gave way to permanent snowfields, scree- and talus-littered slopes, and frozen lakes at the base of remnant glaciers dressing otherwise completely barren peaks. We crossed over Mount Ferry's frigid south shoulder and then hiked around three more miles along a narrow and precipitous ridge. Clawing our way over and around half a dozen small peaks, we finally came to a faint trail on the east side of Peak 5154 ("Fifty-One Fifty-Four")—unnamed peaks are referred to by backcountry travelers by the altitude at their summits—which we took north for another third of a mile. We made camp in the late afternoon at a top-of-the-world spot commanding a grand view of the east side of the Bailey Range.

Our cross-country adventure was over—critically for Bruce, who had a wounded finger that had become badly infected. The next day, we dropped 3,000 vertical feet by trail down a steep, forested slope and crossed the Semple Plateau to ford the unbridged Elwha River. Mitch and Eileen would meet us the following day in the parking lot at the end of the Elwha River Trail and drive Bruce to an urgent-care facility.

I had found a new adventure buddy in Bruce. We exchanged phone numbers and promised we'd stay in touch. Bruce told me I would know when it was he calling, because his first utterance would simply be "Whitaker." There was no logic to it, but it quickly became our mutual salutations. I was now Whitaker. He was Whitaker. It was never confusing except to any third party.

Through the following winter, I pored over dozens of topo maps to decide on my next cross-country adventure—this time with a new stormproof Moss tent instead of a kiddie playhouse. I quickly became fascinated with an alpine area in the northern section of Kings Canyon National Park: the Ionian Basin. Completely above timberline, uncrossed by trails and home to dozens of lakes surrounded by 13,000-foot peaks, Ionian Basin was the most remote area in all of the Sierra Nevada mountain range. I was drawn to it like iron to a magnet.

I shared my excitement with Whitaker. Studying the relevant topo maps together over the phone, we slowly devised an ambitious eighty-mile back-pack trip that would take us twelve days to pull off. The summertime trip would include around twenty-six miles of cross-country navigation above 10,400 feet altitude. Except for a few hours of requisite hiking through interconnecting terrain, we would spend seven consecutive days above timberline. The likely highlight of the trip would be a climb of 12,975-foot Scylla, a vertiginous peak at the south end of the Ionian Basin.

It had taken me several years, during which I had made and learned from my share of mistakes, but by 1986 I had become an able navigator. And despite his relative newness to cross-country navigation—the Bailey Range Traverse had been his first off-trail backpack—Whitaker was a remarkably insightful topo-map reader. Together we painstakingly fine-tuned the itinerary for the trip. Wrapping up weeks of exhaustive planning, Whitaker dryly declared, "We don't need to do the backpack anymore. We already know what it's going to look like from the maps."

We would bring ice axes and crampons. A thirteen-day backpack through the John Muir Wilderness and adjacent Kings Canyon National Park I'd done three years earlier, in August 1983, had firmly impressed on me that necessity. That trip, with my Madre Grande buddy Tony Morel, had culminated in a hair-raising cross-country traverse of the north side of Finger Peak, an impressive 12,400-foot mount perched on the aptly named White Divide.

During that trip, storm clouds spawned by a hurricane off the coast of Baja California had chased Tony and me as we climbed out of Blue Basin up to a windswept col above timberline between Finger Peak and Peak 11587 ("Eleven Five-Eighty-Seven") a half mile to the east. Scanning the north slope of Finger Peak on the brink of the fast-approaching storm, we were overawed. The nearly mile-long route was buried underneath a massive snowfield forbiddingly inclined at about a thirty-degree angle, its frozen run abruptly terminating 900 feet downslope at the lip of a cliff that plunged another 300 vertical feet to the floor of an alpine basin. A slip on the ice-crusted traverse, we feared, could send us quickly skating down the snowfield and over the edge of the cliff. We had not brought ice axes or crampons.

A rational person would've canned the traverse of Finger Peak and retreated down to Blue Basin, especially considering the imminent storm. But the col where we stood was littered with sharp rocks, and we decided to use them as substitutes for ice axes. Grabbing a carefully chosen triangular rock in each hand, we ventured out onto the icy snowfield in the shadow of Finger Peak's sheer north face. Kicking footholds with our booted toes and heels on each and every step forward, our progress was painfully slow and exhausting. The couple times we slipped and fell—as was inevitable—we halted our slide by immediately stabbing our "rock axes" into the glassy snow. We were halfway across the traverse when dark clouds poured over the divide and enveloped us. It began to rain.

Despite our strenuous exercise, we were already very cold when the frigid storm descended on us; we were both sweating profusely from our exertion and drenched inside our rain gear. Now we were inside a rain cloud to boot, in nearly whiteout conditions. Caught in the middle of an exposed and unstable traverse, the ambient temperature plunging close to freezing, there was no way to get out of the elements.

The rain was especially dangerous for Tony, who had discovered during a weaker storm at the very start of our trip that his Gore-Tex rain gear was shot and leaking badly at the seams. As a stopgap, he had fashioned a new rain jacket out of a thirty-three-gallon plastic garbage bag, inverting the bag and cutting holes in it for his arms and head to poke through. In lieu of a hood, he wore a gallon ziplock bag on his head, upside-down. I had taken a hilarious photo of Tony modeling "GarbageWear" in a forested camp several days earlier, but now his attire was no laughing matter. His sorely inadequate clothing had become a deadly serious liability on the stormy north slope of Finger Peak.

The ice-cold rain turned to stinging hail as we finally approached the base of a sheer cliff wall at the far end of the traverse. Climbing up and over a partial break in the cliff face, we were both on the verge of shivering, our limbs and faces numb with cold. Dropping from the crest of the White Divide, alternating snow and boulder fields took us over the next hour and a half 700 vertical feet down to the north shore of Cathedral Lake, where we hastily set up our tent and stumbled inside to warm up in our sleeping bags.

Three years later, the harrowing Finger Peak traverse was foremost in mind while planning provisions for the Ionian Basin trip, and ice axes and crampons assumed prime positions in the packing list. On the morning of August 17, 1986, Whitaker and I drove to a trailhead at Florence Lake in the Sierra. As we donned our backpacks in the trailhead parking lot, I thought about the touch-and-go traverse of Finger Peak and noted Ionian Basin's reminiscent terrain.

"This is a trip we're gonna remember for the rest of our lives," I enthused, then wisecracked, "However short that might be." And with that, we stepped into the John Muir Wilderness, eastbound for Kings Canyon National Park.

It was great to be out in wilderness again, especially with an able and fun partner like Whitaker. We hiked around twenty-one miles by trail over the first few days, east along the broad and rapidly flowing South Fork San Joaquin River, crossing into the national park, and then south up the slotted and sparsely forested Goddard Canyon. Far up the canyon, the trail petered out at roughly 10,400 feet altitude and our cross-country travel began. Another mile of hiking left the trees behind and took us up to boulder-rimmed Martha Lake at 11,000 feet, where we camped in the shadow of the magnificent granite domes and pyramidal peaks of the LeConte Divide. Five days of backpacking continuously above timberline lay ahead.

The next morning, we hiked over a snowbound saddle at 12,400 feet altitude on the south side of Mount Goddard to enter the stunning Ionian Basin. We were now far into a land of rock, snow and ice dotted with deep blue and aquamarine lakes, many still half-frozen. Trees were nowhere in sight, not even in the far distance.

From our camp that afternoon beside twin lakes, the land plummeted just a few stone throws to the south into the trail-less Goddard Canyon. I noted with delight Finger Peak, little more than two miles away as the crow flies, peeking above the tiny icebergs floating in the lakes, evoking memories of my and Tony Morel's roll of the dice three years earlier. That night in the Ionian Basin, I suffered terrible altitude sickness: a jackhammer-pounding headache and stomach-churning nausea.

Luckily, by morning I had acclimated to the thin atmosphere and was feeling better. Whitaker and I took a layover and made a surprisingly easy climb to the summit of Scylla. The view from the slanted summit was jaw-dropping, surrounded as it was by over 100 square miles of trail-less, high-elevation terrain.

The route we subsequently took from camp across the Ionian Basin was snowy enough for long stretches—and the oxygen-starved air between 11,000- and 12,000-feet altitude so energy-sapping—that we could only manage to hike about a half mile per hour, or four miles in an eight-hour day. But I'd be lying if I said it was just the snow, thin air and required navigation that slowed us down.

While packing for the trip at a friend's apartment in the Bay Area six days earlier, Whitaker and I had let discipline and weeks of planning take wing, insouciantly throwing extra candy bars and additional bags of nuts and trail mix into our packs. At the end of our twelve-day backpack, we would walk out of the wilderness with an astounding twenty pounds of leftover food—enough candy bars and peanuts to start a concession stand in the Ionian Basin.

Nevertheless, the trip through the fabulous basin went like clockwork, and it was over way too soon when we crossed over the saddle just west of 13,300-foot Black Giant to camp beside a lake half a mile from the John Muir Trail. The next day, my thirty-third birthday, we took the trail west over the 12,000-foot John Muir Pass and through granitic Evolution Basin.

At the west end of the basin, we left the trail and climbed 400 vertical feet up to the Darwin Bench. Situated at timberline, the bench was populated by stunted trees and granite boulders, none too high to obscure the views in any direction across its span. As Whitaker and I dropped our backpacks to set up camp, we spied a couple of hikers coming toward us from across the bench.

"Looks like we won't have the place to ourselves," I lamented, as I turned my attention to emptying my pack.

Seconds later, I looked up to determine how close to us our visitors would encroach, but they were inexplicably gone—nowhere to be seen, in relatively open terrain. It was as if some invisible force, guarding against intrusion to the place, had spontaneously vaporized them.

"What happened to those hikers?" I asked Whitaker, incredulous. "They were there just an instant ago."

"It's really strange," Whitaker acknowledged, scanning the area. "What can explain it?"

"It's the Curse of the Darwin Bench!" I erupted melodramatically, mimicking the menacing voice-over for a horror-movie trailer and bending the pitch of the word "Curse" sharply upward for sensational effect.

Whitaker cracked up. Maybe it was the ridiculous notion that the beautiful place was cursed, or my pretense's over-the-top delivery. Whatever, that moment sparked the genesis of a playfully absurd and enduring myth, attributing to an imaginary hex the cause of all unexplained phenomena, accidents, equipment malfunctions and even minor misfortune suffered by us in wilderness. The Curse—upper-case letter "C" designated in deference to its alpha dominance—would be henceforth identified by name before the start of each of my backcountry trips as a first step toward avoiding contact with the malevolent spirit behind it, lest we trigger bad luck in wild country. There was a different Curse in each wilderness, collectively a hydra to steer clear of at all costs.

To that end, there were cockamamie ground rules and layers of farcical theories added to the mythology during successive wilderness trips. Rule #1: the Curse is presumed inextricably linked with a geographical place which, to be eligible, must have its name printed on a topo map for the area we were exploring; the Curse took on that place's name, and the more ridiculously antithetical the association was, the stronger the threat. Particularly evil Curses threatening my well-being in backcountry would include the Curse of Puppy Lake and the Curse of the White Branch Youth Camp.

Rule #2 maintained the closer you hike to a Curse's home base—its USGS-named place—the stronger its destructive power and malevolence grows, urging greater caution against violating Rule #3: Never Tempt or Taunt the Curse. Examples of taunting the Curse would include saying things like "That mountain pass doesn't look that difficult" or "It looks like we'll have great weather today." Such remarks would all but guarantee the opposite outcome and draw instant rebuke from your comrades if you uttered them anywhere near the Curse—even within the same zip code.

On trips where the Curse was especially strong, as evidenced by multiple misfortunes befalling us in the wilds, we would promise to say nothing that might be construed as taunting the Curse until we had at least exited wilderness and crossed over state lines, whether by car or airplane—simply being in the air inside state boundaries did not give the all-clear. Some Curses were that tenacious.

Luckily, the Curse of the Darwin Bench would (temporarily) relent after disappearing the two hikers who had nearly trespassed our camp. The following day, Whitaker and I hiked cross-country without incident up alpine Darwin Canyon to Lamarck Col on the craggy Glacier Divide. From the col's dizzying 12,975-foot vantage, Owens Valley lay sprawled in the distance nearly 9,000 vertical feet below us, the suitably named White Mountains in Nevada looming on the horizon beyond. Descending 1,300 feet in altitude from the cirque's crest and back into the John Muir Wilderness, we backpacked through lush alpine meadows dotted with glacial erratic blocks before making camp on a sandy ridge 700 vertical feet above Upper Lamarck Lake.

The next morning, we dropped another 1,000 vertical feet down to Lower Lamarck Lake, racing against a fast approaching thunderstorm. From the lake, we hiked earnestly cross-country up into the Wonder Lakes Basin and toward an exposed 12,000-foot pass we urgently needed to cross over before the electrical storm struck. Weighted down by the ridiculous amount of food we still had remaining in our packs, the 2,300-foot climb took us a few hours—too long. We were still a quarter mile shy of and 200 feet below the rocky alpine pass when the thunderstorm overtook us and hit with a vengeance.

The angry skies erupted directly overhead with deafening detonations of thunder and dazzling flashes of coincident lightning. The rubbly, open terrain offered nothing but low-lying granite boulders for protection. We were completely exposed to the storm—walking lighting rods. Quickly ditching our packs—mine had an external, electricity-conducting metal frame—we threw on our rain gear and ran for the tallest boulders we could find as scattered drops of rain accelerated into a cloudburst in less than a minute. Squatting between two waist-high boulders with my head ducked in the torrential downpour, I tried to keep my feet out of a stream of water that was suddenly flowing downhill between my spread legs.

"This is fucking intense!" Whitaker shouted from a crouched position nearby, as howitzers boomed overhead and black clouds unleashed their electrical fury.

"It's the Curse of the Darwin Bench!" I shouted back in full-on horror-movie voice.

Fifteen minutes later the storm quickly petered out. We weren't out of danger, however, as there was another cell approaching.

"Let's get over the fucking pass and down below timberline before the next storm hits," I urged. Whitaker nodded.

Luckily, the weather held off as we scrambled up to and over the pass and dropped 1,200 vertical feet down the other side of the divide, where we joined the Piute Pass Trail. Storm clouds continued to chase us as we raced over yet another 11,400-foot pass and down across treeless Humphreys Basin. By the time the next storm cell hit us, we'd made it safely into the forested upper reaches of Piute Canyon.

Rejoining the South Fork San Joaquin River late the next day, I stopped to nostalgically gaze south up toward the high country and Goddard Canyon. The Ionian Basin trek had gone swimmingly overall, with just a couple hiccups, the best you could hope for on a twelve-day odyssey including extensive cross-country travel. I reflected with satisfaction on the successful trip and was already looking forward to a solo backpack in Northern California's remote Siskiyou Wilderness, planned for the following week.

I should've quit while I was ahead.

-8-

BAD BETA FOR
THE SISKIYOUS

Despite my growing passion for cross-country backpacking since my baptism in navigation in Anza-Borrego in 1981, trail hiking still held an allure for me five years on. Backpacking off-trail was an exciting adventure, hiking on trails more a tranquil meditation, and I enjoyed both. But also, many beautiful places below timberline in the Pacific Northwest and California were difficult to access except by trail. Nearly a century of wildfire suppression by the US National Forest Service had led to a fivefold increase in historical forest density, and unrelenting bushwhacking cross-country through leg-scratching brush and face-smacking tree branches held little appeal after my first few attempts. If I wanted to visit scenic areas tucked away in dense woodlands, or climb quickly up to alpine areas where the going cross-country was unfettered, hiking by trail was the best—sometimes the only feasible—way to do it.

But many trails were rarely maintained—some so long ago, they now existed on old maps only, having been reclaimed by nature in the many years since a shovel last touched them. Knowing this, I called a ranger station in Cave Junction in the summer of 1986 to inquire about trail conditions in the remote southern portion of the 153,000-acre Siskiyou Wilderness, where I hoped to do a three-day solo backpack trip.

"You'll have a great time," the man answering the telephone cheerily assured me. "The trails are in excellent shape."

Unfortunately, I failed to ask him when was the last time—if ever—he'd hiked the trails in question. I would learn, the hard way, that relying on an unvetted source for so-called *beta*—firsthand info on backcountry conditions—could prove a serious mistake.

The area in the Siskiyou Wilderness I wanted to explore straddled Northern California's remote Klamath and Six Rivers National Forests around twenty-five miles south of the Oregon state line. According to my topo maps, two trails in the area ran in succession along high mountain ridges before the latter of the two dropped over 4,000 vertical feet down to a trailhead on the South Fork Smith River. In order to hike the trails end to end without retracing my steps, I'd have to arrange a shuttle between their trailheads. My then music-business partner Lu Judd generously volunteered to help.

On the morning of September 4, I turned my 1968 Chevy Impala off rural US Route 199 and drove twenty miles up a gravel Forest Service road to the riverside trailhead for the South Kelsey National Recreation Trail. The planned endpoint for my backpack trip, I left my vehicle there to retrieve three days later. Lu then drove me, I riding on the back of his motorcycle with my backpack, another ten miles on logging roads higher up into the Siskiyou Mountains to the ridge-top trailhead for the Boundary Trail, the starting point for my route. There were no tire tracks in the duff at the dirt trailhead save for those made by Lu's motorcycle; nobody had evidently been in this country for a very long time.

I would need to hike thirty-two miles over the following three days to get back to my car. As Lu sped away on his motorcycle, I threw on my backpack and stepped out onto the ridgeline Boundary Trail. Just as I'd been assured by the person manning the phone at the ranger station in Cave Junction, the trail was in excellent condition, with good tread and easy to follow. The blue sky was pin-clear, not a cloud in sight. The scenery along the ridge top, straddling two major watersheds, was gorgeous: as I blissfully hiked, the view to my left was of unspoiled canyons plunging nearly 4,000 feet in altitude to the South Fork Smith River and, to my right, 2,000 feet down to Blue Creek, a major tributary of the Klamath River. I saw no footprints besides my own.

The air was dead still and mute, and by noon the sun felt unusually hot considering my relatively high altitude. In what would turn out to be the second-hottest heat wave of 1986, the tiny thermometer clipped to my backpack read 90°F as I traversed a steep slope north through thick forest. The grade flattened as the trail took me onto a narrow bench cut into the precipitous mountainside. Hiking through a short S-curve along the wooded path, I came suddenly to the edge of a small meadow. A black bear was in the clearing, about twenty-five yards away from me. I must've been downwind from him, because he didn't notice me.

Shelved by the steep mountainside climbing sharply on my right and plunging into a deep canyon on my left, the only level way forward was through the meadow on the bench. Someone—the bear or I—had to surrender the right of way. I'd previously encountered black bears a few times in wilderness, and they had always fled as soon as they noticed me if given enough space. Surely this bear would follow suit, I thought, if I retreated a bit and then gave it advance warning of my approach so as not to spark a confrontation.

I quietly backed up through the S-curve in the trail, gingerly removed my backpack and softly retreated an additional thirty yards. Slowly walking back toward my pack, I shouted in as deep a voice as I could muster, "Hey-yo! Hey-yo, black bear! I'm coming! By the time I get there, you'll be gone! Hey-yo, black bear. Hey-yo!"

Rounding the S-curve, still shouting, I fully expected to see the bear had left. Instead, it had advanced several yards in my direction and was hunched forward like a loaded spring, ready to pounce, its menacing eyes staring intently at mine. My heart leapt into my throat, my sphincter involuntarily dilated and I nearly soiled myself. This bear was not thinking of fleeing. It was thinking of having me for lunch.

I slowly backed away into the S-curve until trees hid me from the bear's line of sight, and then ran in a panic to my backpack. Knowing that bears crave sugars and fat, I grabbed a large bag of gorp and quickly scattered the contents on the ground. My heart racing, I threw on my pack and made a mad dash off the trail and down the steepest part of the mountainside I could find, hoping the bear would take the easy meal (the gorp) and not chase after the difficult one (me).

I dropped several hundred feet in minutes, ignoring the branches lashing at my face and torso. Still afraid I was being hunted, I made a frantic lopsided traverse across the steep slope. When I felt certain I had pushed far enough north to bypass the meadow above me, I climbed quickly back up to the trail and hightailed on it for another five minutes before collapsing in a trembling heap, drenched in sweat, dehydrated and completely out of gas.

I was shaken but unscathed save for a few cuts and bruises. Over the next ten minutes, I drank a quart of water and gobbled up nearly a half-pound of gorp to recover my strength. I pushed north on the trail for another hour, eager to put as much distance as possible between the scary bear and me. I camped that night near a spring, hoping for no further drama.

I continued north on the Boundary Trail the next morning, but now the path was becoming increasingly obscure. Very quickly it became completely overgrown and impossible to find. I figured this was just an isolated stretch of trail that had been reclaimed by nature, and I would locate it again if I pressed on, navigating by map and compass; after all, the person at the ranger station in Cave Junction had assured me the trail was in great condition.

In fact, I soon stumbled again onto the trail. My faith restored, I followed it for fifty yards before it disappeared again into a jungle of undergrowth and closely spaced trees. I would not find it again for another mile. The same lost-and-found repeated itself several times over the next few hours, sending me on a rollercoaster ride of hope and despair.

At this point I would've normally aborted the route. But my car was parked a day and half's journey ahead, not behind me. Retracing my steps back to where Lu had dropped me at the Boundary trailhead was not a good option; I'd have to face the bear again, I'd run out of food and water by the time I reached the trailhead, and the logging roads I'd have to hike back to my car ran along the tops of high and dry ridges for ten more miles with no access to water. I had little choice but to push onward and hope trail conditions would improve.

In fact, they got worse. Where the trail disappeared once again, the way forward was clogged with the densest and highest thicket yet of tanoak and madrone trees, blocking my views out to landmarks and thwarting navigation. Every hour or so, I climbed a tree and shot one-handed field bearings on distant peaks to verify I was still on course and not heading off on some interlocking side ridge into no man's land. The temperature rose to 90°F for a second day, and I couldn't find water. I was getting dehydrated and exhausted while making less than a mile per hour along the vegetation-choked ridges.

The thickets were horrible, but not the worst taken by themselves. The most cruel and disheartening obstacles in my way were the voids wrought by two unmapped landslides—thirty-foot-high sheer drop-offs where the mountainside had previously avalanched and taken out over a half mile of rock and trees downslope, creating pitched chasms each a quarter mile wide. With no way across the two slides, my only recourse was to battle cross-country steeply up and around, soul-crushing detours through tangled thickets that would each take me about an hour in the sweltering heat. I swore if I made it out of this wilderness alive, I would kill the person who told me the Boundary Trail was "in excellent shape."

After twelve hours of incessant struggle, I finally arrived battered and bloodied at Harrington Lake. At last I had water. I slaked my thirst, refilled my water bottles and joined the South Kelsey National Recreation Trail—what at first blush seemed to be a reasonably preserved path back to my car. My biggest problem now was I was almost out of snacks, having donated most of my gorp to Mister Scary Bear the preceding day. Worried I would run completely out of food before getting out of the wilderness, I humped another couple miles west to the top of aptly named Baldy Peak. Pitching my tent on the bare summit as night fell, I crawled inside thoroughly exhausted but with hope renewed. Then came the lightning.

I had almost fallen asleep when I heard the first peal of thunder. I was so utterly wasted, I held off moving the tent off the exposed summit until it became apparent I must, at which point the lightning was almost directly overhead and the rain falling in sheets. Stumbling out of the tent in my rain gear, I dragged the freestanding shelter thirty yards off the mountain's exposed summit, down its steep east slope into thin tree cover, and crawled back inside. The tent, pitched at roughly a 45-degree angle in an unrelenting downpour, held against the violent storm through the night. But with scores of lightning strikes occurring every hour, I didn't sleep a wink.

The next morning dawned bright and sunny. Thoroughly drained, I girded myself to tackle the 4,400-foot descent, in six miles, down to the South Fork Smith River. From the bottom, I would have to backpack eight more miles along the river to get to my car—a fourteen-mile day in total.

In my depleted condition, the hike down from Baldy Peak was brutal but I made it to the river by noon. Now at least I had a dependable water source. But my troubles were not over. Hiking downstream, the trail soon came to an abrupt end. The river had previously flash-flooded and taken out the south bank, completely obliterating the trail. A dense thicket of eight-foot-high poison oak shrubs stood in my way along the newly formed bank and up the encroaching canyon wall.

As anyone who has tangled with the nasty plant in this part of the US knows, this was not your ordinary poison oak blocking my way. Extremely virulent, the last time I had a minor brush with it in the Siskiyous, the resulting itchy rash spread over virtually my entire body and tormented me for a month, defying every conventional remedy. (The eventual cure, a traditional Indigenous-Mexican treatment of last resort, was pouring my first catch of urine on the rash each morning for a few days.) I was not about to go thrashing through the stuff.

I could see the trail resumed again along the riverbank about thirty yards downstream. The river's receded edge looked boggy getting to there, but I was past the point of caring if my boots got wet. Leaping off the three-foot-high embankment into the bog, I didn't realize until it was too late that I was jumping into quicksand. Within thirty seconds, I had sunk in the cement-like mix nearly up to my hips.

It took me a few minutes to pull myself out of the mire. Free at last, I slogged across the rest of the bog—which was much firmer—to where the trail reappeared along the bank. After rinsing my boots and socks in the river, I resumed hiking.

Now at low altitude, it was stifling hot with the temperature soaring into the upper 90s. I had a splitting headache and was very weak and nauseous—suffering from apparent heat exhaustion—and drinking no amount of water would bring me around. Late that afternoon, I literally crawled 250 feet up to my car parked at the South Kelsey trailhead. I don't remember the drive home.

That evening, Lu came to my home, a rented manufactured house on the outskirts of Cave Junction, expecting to hear all the usually glowing details about my wonderful wilderness adventure. He found me lying in a bathtub filled with cool water, barely able to speak and keep my eyes open. His reaction summed up the situation concisely.

"You normally come back from these trips looking like a god," he said. "You came back from this one looking like a whipped dog."

The next morning, I called the ranger station in Cave Junction to offer an update on current conditions for the Boundary and South Kelsey National Recreation trails, so the staff could forewarn other backpackers considering hiking the route. Hearing where I had gone, the ranger I talked with sounded surprised and impressed.

"You hiked the Boundary Trail?" he asked. "That trail hasn't been maintained in very many years."

"Tell that to your workmates," I admonished. I told him about Mister Scary Bear.

"He was probably a 'problem bear' relocated from a popular camping area where he was causing trouble," the ranger surmised. "We move dangerous bears to remote areas where they're not likely to encounter people."

That was the last time I backpacked the Siskiyou Wilderness, but not because I rued it. Unforeseen circumstance would impel me to leave the Illinois Valley a few months later. Professional musician, vagabond, communal agriculturalist, backpacker and wilderness navigator—I was about to reinvent myself yet again.

-9-

HIGHER CALLING

In the late 1980s, the city of Eugene, Oregon, was a melting pot of convention and counterculture, of industrialists and environmentalists. Home at the time to 110,000 at the south end of the verdant Willamette Valley (fifty miles east of the Oregon Coast), the city was a haven for artisans and hippies whose principles stood in stark contrast to what were then the area's predominant logging and wood-products industries. Eugene's counterculture influence extended to the surrounding countryside, including the outskirts of Veneta, a town that lay fourteen miles to the west and supported around 2,500 residents.

In late 1986, my then music-business partner Lu Judd suddenly announced he was sick of the economically depressed Illinois Valley and was going to move—with or without me—to Veneta. Lu owned, and was going to take with him, all of the gear in our expanded 8-track recording studio, equipment that was essential to my songwriting pursuits. If I wanted to continue using the equipment, I'd have to follow him to Veneta. Setting aside my attachments to the bucolic Illinois Valley, I acquiesced to the move. Of considerable consolation to me was Veneta was not too far from alluring wilderness areas in the Central Oregon Cascades that I had yet to explore.

In January 1987, I moved my meager belongings into an apartment in Veneta. Lu moved the recording equipment into a small studio a couple miles east of town, one of several modest buildings on a 10-acre hippie collective bordering the shallow and reedy Fern Ridge Reservoir. Over the following several months, the studio became by word of mouth a favorite place for New Age and folk musicians in our Southern Oregon network to record their music, I serving as engineer—and often de facto producer and accompanist on guitar and bass—on the sessions. A more broad-based clientele from Eugene would soon follow. In my spare time, when I wasn't hiking in the Willamette National Forest east of Eugene, I worked on my own rock and pop music productions. All that studio time was slowly turning me into a bona fide recording engineer.

A couple months after moving to Veneta, I learned of a club in Eugene called the Obsidians, formed for the express purpose of hiking, backpacking, climbing and other outdoor recreation in the Pacific Northwest. Attending an Obsidians meeting, I was instantly hooked and joined the club on the spot. Enthralling slide shows presented at its weekly meetings chronicled members' exploits climbing the tallest peaks in the Oregon Cascades—methamphetamine for my adventuring spirit. When the club offered classes in rock climbing and glacier travel in the early spring, I immediately signed up.

I'd had a couple nascent experiences mountaineering while living in the Illinois Valley, but nothing technical. My first—and very nearly last—was on a Sierra Club outing, climbing Mount Shasta in Northern California.[16] Backpacking 3,600 vertical feet up the massive mountain on the first day of the trip, my climbing party and I arrived in the late afternoon at a small level area perched at approximately 10,400 feet altitude—well above timberline at this northern latitude—where we established a base camp in the snow. The sky was totally overcast, clouds blotting out the snowbound mountain only a few hundred feet above camp, putting the next day's 3,700-foot climb to the summit in doubt. But by first light the next morning, the cloud ceiling had begun to lift, if only a little. I had just finished eating some granola and melting snow in my cook pot for drinking water when the climb leader announced we'd have a go of it.

---

16 Mount Shasta is a 14,179-foot stratovolcano and the second-highest peak in the Cascade Range.

I hurriedly strapped my crampons to my boots, threw on my pack and grabbed my ice axe. Quickly scanning my topo map, I compared its rendition of the mountain to what I could now see of our climbing route above camp. The slope was very steep, gaining in one mile over 2,700 vertical feet up to the cloud ceiling, and the snow was still icy in the shadow of predawn light. The climb leader consented to each member of our team climbing at his or her own pace and rejoining, hopefully, on the summit. We would follow the aptly named Avalanche Gulch climbing route at first but veer off it to our left at around 12,000 feet altitude to climb around the west side of the Red Banks, a line of closely spaced and heavily eroded rock outcroppings that guarded the final approach to the summit like a broken fortress.

I started out at a brisk pace, but the thin air—and my poor acclimation, having been near sea level just twenty-four hours earlier—soon made even moderate exertion debilitating; every three or four steps, I needed to stop briefly to catch my breath. An hour into the climb, around 1,000 vertical feet above base camp, I was methodically anchoring my steps up the slick slope with my ice axe when I heard an anxious voice ring out above me.

"Rock!" came the alert no climber wants to hear.

Looking up, I saw a boulder—three times the size of a basketball but more the shape of an asteroid—hurtling down the steeply pitched snowfield about 200 feet directly above me. There was no way I could run across the icy bluff in crampons to quickly get out of the way of the rock's bounding dive.

"Rock, Michael!" immediately came the second alert, evidently from someone in my climbing party. That boulder had my name on it.

As fast as I could manage without slipping and falling, I stabbed my way across the face of the slope with my ice axe and crampons. After a few steps and mere seconds, the boulder shot past me at chest level, easily at 30 mph, exactly where I'd been standing on the first alert. Had it hit me it surely would've killed me. Luckily, it missed everyone else on the mountain too. I took a few deep breaths, counted my blessings and continued the climb.

A couple hours later, I had cleared the Red Banks and was gasping for oxygen on my way up to Misery Hill, a suitably named false summit a little over 300 feet below and a quarter mile away from the true summit. I was alone now, having overtaken the others in my party. Climbing into the clouds, I gained the false summit in short order and found myself in whiteout conditions. Following my compass heading, I crossed a broad saddle, removed my crampons and executed a scramble up craggy rocks to the summit. A few climbers from another party were already there when I arrived.

The view from the 14,179-foot summit was almost completely occluded by clouds, parting briefly now and then to teasingly reveal a sliver of landscape 6,000 vertical feet below me, only to cloak it again seconds later. I was exhausted but exhilarated, having bagged my first major peak. I quickly ate two large peanut butter and jelly sandwiches to refuel—a mistake. My body's automatic drive to manufacture more red blood cells for my oxygen-starved lungs—on Shasta's summit there is only 58 percent as much oxygen as at sea level—left no energy to digest a stomachful of rich food. Ten minutes later, I had a splitting headache and felt nauseous. I was also becoming increasingly lethargic and chilled in the cold, moist, thin air. I realized I could not linger on the summit. As I prepared to leave, my climb leader arrived to greet me.

"I'm feeling sick and have to go down," I told him. "I can't wait for everyone else to get here."

"I understand," he replied, and then advised, "Go down through the Red Banks. It's safer."

His advice was highly questionable, considering I'd be downclimbing a part of the mountain I was unfamiliar with, through a rockfall zone, alone and in unsettled weather. But I was a newbie to mountaineering, so I followed his counsel.

"See you at base camp," I said, throwing on my pack.

An hour later, I'd made it to a point just above the Red Banks in whiteout conditions and light hail. I always carried my compass attached to a lanyard around my neck so I couldn't easily lose it. Now my prudence would pay off, but less so for safekeeping than for quick access. The clouds enveloping me parted for a few seconds—barely long enough for me to take a compass bearing to base camp over 2,000 vertical feet below. I carefully downclimbed a very steep and narrow snow chute between two of the Red Banks' rust-colored crags, knowing a disabling fall here, climbing alone, would put me in serious peril. As I reached the bottom of the rock outcroppings, the clouds cleared for good—or rather, I dropped below them—making the direction toward camp evident from there on. An hour later I arrived back at my tent, silently rejoicing in what now felt to my lungs like thick air, my headache and nausea completely gone.

Minutes after my arrival, two climbers from another party arrived in camp fresh from the summit, backslapping each other and boasting about their having "conquered Mount Shasta." I found their proclamation to be profoundly pretentious and snickered under my breath.

I wanted to correct them. We cannot conquer a mountain. We step foot on it praying for safe passage, and leave its summit soon after our arrival for mortal fear of staying too long. The mountain remains, unbroken and indifferent to we who were but ants on its hard summit. To suggest we have conquered it—a declaration so easily made after escaping below to safety— is the height of arrogance and pomposity.

Soon after climbing Shasta, and while still living in the Illinois Valley, I climbed 9,182-foot Mount Thielsen. A pointy peak known in rock-climbing circles as the "Lightning Rod of the Cascades," Thielsen's summit is not a place you'd want to be in anything but clear weather. I climbed the volcanic mountain alone on a sunny summer day from a trailhead on Oregon Route 138, a two-lane blacktop high in the Oregon Cascades.

Nearly 4,000 feet of climbing took me several miles first through primeval forest on trail and then cross-country up steep scree slopes to Chicken Point. A rocky shoulder at the south base of Thielsen's needle-shaped summit spire, Chicken Point owes its name not to imagined alpine poultry but to the many people who have dared not climb the peak any higher. Despite the 80-foot pinnacle's large handholds and footholds, most people who brave it do so roped up, for an unprotected slip on the spire would likely result in a fatal fall 1,500 vertical feet down the east side of the mountain—a tragic accident one of my later climbing buddies would tell me he once personally witnessed. Because I was climbing alone, and unequipped with technical rock-climbing gear I wouldn't have known how to use anyway, I free soloed the pinnacle. From the summit, I was delighted to see my old friend Mount Shasta looming on the horizon 125 miles to the south.

A year later, I recognized the Obsidians' mountaineering classes would give me the skills I needed to climb smarter and safer, including on mountains more dangerous than Shasta and Thielsen. Between classes, I pored over the preeminent climbing treatise *Mountaineering: The Freedom of the Hills* (written by over forty experts on the subject) and Royal Robbins's *Basic Rockcraft*. Immediately after completing the Obsidians' course, I signed up for my first alpine adventure with the club: a mid-spring climb of Oregon's highest peak, 11,245-foot Mount Hood.

It was on a Friday night in late May 1987 that I drove with seven other Obsidians in the club's van to aptly named Timberline Lodge, an impressive four-story building made of locally sourced masonry and timber that stood at road's end on the open south slope of Mount Hood. Upon our arrival at the large parking lot outside the rustic lodge, our climb leader, an experienced alpinist named Rick Ahrens, gave the rest of us the lowdown about the next day's climb.

"We want to be off the summit early tomorrow morning before the ice melts on the mountain, to avoid rockfall below the Pearly Gates," he said, referring to the eroded snow- and ice-encrusted rock formations through which we'd be climbing, in a steep snow chute, a couple hundred vertical feet below Hood's summit. "That means we need to start the climb at one thirty in the morning, which is just a few hours from now, so try to get some sleep. Everyone needs to have eaten breakfast and packed all their gear for the climb before one thirty, as we will not leave a minute later."

I tried sleeping in the back of the club's van, but with the bright overhead lights in the parking lot and sounds of vehicles coming and going at all hours—not to mention my excitement over the climb—I didn't sleep a wink. I was already knackered when I switched on my headlamp at the edge of the parking lot to begin the climb in the pitch-black night; a crescent moon would not rise for another couple hours.

The first 4,500 feet of elevation gain was a simple walk up, using an ice axe for greater purchase on the crusty snow. The whole way, I was lost in engrossing conversation about climbing and backpacking with a guy in our party named Tom, who easily matched my fast pace. The temperature was 23°F, and an unrelenting wind blowing 20 to 25 mph across the snowy slope plunged the wind chill to around 10 degrees, forming feathery rime ice on my hair, moustache and clothing. We were in constant whiteout; we could only see about twenty-five yards ahead of us and kept the correct heading toward the summit only by frequently consulting my compass.

The sun was up but still behind thick, ground-level clouds at 6 A.M. when Tom and I reached the Hogsback, a snowy ridge around 800 vertical feet below the summit where Rick had told us our party should congregate to rope up for the final assault. That's when Tom and I first realized the rest of our party had fallen far behind us. We would end up waiting forty-five critical minutes for them to arrive at the Hogsback. Standing idly in sub-freezing temperatures, on snow and in a steady wind inside a cloud, is a recipe for hypothermia. By the time Rick arrived with the rest of our group, I was starting to shiver.

"I'm hypothermic and have either gotta start climbing in the next ten minutes or head down," I told Rick through chattering teeth. I had already put on my crampons and climbing harness.

Exactly ten minutes later I was climbing, tied together with three others on a rope team. We gingerly crossed a scarily thin snow bridge over the yawning bergschrund and front-pointed our way up through the Pearly Gates.[17] Moments after we gained Mount Hood's summit at 8 A.M., the sun broke through the clouds. The 5,300-foot descent back to Timberline Lodge would be far less dangerous than the ride home that afternoon, considering our driver's physical exhaustion and sleep deprivation.

. . .

---

17 A bergschrund is a crevasse that forms near the top of a glacier. Front-pointing is a mountaineering technique in which a climber kicks the two front-pointing spikes of their crampons into the steep slope before them with each step, to maintain traction.

Four weeks after climbing Hood, I joined the Obsidians for a summit attempt on Diamond Peak, another major mountain in the Oregon Cascades, approaching from the north side. The climb was a crapshoot; nobody in our party of seven, including the leader, had ever tried climbing that side of the mountain before.

The day before the climb, I and another guy climbed a rock outcrop near our wilderness base camp to get above trees for a better look at the mountain. We determined our climb leader's planned route—starting atop the Cascade crest to the east of camp before heading north to the mountain—was needlessly circuitous, would waste hours of precious time and expose us to rockfall along a consequently requisite traverse below a false summit. Nobody had brought helmets for protection. A direct approach to the north ridge of the mountain looked quicker, safer and far more likely to succeed.

The leader, who had yet to get a clear view of the mountain through thick forest, refused to consider our advice. We grudgingly deferred to his judgment—more accurately, stubbornness. His agonizingly slow route would end up being a no-go—aborted for safety's sake when we got to the edge of the rockfall zone—leaving the climb out of time and opportunity wasted.

A week after the bungled climb, in the final days of June, I drove north with several other Obsidians for a climb of 10,541-foot Glacier Peak in the Washington Cascades. We camped at a trailhead for the namesake Glacier Peak Wilderness that night and made the arduous hike to the mountain the following day. A seven-mile trek with nearly 5,000 feet elevation gain, the backpack took us through primeval evergreen forest along the White Chuck River and ended with a cross-country haul out of the glacier-carved canyon to camp on the west ridge of the massive snow-white mountain. Anticipating the next day's 3,500-foot climb to the summit would be on a glacier, I had prudently brought my ice axe and crampons. I should've brought a snowblower. A relentless heat wave had thawed the mountain so much, I found myself post holing to above my knees on the final 100 snowy yards up to the summit.

My next climb with the Obsidians that summer, an attempt in early

July on Mount Washington—another "lightning rod" in the Oregon Cascades—didn't even get out of the parking lot. A dangerous storm on the mountain quashed that climb. But there was a silver lining: the hour or so spent futilely waiting around in the early morning for the weather to lift gave me an opportunity to engage one-on-one with an alluring member of our climbing party, a beautiful woman five years older than I named Diana Tvorik.

Diana had been on a couple of the Obsidians' previous outings I'd participated in, including the failed Diamond Peak climb, but we'd had only limited direct interactions. Slim and fit, her ruler-straight, shoulder-length hair was black as a new-moon night, her exuberant and child-like love for the wild outdoors brighter than a summer sun. I was instantly and completely smitten, drawn to her like addict to needle. Within a couple weeks my unrestrained adoration would win her over, but she was a loner at heart. Our relationship over the next four years would be tempestuous, I yearning to see her every day, she demanding alone time incommunicado for days at a stretch—until she missed my affection and would reach out to me with a tenderness and vulnerability that would make me come running to her at once. She was granite and eggshells. We were off and on, darkness and light.

But it was a fairy-tale romance at first, fueled by a heady mix of pheromones and shared wilderness adventures. We successfully climbed Diamond Peak that summer without the Obsidians, and summited Three Fingered Jack—a perilous shield volcano in the Central Oregon Cascades requiring technical gear and know-how—with the club. We spent all other weekends hiking and backpacking in the mountains until, in mid-August, she badly sprained her ankle while we were navigating off-trail deep inside Olympic National Park. Against my protest, she insisted on hiking out on her own steam rather than wait for a rescue team. I carried all of our supplies, but her ankle was nevertheless in a terrible state by the time we got back to the trailhead a couple days later. Her ankle would never be the same. We would do a couple easy backpacks over the next couple years, but my dream of adventuring in wilderness with my sweetheart was virtually over.

. . .

With Diana out of commission, I pivoted to doing epic adventures with my other friends. Whitaker flew out from Chicago to join me on a twelve-day backpack in Kings Canyon National Park from late August into September. The middle half of our eighty-eight-mile trek was far from trails, navigating remote terrain at and above timberline, over dizzying mountain passes guarding far-flung alpine basins, bagging numerous 11,000- and 12,000-foot peaks along the way. This time we packed much less food—forty-eight pounds—than the truckload we had hauled through the Ionian Basin the previous summer. Lesson learned.

Food would nevertheless be our undoing. After two weeks of privation in the wilds, eating nothing but dehydrated meals and gorp, Whitaker and I were both emotionally unprepared to resist the countless temptations civilization offered during the six-hour drive back to the Bay Area. We stopped at virtually every roadside food stand en route, devouring bags of melons, fresh peaches, various pies, bean tortillas, omelets and ice cream and guzzling quarts of fresh orange juice —anything and everything we could get our hands on. By the time we reached San Francisco, we were both sick to our stomachs. We joked about forming a national support group, modeled on Alcoholics Anonymous, for binge-eating backpackers coming off long trips in the outback. Counseling stations would be strategically placed at wilderness trailheads. The organization, we ventured, could also counsel wildlife—including the bear that had entered our camp and swallowed a plastic film canister filled with butt salve.

Upon my return home from the Sierra backpack with Whitaker, I was jonesing to get in some more climbs before autumn snows arrived. An Obsidians member named Ed Lovegren had been on a couple climbs I'd done with the club and now proposed we bag some summits without the group. I leapt at the opportunity. Ed was light years more experienced and skilled in the art of mountaineering than I, he having previously done around 300 climbs, including some routes with legendary climber Tom Bauman that I would've never dared to attempt.

You'd never guess Ed's mountaineering pedigree, though. A totally unassuming fifty-six-years-young soul rocking a shock of gray hair, his easygoing disposition and quick smile immediately won me over. A stocky man, Ed had muscular legs the size of tree trunks and lungs like hyperbaric oxygen chambers; despite his being twenty-two years senior to me, he would consistently equal my blistering pace on the long, steep hike up to a mountain's rope-up point. Always at ease on and enjoying the calculus of the climb, he'd nonchalantly point up to a couloir or rib of rock with his ice axe while suggesting potential routes to the summit like he was discussing arrangements for a tea party. He invariably and summarily described every scenic viewpoint we'd come to as being "elegant." He drove an old beat-up wood-paneled station wagon to trailheads and usually arrived eating iridescent pink cookies I would joke looked radioactive. On remote multi-day climbs requiring backpacking in to a base camp, he'd always bring a carpenter's level to help him precisely assess the most comfortable spot to pitch his tent—an exercise that amused me and his other climbing buddies to no end. I'd heard he was a Republican, an odd match for a hair-on-fire liberal like me, but we never once talked politics; there was no reason to. From the get-go he affectionately called me "Coop," presumptuous shorthand I'd always dismissed coming from others but curiously liked coming from him. I would grow to love him like a brother.

For our first climb without the Obsidians, Ed suggested 10,052-foot Middle Sister, the central one of three closely spaced, glacier-clad volcanoes in the Cascades and Oregon's fifth-highest peak. We would climb it in late September. With my blessing, Ed invited along another climber he'd recently met. That's how I came to know the amazing John Englehart.

John looked like an NFL quarterback. A clean-shaven, handsome thirty-year-old man with properly short black hair, he stood six feet and four inches tall, and his 220 pounds looked to be all muscle. He was fearless as a lion on summit assaults, climbed rock pinnacles as effortlessly as an orangutan and had a bird's innate sense of direction. Modest about his abilities and in speech, he never swore, and he often responded to my irreverent lowbrow humor with a falsely disapproving "Oh brother" under a quiet baritone laugh. John worked in a veneer mill. Ed was a property tax assessor for the county. I was a longhaired recording engineer. Somehow we were a great team. We'd end up doing many climbs together over the next decade plus.

Our climb of Middle Sister on September 20 would be spectacular, but the highlight would arguably occur the night before the climb in our base camp at Arrowhead Lake, five miles in and 2,100 vertical feet up from the trailhead. Perched atop a 300-foot-high cliff, the small subalpine lake offered incredible daytime views two miles east to the glacier-blanketed North and Middle Sisters and open views of the sky in all directions. Night fell shortly after we finished our dinners, plunging our camp into total black; the nearly new moon would not rise until after four o'clock the next morning. We were idly chatting on the lakeshore in the dark when suddenly a meteor came racing across the sky along a virtually perfect horizontal trajectory, only a couple hundred feet off the ground, wobbling slightly as if drunk and so close to us we could hear it sputtering and fizzing. For about five seconds, the spitting ball of fire lit up the wilderness for miles around us nearly as bright as on a morning just before sunrise, before extinguishing and disappearing in midair. The close-up extraterrestrial visitation left us slack-jawed and yammering excitedly.

The following morning, we ascended Collier Glacier to take Middle Sister's icy north slope up to her rocky summit, a 3,100-foot climb from camp. Rather than retrace our steps on our descent, we downclimbed the northwest-trending Renfrew Glacier so we could enjoy the different scenery it held.

John, Ed and I would finish 1987 on a high note, doing back-to-back climbs from a wilderness base camp in the Oregon Cascades in early October. We summited the highly eroded stratovolcano Broken Top one day—a technical rock climb—and the more straightforward South Sister the next. By the time we returned to the trailhead, we had logged 15,000 feet of elevation change in three days. It was the grand epilogue to my first nine months of adventuring since moving to Veneta. I felt like I'd had my fill and was ready to take it easy over the coming winter.

Returning home from the mountains, I found in my mailbox the inaugural issue of *Home & Studio Recording* magazine.[18] The editor's column

---

18 *Home & Studio Recording* magazine would later shorten its name to simply *Recording*.

invited new writers to query the monthly publication about possibly contributing to it. My audio-engineering chops had become refined enough that I thought I might have something of value to say. Thinking it would be fun to see something I'd written in print, I sent the magazine's editor a letter expressing my interest. I scribbled four ideas I had for articles on a slip of paper and placed it next to my phone so they'd be handy if and when the magazine called.

Six months later, in early April 1988, I had just returned home from a solo backpack trip in the partially thawed Oregon Cascades when I got a phone call from Amy Ziffer, the editor of *Home & Studio Recording* at the time. She asked me what writing I'd previously done. I told her none, save for in my high school's newspaper nearly two decades earlier. Undaunted, I grabbed the slip of paper by my phone and rattled off my four ideas for articles. She liked one of them and asked if I could get the article to her in the next couple weeks. I didn't even ask if I would get paid for my work—I didn't care; the whole thing was a lark. The next month, my article detailing how to execute an arcane analog-recording technique—"spot erasing"—was published in the magazine. Little did I know that piece's publication would launch the start of a decades-long career, writing over 500 articles—product reviews and how-to articles on audio engineering—for leading national and international magazines serving the recording industry.

In between backpack trips that summer, I climbed Mount St. Helens with Ed Lovegren and the Obsidians. Standing on the exploded volcano's shattered south rim, I gaped at the steaming fumaroles in the crater floor. In the distance to the north loomed colossal Mount Rainier, the highest mountain in the Cascade Range. Climbing to Rainier's 14,411-foot summit was on my bucket list, but I had looked into its terrifying crevasses, some 200 feet deep, from a safe distance during backpack trips on the mountain and did not want my name added to their substantial kill list. I felt I needed to acquire more skills before taking on that scary peak.

Five weeks later, I attended an advanced course in glacier travel that included instruction in crevasse rescue. The three days of intensive hands-on lessons were held on the Hayden Glacier on the east side of Middle Sister. Every day, my classmates and I climbed onto the ice from base camp, established just below the glacier, to learn and practice new techniques. Over breakfasts and dinners in camp, the instructor taught us how to tie unusual and helpful knots. On the last day of lessons on the glacier, he demonstrated how to set up a Z-pulley system for hauling a fallen, injured climber out of a crevasse. But for me, the climax of the course was when he had each of us rappel forty feet down into a crevasse—on a rope secured from above—and then practice getting out of it on our own steam, using two *prusik knots*.[19]

Hanging from a rope deep inside a crevasse was a surreal experience. My limbic brain was screaming to get out of that claustrophobic death trap of perpendicular white and pastel blue ice, and I could feel its smooth, frigid walls quickly sucking the heat out of my body. But the novelty of being inside such a nightmarish space was also perversely exciting. Not that I wanted to linger. Prusiking back up toward the blue stripe of sunlit sky above and pulling myself over the lip of the sheer crack, I was glad to be out.

Unfortunately, I would never get the chance to climb Rainier. But my next climb was hardly a snore. On September 10, three weeks after my crevasse-rescue course, Ed Lovegren and I made a risky attempt on Mount Washington. Ed had climbed the mountain around thirty times before, but his acumen hardly guaranteed success that day—an easterly 60mph wind was blowing sideways across the narrow north ridge that was our approach to the summit pinnacle. By the time we got above the last stunted trees that provided a partial windbreak, we were literally crawling on our hands and knees along the ridge top to keep from being blown off the mountain. After about an hour, I'd had enough of our babyish scrabble.

"This is ridiculous," I shouted to Ed over the gale.

I raised myself tentatively into a squatting position. The wind immediately picked me up and blew me two feet off the west side of the ridge. Ed cracked up. I went back to crawling.

A couple hours later, we'd made it to the Notch, a narrow and usually

---

19 Prusik knots are short loops of rope that are wrapped around a vertically descending climbing rope in such a way that allows the climber to ascend the rope using specialized maneuvers called prusiking.

windy gap between the summit pinnacle and a large gendarme on its north side, where we needed to rope up for the vertical climb up to the summit. In the cold shadow of the pinnacle, Ed looked up at the high clouds racing overhead and yelled to me over the din of the howling wind.

"*I* don't want to lead it, do you?" he asked. "You'd be like a fly on a wall during a hurricane."

If Ed, a far more experienced climber than I, didn't feel safe to lead the pitch, I certainly didn't want to attempt it. We retreated back to the trailhead. Mount Washington had for a second time denied me.

A careless accident stymied my outdoor adventuring the next year, 1989. Early in the year, I slammed the heavy driver's-side door of my 1968 Chevy Impala closed in haste and accidentally clipped the inside of my right kneecap in the process, unknowingly tearing my medial meniscus. I would continue to backpack and climb right up until the day before I had surgery to remove the torn cartilage—a year and a half after the injury—but my disability slowed me down in the interim.

In the first July following the accident, I aggravated the injury by hiking nine miles and 3,200 feet up in elevation, carrying 60 pounds of backpacking and climbing gear, to an off-trail camp at the base of Mount Jefferson, Oregon's second-highest peak. The backpack to camp was the prologue to climbing the mountain at three thirty the next morning with the Obsidians. If only. I was left woefully stranded in camp with a painfully swollen knee while my companions made the grueling summit attempt.

I had a warming campfire waiting for my exhausted companions when they returned to camp eighteen hours later, right before night fell. Their quest had failed, falling just short of the summit due to steep ice that was too thin to allow securing ice screws for protection. I felt guilty that I was secretly happy. Having missed out on the climb, at least I would be spared their celebrations.

A month later, wearing a knee brace to stabilize my torn cartilage, I finally summited Mount Washington, a peak that despite its rigors was far less demanding than "Mount Jeff." Ed Lovegren, John Englehart and an ebullient, curly-haired blond woman named Karin Thompson were my companions on the climb, which was Karin's first. (She and I had before then become platonic backpacking buddies, with Diana's blessing.) The mountain was shrouded in clouds during our approach, and a cool 20mph wind was blowing through the Notch when we arrived in the shadowy gap to rope up for the first pitch up the nearly vertical summit pinnacle. But by the time we got up to the rocky summit, the sun had broken out and the precipitous 360-degree views of the world sprawled 3,000 vertical feet below us were on full, intoxicating display.

Returning home, big changes were coming to my professional life. An alt-rock band named Red Over White I'd been recording in Veneta told me about an empty recording studio on the outskirts of Eugene—the largest studio in the greater Eugene-Springfield area—that was being underutilized by various bands as a rehearsal space. I made the building's owner an offer to rent it—she would not grant me a lease—arguing it would save her the trouble of dealing with serial parties. I borrowed a large amount of money on a credit-card account, tendered first and last months' rent payments on the studio and made my business partner Lu an unsolicited offer to buy the recording equipment he owned. Seeing I was determined to strike out on my own, he reluctantly accepted. On September 1, 1989, I moved the recording gear into my new studio, immediately added a 16-track tape recorder and placed advertisements in a local newspaper announcing the opening of Michael Cooper Recording.

It was a gargantuan step up for me. The studio's expansive main recording space had a twenty-foot-high vaulted wood ceiling and two adjoining soundproof isolation booths. A control room (command center for recording equipment and engineer), spacious walk-in microphone closet, lobby, large storage area and loading dock complemented the facility. Unfortunately, the timing couldn't have been worse to start a new business with a high-interest credit-card loan: just ten months later, the US economy would slide into recession.

But the business was all mine—to succeed or fail—and I was exuberant and highly motivated to make it prosper. Patronage was good at the start, and my love life was also thriving: the month I opened for business, I also moved in with Diana. The house she owned on the south side of Eugene was a convenient twenty-minute drive from the studio, and I would finally get to greet each new day with my sweetheart by my side. Life was good.

Seven months later, in the early spring of 1990, my hoped-for song-writing career also started to show green shoots. A duet I'd written and demoed won a regional songwriting contest and caught the attention of Peter Afterman, a music supervisor for innumerable Hollywood movies. Afterman loved my song and told me the producer for *Fire Birds*, a movie starring Nicolas Cage and Sean Young that was scheduled for release in early autumn of that year, had authorized its use in the film's soundtrack during the main love scene between the male and female protagonists. Superstar Phil Collins was on board to sing the male lead in the recording. All that was needed was to find a songstress whose touring schedule did not conflict with Collins's to sing the female lead. I was soaring on an emotional high.

A few days later, Disney bought the distribution rights to the film and moved its release date several months earlier to May 25, leaving no time to reconcile two recording artists' schedules with singing a duet. Another song was quickly chosen for the movie's love scene. In a telephone call, Afterman assured me my song would deservedly find a home in another movie soundtrack. I never heard from him again.

I got off on several backpacks during the first half of that year, 1990, but the torn cartilage in my right knee increasingly limited the kinds of trips I could do; if I would ever climb gnarly peaks like Mount Jefferson, I would first need corrective surgery. On June 25, the day after I came home from a three-day backpack with Karin Thompson, I went under the knife. The operation was a terrific success: less than seven weeks later, I was back-packing again with Karin in the Mount Jefferson Wilderness, the first of a half dozen more wilderness trips before year's end. I had plenty of time for outdoor adventures—the economic recession that started that year had slowed business for my new recording studio to a worrisome trickle.

But the most important thing to me was my repaired knee was no longer holding me back from doing hardcore wilderness trips. On the last day of September 1990, John Englehart, Karin and I set out to climb 10,090-foot North Sister—the most dangerous of the Three Sisters volcanoes—from a base camp at Arrowhead Lake, two miles directly west of the mountain. Our first objective was to cross the intervening Collier Glacier, whose pitched river of fissured ice paralleled the west base of the peak and stood in the way of our summit attempt. We planned to traverse the glacier near its smooth and higher south end in order to avoid its dangerous crevasse field farther north.

The weather was in our favor; it was an unusually warm and sunny day for an early autumn climb. John had successfully climbed North Sister three years prior, he knew the route and he was a much more skilled climber than Karin and I, so he was automatically designated climb leader. He had demonstrated a flawless sense of direction on all our previous climbs, never once consulting a compass, and I had implicitly trusted him not to lead us astray on what turned out to be successful ascents all. But this time, a half hour into our climb up toward the out-of-view Collier Glacier, I felt compelled to tell him I thought he was angling us too far to the north, toward Collier's crevasse field. John assured me we were on course, and I reluctantly deferred. A half hour later, we topped the glacier's lateral moraine for our first look at the ice, around fifty feet below us. Stretched out before us like a hollow coated in shattered white enamel was the crevasse field, just as I'd feared would be the case.

Hiking around the crevasse field from our off-course position would require a lot more time and effort than we wanted to expend. John and I decided we'd instead trade boot-axe belays to travel directly across it,[20] skirting open crevasses and protecting against any that might be hidden or below a potential slip and slide. It turned out to be a good decision, as we all made it across the ice safely. The subsequent rock climb on North Sister went smoothly until we reached the bottom of the Bowling Alley, a sobering couloir just below the summit that had a notorious reputation

---

20 To set up a boot-axe belay, a climber drives the ice axe's spike—the sharp metal tip at the end of the shaft—as deeply as possible into ice or snow and then wraps the climbing rope around the shaft and their booted instep in an S-curve to create friction. Unreliable on hard ice—one might only be able to anchor the spike a couple inches deep—the boot-axe belay's super-quick setup nevertheless makes it a valuable technique when fast travel is necessary and no other alternatives are available.

for funneling rocks down onto climbers. A vertical rib of rock on the right side of the Bowling Alley—outside the chute—looked safer to climb at first glance, so we decided to climb that instead. We quickly discovered every handhold and foothold on that pitch was coated on top with verglas, a thin layer of ice. A slippery and nerve-racking free solo climb took us up to the summit, where truly spectacular views of other major peaks I'd climbed in the Cascades the previous three years—Mount Washington, Three Fingered Jack and Mount Hood to the north, and Middle and South Sisters and Broken Top to the south—left me grinning from ear to ear. Also commanding the northern horizon was Mount Jefferson—the most challenging and dangerous of the ten tallest peaks in the Oregon Cascades—looking terribly stern and defiant, taunting me for my utter failure to climb it in 1989.

Now came the most perilous bit, as most climbing accidents occur on the way down a mountain. Climbing down ice-encrusted rock is especially dangerous because the slightest overhang can make it impossible to see where you can securely place your feet. For this reason, we all took the Bowling Alley down from North Sister's summit. Thankfully, the mountain did not throw any strikes or spares. But a crushing downfall would break me the next year.

Michael Cooper rappelling off Three Fingered Jack (summer 1987)

John Englehart (left) and Ed Lovegren on Mount
Washington's summit (August 19, 1989)

"Whitaker" (Bruce Schumm) sits atop Red Point during
the twelve-day backpack with Michael Cooper in Kings
Canyon National Park (August-September 1987).

-10-

BOOMERANG

From its very beginning, 1991 looked like it would be a tough year. The economic recession that had begun the previous summer was now reaching a fever pitch and sending my business into a death spiral. For seven consecutive weeks, the phone at my commercial recording studio did not ring once. I picked up the receiver every few days to confirm it still had a dial tone.

Throughout my business's deepening downturn, wilderness was my dependable distraction and succor, the place where I would de-stress and gain a broader perspective on life. No matter how bad things got back home, I always had wilderness to turn to. But that too was about to change.

Aside from a few short backpack trips that spring, I spent all my time trying to shore up my failing business with fruitless advertising campaigns, teaching lightly attended classes in recording engineering, pro bono speaking engagements at music stores and the University of Oregon, and other targeted community outreach. Consumed with my business's survival, I neglected maintaining good physical condition.

I bit off more than I could chew in late June, when I joined the Obsidians on a very strenuous day hike culminating in a rock scramble to the top of Rebel Rock in the Three Sisters Wilderness. My left knee was mysteriously painful during the uphill first half of the fourteen-mile hike, a red flag. I tried to push through the pain—a mistake. It wasn't until a few hours later, when I tried standing up after a long lunch break atop Rebel Rock—seven miles from and 3,500 vertical feet above the trailhead—that I realized just how seriously I'd trashed my knee on the hike in. The long, steep slog back down to the trailhead was torture; I only made it back on sheer willpower, limping in severe pain with every step. I would be disabled for the next twelve months, unable to walk more than a city block. Wilderness was now beyond my reach.

To make matters worse, I had just ended my relationship with Diana. Not because I loved her any less but because I felt I had to. She had grown increasingly unhappy and distant over the past winter. When she told me in the spring she doubted she loved me, I knew I had no future with her and must extract myself as a matter of self-preservation. I moved out of her house and into a 400-square-foot one-bedroom apartment—all I could afford with my recording studio on the rocks. Crippled, lovesick and teetering on the brink of financial ruin, I sank into an increasingly deep depression.

Over the next twelve months, I consulted six different healthcare professionals—including sports-medicine doctors, an orthopedic surgeon and a Rolfing therapist—about my painful knee. None could help me, or even had a clue as to the root of my now chronic disability. Pain having forced me into a sedentary lifestyle, my leg muscles progressively shrank and grew weaker as the months dragged on. By winter I had all but lost hope I would ever be able to hike, backpack and climb again, or even do much walking about town. On a sunny day in June 1992, a full year after my injury and with no improvement or hope on the horizon, I drove up to Waldo Lake in the Oregon Cascades, sat on a picnic bench looking a mile across its wind-tossed waters to the untrammeled wilderness on its opposite side, and wept.

I bemoaned my sorry physical state with a friend, Harmony Rocha, the next day. A masseuse in the Swedish tradition, she'd heard glowing stories about another massage therapist in Eugene named Rich Phaigh (last name pronounced *fay*) who had reportedly helped many people with intractable pain and disability. She gave me his phone number. Having gotten my hopes up and then quickly dashed while meeting with multiple other healthcare providers, I halfheartedly told Harmony I'd think about calling him.

A few days later, I phoned Phaigh. I recounted the details surrounding the onset of my injury, rattled off the credentials of the six other healthcare practitioners who had failed miserably to help me, and said I was not optimistic he could.

"What have you got to lose?" he replied, his tenor both philosophical and confident. "Schedule just a half-hour session, and see if it helps."

A couple days later I showed up for an appointment at his house, where his practice had been temporarily relocated. His wife suggested I wait in the backyard to enjoy the beautiful, sunny day while he finished treating another patient. Stepping into the yard, I was aghast. The lawn was strewn with around a hundred empty beer cans and at least as many cigarette butts. Unbeknown to me, the Phaighs had recently hosted a large party; I automatically presumed Rich had all by himself consumed the entire stash whose evidence lay before me. "Jeezus," I muttered under my breath. "What can this guy do for me? Maybe *I* should be helping *him*."

Five minutes later, the extolled masseur appeared. A handsome, clean-shaven and stocky man my age, his huge muscular hands evidenced his profession. His thick, brawny fingers were like jointed telephone poles, his fingertips flattened into hammerheads. No ordinary masseur, the foundation of his practice (started in 1973) was eight years of study with osteopathic physicians, taking dozens of courses in which he learned how to analyze joint function and skeletal alignment. But his was no rote implementation of *x* treats *y*. An unmatched ability to evaluate complex causations twice- or thrice-removed from manifest symptoms informed the intricate ad hoc sequence of treatment modalities he chose to apply to each patient. To say Rich Phaigh was a massage therapist was like calling a Lamborghini a car.

He spent the first ten minutes of our half-hour session observing my physical form and function while I stood, stepped forward and back, and bent this way and that, and then examined my injured left knee, flexing and palpating it.

"Increased Q angle," he said, talking to himself, then explained, "Your patella, that's your kneecap, is pulled laterally out of proper alignment, or to the outside of its normal position. And you have deep scarring all around your kneecap but especially in the suprapatellar tendon, where the scar tissue goes all the way down to bone."

Over the next twenty minutes, he realigned my kneecap using a combination of techniques and did deep, transverse friction massage on my injured tendons, an extremely painful process meant to liquefy and eliminate the scar tissue. At the end of our half-hour session, I didn't know what to think except that it had been brutal.

"Go walk a half mile immediately," he said.

"I can't walk more than a city block," I replied, shaking my head in disapproval of his presumption. "Haven't been able to in over a year."

"Walk a half mile," he insisted. "Let me know how it goes."

I did walk that half-mile—to my utter amazement, totally without pain. To me it was nothing short of a miracle, a first glimpse of merciful light after a horribly dark year. Now I allowed myself to dare hope I could eventually get my adventuring life back. It was a turning point.

It would take many additional painful sessions of deep friction massage to completely eliminate the scar tissue around my knee, but each one brought improvement. And they were oddly fun; Rich had a terrific sense of humor, way more irreverent than mine, and I spent as much time laughing on his massage table as I did groaning. We quickly became great friends.

Slowly I began the long road back to recovery, rebuilding muscle doing therapeutic exercises Rich prescribed and gradually conditioning my knee tendons to tolerate first hiking—progressively increasing distance and elevation gain—and then weight bearing. I was on a laser-focused mission; if a recording session in my rebounding studio didn't end until midnight, I'd do my exercises at midnight. Every other day without fail I went hiking, a little farther or a little higher than I had two days before, scheduling work around my overriding hikes. Finally in May 1993, after eleven months of Rich's treatments and my exercising with military discipline, I was able to resume light backpacking in my cherished Cascades wilderness, an exuberant return that felt to me no less than a spiritual rebirth. Every step I took in the wilds that spring was sheer ecstasy, accompanied by deep gratitude for being allowed to return "home."

In May that spring I also started writing for *Mix*, the preeminent magazine for the global professional-audio industry. It was my third win in a growing journalism career for the wider audio industry, as I had already started writing four months earlier for *Musician*, a New York City-based magazine serving the eponymous readership. And there were more green shoots: my recording studio's business was flourishing again. I had a new girlfriend, Linda, who played guitar and enjoyed hiking and backpacking. Love, health and money were all on the rebound. Life was once again full of promise.

My initiative to write for *Musician*—a widely read magazine that would nevertheless go under six years later—would ultimately prove to be more momentous for my adventuring than for my writing career. My first article in the magazine had been published in March. The following month, the magazine hired a new Senior Editor, a man named Ted Greenwald. Reviewing my résumé soon after his hiring, Greenwald noted I had listed my personal interests at the bottom, something I had presumed was common practice but which he found odd. First on my list was "backpacking and mountain climbing." When Greenwald subsequently called me in June to get better professionally acquainted, he mentioned he too enjoyed backpacking and had hiked the Appalachian Trail from Georgia to Maryland, a feat that impressed me. I told him I was planning an epic backpack in Southern California's Joshua Tree National Monument for the following winter and invited him along. That invitation would be the genesis of a decades-long friendship, doing increasingly extreme and daring cross-country backpacks together through some of the most remote areas of the Desert Southwest.

-11-

DDM 1

During the recording session Lu Judd and I did with singer-songwriter Ashley Cleveland at Santa Cruz's Bear Creek Recording Studio in early 1982, I quickly became friends with the studio's gregarious owner and recording engineer, Justin Mayer. A kindred spirit in both music production and counterculture lifestyle, Justin and I would in ensuing years occasionally take songwriting and backpacking vacations together. In early February 1991 he introduced me to a friend, the free-spirited Dave Gordon. Later that month, the three of us spent four days camping at obscure, primitive hot springs in Saline Valley,[21] a deep trough in Southern California's Mohave Desert.

A tall fit fellow with a clean-shaven face and short brown hair, Dave Gordon lived for backpacking and aspired to a career as a national park ranger in the Sierra Nevada's backcountry, a dream he would realize three years later. His terrific sense of humor was accentuated by an odd laugh—a series of guttural, gasping spasms that sounded eerily like a donkey braying—I found terribly amusing. We quickly became friends.

During the Saline Valley camping trip, Dave and I fantasized about doing a long backpack the following winter in Joshua Tree National

---

21 Saline Valley would be annexed to Death Valley National Park three years later, in 1994. To protect the springs, they do not appear on any National Park Service maps.

Monument,[22] a park 200 miles to the south comprising nearly 800,000 acres straddling two deserts: the high-elevation Mohave and low Colorado. Several months later, my knee injury on the Obsidians' Rebel Rock hike would shelve that adventure until some then-indeterminate future date.

Three years later, my knee completely healed, Dave and I convened with Ted Greenwald at Dave's parents' house in Covina, a suburb twenty-two miles east of Los Angeles, to organize a stockpile of dehydrated food and water-filled plastic jugs for a nine-day backpack in Joshua Tree; the food and water were to be apportioned and buried under rocks in four caches in the desert. Ted and I had just come from the 1994 Winter NAMM Show at the Anaheim Convention Center,[23] which we were attending as members of the press; with my first article published in *Electronic Musician* that month (January), I was now writing for four magazines for the audio industry, mostly penning articles about new pro-audio equipment and recording techniques.

The NAMM Show was my first opportunity to meet Ted in person. A compact, rugged and clean-shaven man six years younger than I, he wore his straight, shoulder-length brown hair in a neat ponytail and worldly responsibilities steadfastly on his face, though the latter hold would mercifully evaporate once we'd escaped into the liberating backcountry. When discussing business matters, such as *Musician* magazine's editorial direction, for which as Senior Editor he was partly tasked, he was eminently articulate and his gaze often intense, engendering respect. Nevertheless, once in wilderness he'd deftly add to the group's typically inane or ironic humor, sometimes contributing unexpected witty counterpoint to serious discussions where jest was otherwise void. He often met my announced assessments of dangers we might encounter along our risker off-trail routes with understated rejoinders—sometimes preceded by an ostensibly resigned exhale—that seemed sober on their face but which were hilarious

---

22 With the passage of the California Desert Protection Act of 1994, Joshua Tree National Monument became a national park in October that same year.

23 NAMM is short for National Association of Music Merchants. The trade organization's annual winter convention is the largest event in the US for musical-instrument and pro-audio manufacturers, consistently hosting hundreds of exhibits.

in context. I would always laugh in response, and then wonder in retrospect if that was his intent or he was trying to be serious.

On January 26, 1994, the fifty-mile Joshua Tree backpack was launched. Ted and I started out without Dave, who due to prior commitments planned to rendezvous with us on a trail inside the park on the third day of the trek. Ted and I left our rental car at the mouth of Berdoo Canyon, on the park's southern perimeter. To deter thieves from breaking into the vehicle while we were away, we left a note attached to the windshield implying that, should they attempt to do so, they would risk being assaulted by rednecks manning blazing guns: "Dave: Be back in a couple of hours. Hunting has been poor. (Signed) Michael, Ted, Jim, Curt." The ploy would succeed in keeping the car undisturbed but unexpectedly backfire: when we returned to the vehicle eight days later, we found a note from the local sheriff attached to our windshield, demanding we call him. He would sternly reprimand us about illicit hunting inside the park before we explained our deceit.

Due to a late start, limited winter daylight hours and extraordinarily heavy packs, it took Ted and me a couple days to backpack eight miles and 2,500 feet in elevation up Berdoo Canyon and into the interior of the Mohave Desert section of the park, during which time a vigorous cold front moved into the area. On the chilly second night out, we smoked a joint in our makeshift camp perched at the high end of a large desert plain and stared in wonder across the open flat at the other-worldly Joshua trees set ablaze by a full moon. Suddenly, a man lurched toward us through a stand of creosote bush, waving his flashlight aggressively and announcing his authority with a spitfire volley of words: "National Park Ranger! Is that wacky-weed I'm smelling?"

It was Dave, braying with his inimitable laugh and joining us a day ahead of schedule. How he found us in the middle of the night and miles away from our planned rendezvous, I'll never comprehend.

As surreal as our moonlit desert panorama was that night, it would not be the scenic highlight of the trip. That would present two days later, during our traverse of Queen Valley. Hiking west across the broad, arid valley, we spied what incongruously appeared to be dozens of gigantic candle flames burning in the foothills of the Lost Horse Mountains in the distance. As we drew closer, the flames revealed themselves to be the golden flowering tops of twenty-foot-high chaparral yucca;[24] the fiery inflorescences alone were up to ten feet tall. Commonly called "our Lord's candle" in allusion to the inflorescence's appearance, we would pass hundreds of the spectacular blossoming plants while backpacking through the mountains the following day.

But this was no relaxed sightseeing tour. Our packs were terribly heavy, up to 70 pounds each due to each person needing to carry three gallons of water between the most distant caches, which were by necessity—dictated by road access—spaced roughly three or four days apart from one another. More arduous still was the winter weather: for nearly a week, temperatures that rose only into the 30s and 40s Fahrenheit were accompanied by a constant 25-to-45mph wind, creating wind chill in the 20s to low teens every minute of each day. Nights were worse, sometimes plunging to below 0°F with wind chill, and we routinely sought out the lee side of large juniper trees for shelter from the unrelenting gale. Dave's single-pole Chouinard tent would not stand upright on loose desert sand in the unceasing onslaught, leaving us no recourse but to sleep out in the open, each wearing up to six layers of clothing inside our sleeping bags. On our fifth frigid night out, hunkered down in the Lost Horse Mountains in a hammering wind after a long day imitating pack mules, Dave summed up the trip bluntly.

"Nothing like a desert death march," he groaned in his sleeping bag with evident perverse pleasure.

The appellation stuck: we'd later refer to that first backpack adventure in Joshua Tree National Monument as Desert Death March 1—DDM 1 for short—the first of many such expeditions to follow. Each DDM would up the ante—eventually with dire consequence.

. . .

---

24 Chaparral yucca (*Hesperoyucca whipplei*) usually takes at least five years to flower, which it does just once before dying.

That year, I would spend over two cumulative months exploring wilderness areas in California, Oregon, Washington and Arizona. In mid-May, Dave joined me for a cold, weeklong backpack in the remote Wenaha-Tucannon Wilderness, a 177,423-acre playground of high ridges and deep river canyons in a section of the Blue Mountains that straddles the border between Eastern Oregon and Eastern Washington. The weather saw to it we'd be completely alone throughout our forty-seven-mile trek: it rained every day, sometimes accompanied by chickpea-size hail and lightning. We made hot teas from wild yarrow, mullein leaves and elder flowers to warm ourselves each night.

In camp at the end of the sixth stormy day, our boots and pant legs were soaking wet from having hiked along dripping overgrown trails in the high country. Dave changed into spare dry pants and sandals. I deferred, saying I was comfortable enough, which prompted a braying Dave to bestow on me the dubious honorific "The King of Foot and Leg Discomfort," a title he enjoyed renewing at every opportunity.

In late July that same year, I drove up to the Oregon Cascades on two hours sleep after a late-night recording session to join Ed Lovegren, John Englehart and two other guys on a climb of Mount Washington. It was my first climb in four years and second time gaining that lightning rod's tight, rocky summit, which to our surprise we had to share with hundreds of newly hatched flying ants. During the approach, Ed dropped his helmet in the Notch, the narrow gap at the base of the summit pinnacle. Before he could grab it, it rolled, picked up speed and then bounced all the way down the steep rock chute and massive scree slope below us—fully 1,000 vertical feet—before coming to a stop. We recovered the helmet later on our way down the mountain. It looked like it had been on 500 climbs and in several car accidents.

Insects were unwanted companions again when Ed and I climbed Diamond Peak in October. On our approach to the mountain along a trail through deep forest, angry yellow jackets stung my left hand twice in quick succession. By the time we got off the summit several hours later, my hand was so swollen I could barely see the lowest knuckles.

Such mishaps are bound to happen if you spend enough time in wilderness. They're usually isolated, fleeting and inconsequential, and good fortune returns just as quickly as it left, well before a trip is over. Then there's the outlier, the trip that breaks the law of averages, where persistently bad luck, freak accidents, rampant injuries, life-threatening illness and nature's unforgiving side all collide to create multiple trials of survival. Such was the mayhem I witnessed on a 280-mile rafting expedition through the Grand Canyon.

Ted Greenwald (left) and Dave Gordon in camp
during Desert Death March 1 (January 1994)

-12-

GRAND CANYON

Driving back to Southern California from the sixth annual Rainbow Gathering in New Mexico in the summer of 1977, I took a short sightseeing side trip to Grand Canyon National Park. A twenty-four-year-old hippie raw foodist who'd been raised in suburbia on Long Island, wilderness was completely foreign to me at the time. Standing on the manicured south rim of the Grand Canyon in a scrum of chatty middle-class tourists snapping photos just steps from an asphalt parking lot, I peered into the awe-inspiring chasm at the Colorado River raging along its bottom a vertical mile below me and wondered what it would be like to raft that twisted ribbon of blue and white water.

Seventeen years later, I would find out. A friend of mine from Cave Junction, Tom Nevling, had been on a waiting list for seven years to get an immensely oversubscribed permit to raft the Colorado River all the way through the fabled national park, a journey of 280 miles. When his number finally came up in 1994, he invited me—and fourteen other friends and third-party acquaintances from all over the West—to join him on the twenty-one-day wilderness expedition. I jumped at the once-in-a-lifetime opportunity. Nevertheless, having seen terrifying video of the monster rapids in the canyon—and having nearly met my end on the Owyhee River nine years earlier—I was nervous about the trip. I'd never been comfortable on or in water. Taking on the Grand Canyon was as much about challenging myself and vanquishing demons as it was witnessing epic scenery.

Tom was the perfect person to lead the trip. A bespectacled, muscular man with short brown hair, he had a humble, laid-back and quietly humorous persona that belied his skill at the oars. He was a supremely experienced whitewater rafter, having run several of the world's most challenging rivers in the US, Canada and overseas. When I lived in Cave Junction in the early 1980s, he took me down the sphincter-puckering Class V Upper Klamath River with aplomb. If there was anyone I'd want to raft the Grand Canyon with, it was Tom.

The expedition would launch during Arizona's summer monsoon season, when oppressive spells of pasteurizing sun and sweltering nights over 90°F would be broken by frequent violent thunderstorms, creating drenching rains and powerful flash floods that would send the area's innumerable scorpions and rattlesnakes and poisonous red ants running for shelter. Ours would be a trip *on* the river, not above it: unlike in the huge elevated commercial pontoon boats that carry tourists securely through the canyon perched high above the rapids, we would run the river in four inflatable rafts fitted with oars and a single paddle raft,[25] each only large enough to accommodate, in addition to supplies, three to five people. Over the course of three weeks, we would run more than 100 sizeable rapids—the most formidable having waves up to ten feet high—squeezed between towering cliffs and thundering through hundreds of miles of wilderness mostly inaccessible other than by boat or helicopter. Our only lifeline would be the ground-to-air transceiver we'd bring along for radioing for help in an emergency—a white elephant in the most remote and deep and narrow sections of the canyon, where radio signals could not escape the confined slot to reach the infrequent aircraft flying over the park.

---

25 The large rafts that carry virtually all the equipment and supplies on an expedition are steered and propelled by a single person using two opposing oars secured to the boat by hardware; one or two additional passengers may be all such a heavily loaded boat can accommodate. The smaller and less substantial paddle rafts are maneuvered instead by a group of people, typically five in number, each person using a single paddle; such rafts offer little extra space for stowing supplies.

On August 14, 1994, Tom and I and the fourteen other expedition members converged at Lees Ferry, a rare river access point on the northeast border of the national park, to organize the huge amount of equipment and supplies needed for the expedition: oar boats and paddle raft, oars, paddles, repair equipment, pump, winch, carabiners, dry bags, life jackets, rescue ropes, around a half ton of food, coolers filled with dry ice (for preserving perishables), propane tanks, stoves, folding tables, canopies (for preparing large group meals in shade), cook pots and utensils, water filters, sanitizing bleach, first aid, lanterns, tents, sleeping bags and pads, day packs, clothing, five-gallon plastic buckets (for collecting river water, and bailing water out of swamped boats), waterproof ammo cans (for storing at-the-ready cameras, sunscreen and other sundries), Rocket Boxes,[26] a toilet seat and toileting supplies, tarps, and nets to batten down loose items piled in the boats. It would take fourteen hours of work—until mid-afternoon the following day—to get everything unpacked from vehicles, sorted, reorganized and secured in the watercraft before we could "put in."

Outfitting a river expedition is nothing like packing for a backpack trip—if you can float it, you can take it. Space, not weight, is the only limitation, although a heavy boat is much harder to steer through rapids than a light one. One of the expedition's members had refined outfitting his raft to an art form: Roger, a modest and disarmingly forthcoming guy sporting glasses and slightly receding blond hair, brought along a solar panel, camcorder, tripod, French horn, music stand, sheet music, digital recorder and a solar shower. He and Erica, a likeable young flautist with curly dark-brown hair falling to her shoulders, would serenade us after dinners in remote riverside camps with classical-music duets, a delightful juxtaposition of lilting woodwind and shushing canyon wind, of muted brass and rushing water.

---

26 A Rocket Box is a military-surplus metal ammo can, rectangular in shape, with a hinged cover that clamps securely shut and is sealed with a rubber gasket. Rocket Boxes are used as portable toilets on rafting trips for which, for ecological and sanitary reasons, solid human waste is required to be stored and transported for later removal from the riparian area at the end of the trip. A Rocket Box used for this purpose is sardonically referred to as a "groover" because, unless a toilet seat is mounted atop it, the hard, rectangular top edges of the box leave temporary grooves in a person's backside while sitting on it to do their business.

Ours was a motley crew, mostly but not wholly harmonious. Tory, Heather and Keech were an inseparable trio of amiable and fit counterculture types in their early twenties whom, along with Tom, I gravitated to the most. Everyone else was in his or her thirties or forties. Art was unflappable and clearly the most talented river runner in the group, even more masterly than Tom; he was by turns friendly and aloof, and had limited patience for the less skilled. Jim, a stocky man rocking a very thick dark-brown moustache and short, curly hair under a white wide-brimmed hat, was reliable and fastidious, seemingly constantly preoccupied with organizing his raft and supplies. Jude, a woman with streaks of blond through sandy hair, could be rude. Bespectacled Patti was petite, quiet and unassuming. Donnie, a slender woman with short brown hair, struggled with her devoutly religious mores and would question them by the trip's end. Joe and Lee, a religious married couple from Utah, got quietly along with everyone and were liked by all. Jon and Patricia were the opposite, a quarrelsome and uncharitable couple from Oregon whose relationship would self-destruct before the trip's end on account of Patricia's overt flirting—unreciprocated—with Tom.

Those who hadn't brought a raft engaged in musical chairs for rides among those who had, or manned the paddle raft. Newbie to rowing that I was, I would only take the oars through quiet pools, riffles and, after dozens of miles of practice, easy Class II+ rapids with waves no higher than four feet and very few rocks; my attempting anything more difficult would've been disastrous. Mostly I just rode as a passenger through the bigger rapids, bailing water out of a flooding raft when I wasn't hanging on for dear life.

Frankly, I was afraid to ride in the paddle raft, which because of its much lighter weight and smaller size was the most vulnerable to flipping over, and I avoided it. Despite its transit through roasting desert, the Colorado River's water is a frigid 46 to 50°F in the north section of the Grand Canyon, and I remembered vividly from my experience on the Owyhee what being in very cold water does to the human body. Furthermore, river flow in the Grand Canyon runs a frightening 10,000 to 20,000 cubic feet per second—depending on how much water Glen Canyon Dam releases just upstream of Lees Ferry—which in comparison makes water flow on the Owyhee look like that from a garden hose. To me, riding a tiny rubber paddle raft through the Grand Canyon was as safe as taking a hot-air balloon to Mars. In fact, our expedition would end up suffering a cascade of accidents far beyond those I imagined might stem from the paddle raft's instability—world-class rafter Tom would tally more mishaps and injuries on our single expedition than had occurred on all his many previous river trips combined.

But for the first six days, the Grand Canyon was enchanting. From our riverside camp at the sheltered mouth of Red Wall Cavern, we saw flash floods spawned by faraway thunderstorms turn the Colorado River into orange-brown soup carrying small trees and other debris downriver; lounging at night on the cave's fine-sand beach after dining on potato soup, corn and sea bass, we watched lightning set the towering, sheer walls of the chasm alight and listened to its thunder boom and echo up and down the massive canyon. In another camp, we watched flash floods simultaneously burst out of the mouths of three U-shaped canyons terminating high up on the opposing faces of sheer orange and red cliffs, creating rusty red to dark brown waterfalls 900 feet high. Ring-tailed cats—exceedingly cute little creatures that look like slender, shorthaired juvenile cats, each with a long, ringed raccoon's tail—visited our camps at night. Bighorn sheep drank from the river's edge as we floated by in our boats. On a layover, we bathed nude in a placid pool of cool water below a beautiful waterfall in Saddle Canyon. We hiked to the top of a huge talus slope at Nankoweap to view Anasazi ruins, primitive grain storage rooms that had been gouged out of the cliff faces around 900 years earlier. We all took a warm mud bath together where the Little Colorado River joined the main canyon.

Still, hardships tested and dangers threatened even just a few days into the trip—forerunners of things to come. Running the "Roaring 20s" rapids below river mile 20, I quickly went from wretchedly hot in the 110-degree heat under a broiling sun to shivering cold in canyon shadows after being drenched by frigid waves swamping the boat, a sequence repeated throughout the day. The first raft through each rapid would wait below for the next to come through, rescue ropes at the ready in case a boat flipped; in such an event, a few minutes in the bone-chilling water would be all it would take to render the overboard completely helpless, their lives hanging in the balance.

Outside help could not come quickly enough to remedy any lapse in our precaution: the nearest trail out of the canyon—climbing 6,000 vertical feet up to a dirt road on the little visited North Rim—was eighteen miles away.

And yet, this was apparently the easy water, the safe. I overheard the most experienced rafters in our party talking nervously about Adrenaline Alley, a treacherous thirty-mile stretch of river we'd be running a few days later that had waves twice as high and rapids twice as long as those in the Roaring 20s. I hated to admit it, but I was scared.

In fact, our introduction to Adrenaline Alley was inauspicious. Jon steered a raft into the canyon wall while running Adrenaline's first stretch of whitewater, Unkar Rapid, tearing a huge hole in the side of the Sotar self-bailer that took three and a half hours to repair.[27] We couldn't help but fear this was an omen, especially because Unkar was easy compared to the upcoming Hance Rapid.

The first technical rapids of the trip, the boulder-strewn Hance scared everyone, except maybe Art; I was half-convinced running it would be my last moments alive. Joe, Lee and I prayed together in an eddy above the rapids, I deferring to their denominational pleas to Jesus I would've normally discounted, on the remote chance they might have some pull with a higher power, *any* higher power. Thankfully, Joe ran Hance perfectly except for dropping into but then quickly punching out of a huge hole at the bottom of the run.[28] I could've taken my pulse in my elbow in that hole.

Nobody flipped or fell overboard on Hance, an important psychological hurdle. We all ran more than a half dozen other rapids in the upper stretches of Adrenaline Alley that day without incident, our triumphant warrior cries bouncing off the sheer canyon walls with each successful run. But the biggest and most dangerous rapids were still to come.

---

27 A self-bailing raft has openings fashioned around the perimeter of its inflatable floor that allow excess water to automatically drain in seconds, foregoing the need to bail water with a bucket.

28 One of the most feared hazards in whitewater rafting, a hole is formed when water flows over an obstacle such as a boulder, drops on the far side to a level lower than the surrounding water and then reverses direction back onto itself, often submerging and preventing objects in the hole from escaping.

We did a long, nervous scout the following day along the water's edge at Granite Rapid, by far the most terrifying water yet. Tom concluded we should avoid the boulder fields on the left and center of the river, running instead the long chaotic train of ten-foot waves, huge holes and laterals down the right side.[29] Moments later we rowed out to the top of the rapids, our tight faces breathing hard with runaway fear. My heart was racing as the raft I was in rode up the first ten-foot wave, caught air at the top and then plunged into the deep trough on its far side. I had just enough time to take a deep breath of air before the next ten-foot wave crested and crashed down on my boat mates and I, completely submerging the boat and us. Moments later, the raft lumbered out of the violent, numbing water just in time for the next ten-foot wave to completely bury us, followed by the next. Somehow, inexplicably, we punched through, as did all our other oar boats. Totally drenched and shivering, and all our rafts save for the Sotar self-bailer swamped, we bailed water while watching the small paddle raft enter the top of the run. And then it happened.

From our positions in riverside eddies about a quarter mile below the rapids, we saw the paddle raft disappear behind a towering wall of water about a third of the way through the run. When it reappeared, it was upside down, with loose paddles and flailing bodies chaotically tossing about in the maelstrom. A split second later, the next monster wave completely engulfed them.

"They're over!" Tom yelled. "Get into position! They're gonna be cold!"

We quickly rowed out into the river, spreading our four boats evenly across its span, rescue lines poised in nervous hands, waiting for bodies in the vicious current upstream to come to us. Three of our overboard companions reappeared, clinging to the overturned paddle raft and attempting to climb atop it. A fourth person, Jon, was too far away from the raft and desperately swimming for his life. The three with the raft managed to flip it and haul themselves back in. Tory threw a rescue line to Jon and pulled him into his boat.

---

29 A lateral is a large wave or hole that forms due to water hitting an obstacle at an angle.

"How many were on-board the paddle raft?" someone yelled over the roar of the river.

"Five," someone yelled back.

"Five?" someone else anxiously questioned. "Are you sure? I see only four. Who's missing?"

"I see Roger, Jude, Donnie and Jon," I hollered back. "Oh my God, where's Erica?"

Seconds later, a black helmet came rushing toward us in the current. It was Erica's. Over the next ninety seconds, we secured the four found survivors—but still no sign of Erica, the much-liked, curly-haired flautist who had with Roger serenaded us in our camps. Talk became desperate. The swift current should've brought Erica to us long ago. Now the expedition was no longer a fun adventure, but suddenly grim black misery, our worst fears of Adrenaline Alley becoming harsh reality. People started praying out loud. Lee was nauseous, Heather weeping.

Just as we were all about to give up hope, someone spotted a person staggering onto shore about a quarter mile or so upstream. It was Erica. Miraculous Erica. Fifteen minutes later she would meet the rest of our party at a midpoint along the river's bank. She was unhurt, but shaken.

Amazingly, most of the gear from the paddle raft was recovered. To their credit, the paddlers insisted on immediately going on before they had time to digest their close call and psyche themselves out. The rest of that afternoon, we tackled the remainder of Adrenaline Alley, one of the three most feared whitewater runs in Grand Canyon along with Crystal and Lava Falls Rapids. Having had enough terror for one day, we camped upstream of Crystal.

We nervously scouted Crystal Rapid the next morning for fully forty-five minutes, agonizing over the possible routes through the cauldron of roiling water. The river was a terrible monster here, like an entire ocean funneled and amplified between cliffs, with mammoth holes on river left, a boat-ripping rock garden at the center of the river below the rapids and terrifyingly gigantic waves on river right. Nobody was eager to be the guinea pig to run it first. Art and I volunteered, he at the oars and I consigned to bail water. Our companions would watch from onshore to see if Art's line through the chaos worked, and learn from our mistakes.

My heart was beating at double time, my breathing hard and fast, as I crawled into Art's raft. Our companions gave us encouraging thumbs up, and I could see the concern and respect for us in their eyes. But unflappable Art ran Crystal perfectly. The next three boats also came through Crystal okay. But oarsman Jim, with boat mates Tory and Jon, was pulled by the powerful current too far left. We watched, transfixed in horror, from the bottom of Crystal as Jim hit the biggest hole and got hurled out of the boat into it. Tory quickly pulled him back in while Jon grabbed the oars, but the diversion cost them valuable time to course correct as they punched through the hole, and they ended up running right into the rock garden below and got wrapped. They managed to free themselves, only to get wrapped once more on the next boulder downstream. Breaking free again, they finally finished their harrowing run to rejoin us below the rapids.

That evening in camp, Tom and I spoke.

"You were brave to volunteer to run Crystal first," he said.

"Bravery had nothing to do with it," I replied. "In all honesty, I figured my best chance to make it through alive was to run it with Art."

The next day, our tenth on the river, the paddle raft flipped again while running Specter Rapid. This time the occupants managed to stick with the raft, but the incident was nevertheless traumatic for all, especially those who went overboard. The mood turned festive that evening, as my friends and I passed around a bottle of whiskey to celebrate my forty-first birthday. Little did we know our party's fortune would turn grim again just a few hours later.

I awoke at six o'clock the following morning to the sounds of Tom's urgent voice and a woman wailing in pain.

"Mayday, mayday, this is the Nevling party in the Grand Canyon. Does anybody read me?"

Tom was shouting into our ground-to-air transceiver. Lee lay howling at his feet on an inflatable mattress, her concerned husband Joe and a half dozen other group members by her side. She had awakened at 3 A.M. with acute abdominal pain and, in the three hours since, it had only grown progressively and exponentially worse.

Tom's urgent maydays were returned only with static for the next half hour. Lee's pulse rate dropped into the forties. Her complexion was ashen. We suspected she had appendicitis, or possibly a tubal pregnancy. It was apparent to all that she needed immediate evacuation from the canyon to a hospital. But we were at the bottom of one of the most remote sections of the Grand Canyon, where our transceiver was apparently worthless.

Jim and I volunteered to climb up the south side of the canyon with the transceiver, in hopes of transmitting a signal out of the chasm. Over the next hour we gained around 700 vertical feet on a steep but accessible slope, stopping frequently along the way to send out maydays that were consistently met with static. A couple hundred feet farther above us were sheer palisade walls. I climbed alone up to their base to scout, in vain, a way up the cliffs, hoping we could eventually attain the canyon's rim still thousands of feet above us. The footing below the cliffs was dangerously insecure, the slope below me very steeply pitched, and I was beginning to run low on water. I regretfully descended back to Jim, who was feverishly working the various frequencies on the transceiver.

"Mayday, mayday," Jim urged. "Nevling party at river mile 130. Unstable medical condition. Need immediate evacuation. Do you read me?"

Suddenly the static broke.

"We read you, Nevling party," came the desperately hoped for reply.

We had contacted a commercial aircraft that happened to be flying, somewhere out of sight, within our transceiver's range.

"We'll forward your mayday to the National Park Service," the pilot continued. "Good luck."

Ecstatic, Jim and I hurriedly scrambled down the side of the canyon and back to our party on the river's edge with the good news. An hour after our return, we began to hear the muted sounds of helicopter rotors. A white helicopter, the acronym NPS emblazoned in large black letters on its side, appeared over the south rim of the canyon. I flashed the mirror on my compass to catch the pilot's attention, and he guided his craft to our orange emergency panels arranged in an "X" on our cleared landing site. Once landed, two medics, a man and a woman both thirty-something, took Lee's vital signs and started her on IV fluids.

"It's good you had the common sense to go higher," the male medic told me, after hearing of Jim's and my climb up the south wall. "Sometimes the only way to get a mayday out of the canyon is to climb to higher ground."

The medics could not determine what was wrong with Lee, only that it appeared to be serious. With the support of four from our party, they carried her on a stretcher onto the helicopter, to be flown to a medical facility on the park's South Rim. Despite her grave condition, Lee insisted her husband Joe stay with their raft to complete the expedition. A couple minutes later, the helicopter disappeared with Lee over the south wall of the canyon, its thrum went silent, and we were all left stunned and speechless beside the rushing river.

There was nothing to do but continue on down the river and hope for improved fortune, but the latter was not to be. Later that same day, Jim shot past the eddy at our planned campsite above Tapeats Rapid and got firmly wrapped on a huge boulder. Using ropes and the winch, it took three and a half hours to free his raft.

That evening in camp, we all talked about how much we were looking forward to a hike we'd planned to take three days later in famously picturesque Havasu Canyon, widely considered the most beautiful place in all of Grand Canyon. We desperately needed the break. Except during layovers, every day had been exhausting: we'd awake at 6 A.M. for breakfast, schlep the cooking and camping gear back into the boats, run the river for eleven or twelve hours, unload, bleach and filter gallons of river water in buckets, and eat dinner in the dark at around eight or nine in the evening. Then repeat.

On our fourteenth morning on the river, we wearily pulled our boats to shore at the mouth of Havasu Canyon, just as a woman carrying a backpack came down to the water's edge. To our astonishment, it was Lee. Over the previous seventy-two hours, she had passed a kidney stone at the South Rim's medical facility, borrowed a backpack from a friend in Flagstaff, bought supplies at a camping store, caught a ride to the head of Havasu Canyon and hiked twenty miles—in just twenty hours—to arrive at the river's edge exactly to the second as our boats pulled in. Everyone was stunned by her strength and sheer determination, and joyous to have her rejoin the expedition.

Our joy was short-lived. During that morning's hike alongside Havasu Creek's breathtakingly beautiful turquoise waters, Roger fell off a rock ledge and broke his arm. He insisted he would not leave the expedition to seek medical attention but would continue on as a passenger in one of the rafts with broken arm unset, an incredibly gritty decision. We put his arm in a sling on the spot and assisted him on the hike three and a half miles back to the rafts, crossing the swift creek six times and executing numerous pitches over boulders en route. In the boats once again, our party continued rafting downriver until just before dark, making camp in a spot we later realized was crawling with numerous poisonous bark scorpions. Related to the scorpion that had stung me in Yelapa, Arizona's bark scorpions are far less venomous but still potentially lethal. I was really anxious.

But not as anxious as I was the following day when we prepared to run Lava Falls Rapid, universally feared in equal measure to Crystal Rapid. Scouting the run from an overlook, the deafening roar of violent white-water—in chaotic upheaval every inch from bank to bank—amplified our terror as we surveyed its disorderly monster waves plunging into massive holes in the center of the river and on river right. River left was strewn with boat-eating rocks, leaving only a narrow slot to run between the nightmar-ish holes. So primal was our fear while scouting Lava Falls that, during the walk back to our boats, fifteen of us—all except Art—urgently ran en masse into the nearby bushes to empty our bowels.

But despite the intimidating run-up, I unexpectedly ended up loving the run through Lava Falls, even the ten-foot wave that hit with a force that threw me a foot backward in the raft as I held fast to keep from being swept overboard. All five boats made it through Lava Falls, although the paddle raft ironically ended up flipping in Little Lava Rapid immediately below. With that flip, eleven of our party of sixteen had been swept overboard during the expedition.

The river was taking its toll in another, unexpected way. Over the prior two-plus weeks, my decision to bring sneakers instead of sandals to the Grand Canyon came back to haunt me. My footwear's poor drainage and aeration resulted in my left foot developing a severe case of "boat rot," a painful fungal infection that now left my toes bright red with raw flesh, the skin eaten away. Every night in camp, I soaked my foot in a bucket filled with diluted bleach to kill the fungus. My foot rotted so badly, I started riding through lesser rapids with my left leg lifted high in the air in order to keep the foot as dry as possible. Everyone else soon started mimicking me, lifting their left leg while riding through whitewater. It became vogue.

Again the fun was short-lived. The raft Patti was in went into a huge hole while running Kolb Rapid. The momentum of the boat's bucking stern, where Patti was seated, threw her violently forward, smashing her chin into a metal Rocket Box and also injuring her thumb. The same hole temporarily captured two other boats in turn—Art's and mine—nearly capsizing them. My raft—this time with me at the oars—nearly capsized again on Little Bastard Rapid when it got stuck momentarily in a sleeper hole.[30] That night in camp, a bark scorpion crawled up Jude's arm but thankfully did not sting. By then fully half of our party had gotten injured or fallen seriously ill.

After almost three weeks of physical exertion and never-ending drama, everyone was so thoroughly exhausted that we would doze off in between running rapids. Deep asleep as I floated downstream through quiet pools, the slowly growing roar of an approaching whitewater run would pull me back to consciousness. So fatigued and inured to the river I'd finally become, I would sometimes wait until the roar of the river was thunderous and we hit the first wave before rousing myself to an upright position. Roger one-upped everyone's growing insouciance, sometimes manning one oar through rapids with his good arm—his broken one in a sling—in tandem with a boat mate at the other oar. We'd all become certified river rats, battered by the Grand Canyon but not broken (except for Roger's arm). But still the mishaps kept coming.

On our eighteenth night on the river, it was my turn to cook dinner for the group. Being thus preoccupied, I hadn't noticed where the groover had been situated for the night, out of sight from the tents and kitchen area for privacy's sake.

---

30 A sleeper hole is formed by a rock that sits barely under the water, making the hazard less discernible.

"It's upriver past the tall grass, a couple feet from the bank," Tom informed me as I finished washing everyone's dishes well after nightfall.

The night was pitch black, a nearly new moon not due to rise until around 3:30 A.M. I had a mild case of heat exhaustion—nausea, dizziness, pronounced fatigue and shortness of breath—from the afternoon's over-100° heat. At midnight, I went urgently looking for the groover in my weakened state. My flashlight lit up the waist-high grass as I stumbled through it, blinding my view of everything immediately behind the tall blades to dimensionless black. In my haste and lightheadedness, I walked right off the steep embankment hidden by the tall grass and fell three feet onto a rattlesnake, prompting its tail to rattle angrily just a foot from my right ear. The snake was stunned by the impact and trapped under a thick matt of crushed grass for as long as it took for me to scramble quickly back to safety at the top of the embankment, unhurt.

Venomous bites and stings were an ever-present danger in the canyon. Our camps had been infested throughout the expedition with thousands of poisonous red ants, and half of our party had already suffered the insects' non-lethal but painful bites. On our nineteenth morning on the river, it was my turn, and I had the worst reaction of all. Bitten on my right foot's arch, the pain and swelling were so intense that I could not tolerate having the wound site out of the mercifully numbing-cold river for more than a minute at a time. Despite taking codeine and smoking marijuana that evening, I was still in intolerable pain. Soaking my throbbing, swollen foot in a bucket of cold river water helped, but only for around five minutes, by which time my body heat warmed the water a few degrees and killed its anodyne effect.

My only recourse was to sleep atop a small ground cloth on the muddy edge of the river with my right foot in its pain-relieving water. But the water level, restricted by Glen Canyon Dam above Lees Ferry, progressively dropped throughout the night, forcing me to wriggle down the muddy bank every ten or fifteen minutes to keep my foot in the receding water. At 11:30 P.M. a thunderstorm blew in, adding to my misery. I pulled on my rain gear, hiked up my right pant leg in the river water, and dragged the muddy ground cloth out from under me and over my head and torso, all it could cover at once. I spent that entire night nursing my foot in the river, lying in the mud like a dying water buffalo, lightning flashing above the craggy canyon walls and rain intermittently pummeling me.

My foot was still swollen the next morning when Keech got stung on the abdomen by a bark scorpion. Joe quickly used a Sawyer Extractor Pump, a piston-like first-aid device, to suck the venom out of his wound. His fast response saved Keech from the worst aftereffects, leaving only the site of the sting numb and the lymph glands in his groin a bit painful.

That was the last damage the Grand Canyon would inflict on us. But while it had severely tested us all, we would nevertheless leave the canyon not with aversion but in awe of its incomparable beauty and indomitable wildness. On the twenty-first day, the expedition came to a bittersweet end shortly beyond where the canyon widens and dramatically shrinks in height. The Colorado River's mighty flow first slowed, then became crippled and finally brought to a smothering halt as it emptied into man-made Lake Mead, where we took out our boats.

We spent our first night outside wilderness in a sleazy hotel in Las Vegas, bewildered by its flashing neon lights, noisy slot machines, cigarette smoke-filled game room, leather-skinned gamblers and gaudy hookers. It was a shocking and disturbing return to so-called civilization. The Grand Canyon already felt impossibly far away, farther than in calculable miles, like a dream quickly fading upon awakening. I felt sad.

Thankfully, I had three more planned wilderness adventures back in Oregon to look forward to as a consolation later that summer and fall. And a dozen more trips already penciled in on my calendar for the following year. The year 1995 promised to be terrific fun. And it was—until it wasn't.

Michael Cooper in the Grand Canyon (August 17, 1994)

-13-

WILDERNESS BROADCASTS

As Desert Death March 1, aka DDM 1, drew to a successful close in February 1994, Ted Greenwald, Dave Gordon and I made a pact to follow it up the next winter with DDM 2 in another desert. Ted and Dave readily deferred to me to plan the backpack's locale and cross-country route. In fact, I was the lead planner for most of the backpacks I did with friends, if for no other reason than I loved studying topo maps more than they did and would exhaustively search for hidden attractions that would extend a backpack's scenic potential. Even for ostensible trail hikes in the Pacific Northwest, I would catalog all the unnamed peaks, unmarked cliff tops, secluded canyon rims and hidden waterfalls the trails neared but did not quite access, and then devise cross-country side trips to each to enjoy their climactic views.

Those were short detours. Getting to remote viewpoints two days' hard journey from any trail in waterless desert mountains took planning—and navigation skills—to a whole other level. For those backpack trips—the Desert Death Marches that began in the mid-1990s—I was if not the sole navigator then the de facto lead. I had become expert at reading topographic maps, so familiar with their cipher that I would often commit their tortuous contour lines to eidetic memory. I began to recognize what I called "inferred" features on topos, where the subtle alignment of relatively widely spaced contour lines suggested a low-lying ridge or a dry waterfall lay hidden between them, informing my route planning. Navigating in the backcountry, I incorporated altimeter readings with my map-and-compass work, using elevation as third-dimension data points to negotiate mazes of diverging canyons where planar triangulation was virtually impossible. For desert backpacks, I deliberately and meticulously devised the most hardcore but likely doable routes—and escape routes to water caches in case they proved to be dead ends.

Knowing my obsessive attention to detail, my backcountry buddies would inevitably ask me a question about the topography that lay ahead, such as our elevation gain to the next mountain pass. This would immediately prompt my whipping out a topo and launching into a pretend wilderness-wide radio broadcast, always with this needlessly long introduction: "I'm glad you asked that question. Good afternoon, ladies and gentlemen, and welcome to this edition of [pretentious pause] . . . Map Talk. Your host: Michael Cooper. Guest speakers: [names of backpacking companions]." After making everyone endure this compulsory lead-in, I'd answer all questions seriously.

It was not unusual for several episodes of Map Talk to abruptly broadcast each day during a wilderness trip. And in truth, most of my companions enjoyed the farcical preamble and looked forward to the useful and detailed information that would immediately follow. Not so, my sister-in-law Eileen. On family backpacks in the Pacific Northwest, Eileen would groan and protest before "I'm glad you asked that question" progressed to the last syllable, but there was no way to shut the broadcast off once her question carelessly slipped her lips. Map Talk became required listening for all who were trapped in the outback with me. I was, Eileen would complain, terribly consistent.

In fact, I once deviated from Map Talk. The exclusive departure came during a backpack with my younger brother Mitch in Oregon's Rogue-Umpqua Divide Wilderness in May 1993. Camped along the rushing Castle Rock Fork of the Umpqua River on a night as black as charcoal, Mitch and I stayed up past midnight quaffing a bottle of Chardonnay down to the last drop. After stumbling into our tent for the night, we discovered an enormously bloated tick was tenaciously attached to the right side of my neck. Tweezers would not remove it.

"You're gonna have to dig it out with this," I said to Mitch, handing him a large blunt sewing needle from my repair kit.

It would not be easy surgery. First of all, the tick was embedded a mile deep in my neck. Second, we were both quite inebriated (a plus for me, as I was not otherwise anesthetized). Third, Mitch was by nature a kind and cautious soul, and he was pained to gouge me. The surgery would be tougher for him than for me.

"Shit, it's really embedded deeply," he lamented as he dug into my neck with the sewing needle, a headlamp illuminating his bloody handiwork. "I can't even see the head."

His face inches away from my neck, he excavated fitfully around and under the tick's front end for the next forty minutes, but to no avail.

"How the hell am I going to get this tick out?" he groaned.

"I'm glad you asked that question," I announced loudly. "Good evening, ladies and gentlemen, and welcome to this evening edition of . . . Tick Talk. The host: Michael Cooper. Guest surgeon: Mitch Cooper."

We both laughed—and then the tick's body broke off, leaving the head completely buried inside my neck. Two years later, at the start of DDM 2, the lump had still not been fully absorbed.

For DDM 2, Ted Greenwald and Dave Gordon and I planned to explore a remote area in the center of the roughly 600,000-acre Anza-Borrego Desert State Park. Our itinerary would take us through the Vallecito and Tierra Blanca Mountains, an area centered about twenty-five miles south of where Tony Morel and I had first cut our teeth in the art of desert backpacking fourteen years earlier.

The planned forty-two-mile route—over 80 percent of it off-trail—would launch on February 12, 1995, and, I figured, take us seven days to pull off. I really needed the weeklong vacation, for the upgrade of my commercial recording studio to 24-track digital production capabilities the preceding fall had resulted in an avalanche of new business and I was working ninety-five grueling hours a week to meet the demand. Dave, who a year earlier had finally realized his dream to become a wilderness ranger in the backcountry of Sequoia National Park and now sported a full beard and moustache to suit his feral persona, was relishing having a winter adventure while on seasonal furlough. So it was especially disappointing to both of us when Ted suddenly announced little more than a month before DDM 2's scheduled launch that, due to numerous work and family obligations, he could not afford to take time off for the backpack. He sounded sad, but resolute and impervious to persuasion.

In response, Dave and I activated what would come to be known as the Greenwald Maneuver. Rather than pleading with and overtly pressuring Ted to change his mind, the reverse-psychology stratagem entailed Dave and I succinctly expressing our disappointment that he couldn't make the trip and then telling him we were going to do it without him. The Maneuver had the intended effect: a few days later, Ted called to say he'd worked out his impediments and would join us after all.

The route for DDM 2 would end in an area named Elephant Trees. Continuing the yarn that all misfortune on backpacks is caused by a Curse—a malevolent spirit whose energy emanates from a place officially named on one of our maps—I forewarned Ted and Dave about the Curse of the Elephant Trees, a hex freakishly part animal and part vegetation. We came to the desert prepared for unusually rainy weather, as the Curse had already firmly established an El Niño weather pattern over all of Southern California, hardly the limit of the Curse's baleful reach.

Weather during our first day in the backcountry was deceptively benign: partly cloudy and pleasantly cool. Hoisting our 60-pound packs, we hiked by trail through Little Blair Valley to the site of ancient Native American pictographs in Smugglers' Canyon. Leaving the trail and continuing cross-country to the head of the canyon, we dropped our packs and climbed Whale Peak, a roughly 2,000-foot vertical ascent. From the 5,320-foot summit, clad in a contrasting mix of pinyon pines and cacti and massive rock slabs, a sweeping 360-degree panorama enthralled us: the land-locked Salton Sea to the east, mountains in Mexico to the south, the Santa Ana Mountains to the west, and the majestic Santa Rosa Mountains and snow-capped San Jacinto Mountain to the north. On our way down from the summit, Ted fell and landed on his tailbone on a large boulder but miraculously suffered only minor injury. We bivouacked that night in Smugglers' Canyon under stars and among scattered short juniper trees, spiky "Spanish bayonet" yucca and thorny ocotillo. It was around 40°F and very windy—a cold front was moving in.

We backpacked down Smugglers' Canyon the following day, circum-navigating a few dry waterfalls—the first around forty feet high—en route. We crossed the two-lane asphalt County Highway S2, then named the Old Overland Stage Route,[31] in very light rain showers to pick up our first water cache on the edge of Vallecito Creek's dry wash. That night we camped under a waxing moon in the aptly named Moonlight Canyon.

The following morning, the Curse of the Elephant Trees unleashed its fury with zero restraint. Around an inch and a half of rain—over 20 percent of the average annual total for the area during the 1990s—drenched us as we backpacked cross-country through the Tierra Blanca Mountains to arrive at our second water cache off S2. The rain pounded us in wind-driven sheets as we removed virtually all our supplies from our backpacks, exposing and soaking the lot; however regretful, this exercise was necessary in order for each of us to properly position deep inside our packs three plastic gallon jugs filled with water—over 25 pounds of newly added weight—so they'd be closest to our hips and centers of gravity while hiking. Everything but our sleeping bags, which were stuffed inside thirty-three-gallon plastic trash bags, got thoroughly drenched in the process. The most remote stretch of our route—three and a half days of cross-country travel north through the rugged Vallecito Mountains—lay before us as we hoisted our now sodden 70-pound back-packs and lumbered off into the drowning deluge. The conditions were so extreme, Dave and Ted briefly suggested we abort the expedition. I convinced them to persevere, promising our fortunes could only improve.

That evening we were all so sore and exhausted that we incautiously set up our tents in a flood-prone wash at the foot of the mountains,

---

31 The Old Overland Stage Route, known today as the Great Southern Overland Stage Route of 1849, chiefly follows the path of the Butterfield Overland Mail stage-coach service that carried passengers and mail west from Memphis, Tennessee, and St. Louis, Missouri, to San Francisco from 1858 to 1861, passing through the deserts of Southern California en route.

willfully disregarding lingering showers for the comfort of lying on soft sand. Scanning frequencies on a small hand-held transistor radio around midnight, Dave heard a flashflood warning issued for San Diego County. We grudgingly moved our tents in the rain to higher ground outside the wash, a wise precaution: when we continued farther up the wash the next day, we saw unmistakable signs a flash flood had come within a half mile of our camp.

The storm mercifully broke by morning, partly cloudy skies returning as we hoisted our still ridiculously heavy packs. Surveying the terrain ahead on our map, several washes—broad and shallow at their mouths but dissected higher up into a confusing maze of deep, forking branches—led north into the rocky Vallecito Mountains from our low camp. Only one, June Wash, led up to a pass I deemed to be the only feasible route through the steep mountains. But navigating by map and compass, Dave had unknowingly led us off-route into the wrong wash during the previous day's powerful storm.

It was an easy mistake to make in complex terrain occluded at the time by clouds, and with long distances to the few visible apexes of mostly opposing peaks in the Vallecito and Tierra Blanca Mountains compounding parallax error.[32] Although the first (highly inaccurate) commercial GPS units had come to market several years earlier,[33] neither Dave nor I owned one but preferred instead to use old-school analog tools and navigation techniques. (Ted had not yet learned how to navigate.)

---

32 The farther away landmarks are from a navigator's position, the more any slight inaccuracies introduced while taking field bearings are compounded. Mistakes can be caused by parallax error affecting the perceived bearings to landmarks used when triangulating. And when the only usable landmarks are virtually opposite rather than approaching ninety-degree angles to one another, triangulation becomes literally impossible, greatly complicating navigation.

33 In a program dubbed Selective Availability (SA), the US government intentionally degraded the signal used by commercially available GPS units in the 1990s so that they were only accurate to within roughly 300 feet; SA was implemented at the time out of fear accurate commercial units could be used in a military attack on the US. On May 2, 2000, SA was discontinued. With additional enhancements, today's GPS units can be made accurate to within roughly ten feet.

Dave's navigation error wasn't immediately obvious. After hiking a mile north in the wash we'd camped in the night before, he and I realized it was gradually veering away from our essential mountain pass. We climbed out of the wash up to a short ridge top and took some field bearings. After much debate, I convinced Dave we were a third of a mile east of June Wash. We quickly course-corrected. By sundown we made the mountain pass, where we carefully pitched our tents to avoid deceptively fuzzy-looking but dangerous cholla, a cactus that wields thousands of small barbed spines that are notoriously difficult to remove from its easily impaled victim. The pass was but a narrow strip of level ground, the vast stony desert dropping off just feet away to the north and south of our tents. We were in the blissful middle of no man's land, no footprints but our own breaking the virgin desert sand.

Backpacking the next morning down a ravine on the north side of the pass, we happened upon a slowly dripping seep—unmarked on our map, and probably only trickling due to the recent storm—that was productive enough for us to fill a few quart-size bottles with precious water. As we broke out of the mouth of the ravine and onto arid Hapaha Flat, my earlier breakfast—or maybe it was the desert seep's untreated water—rebelled and I began to get intense stomach cramps that stopped me in my tracks, doubled over in pain.

I brewed up a pot of ginger root tea in the shade of a large smoke tree where, to our astonishment and delight, a pair of friendly desert hares tentatively joined our company. The tea set me right, and we continued north across the sun-bleached flat and up a difficult canyon filled with room-size boulders to reach at dusk the remote "East Harper Plateau," our shorthand for the unnamed, boulder-choked high ground east of Harper Flat.

As Dave and Ted set up camp, I went off to "recce" our way off the far end of the plateau and take some compass bearings. Jumping from one large boulder to another in the dimming light, I failed to see the rigid, spear-tipped blade of a large desert agave aimed directly at me. My right knee hit it with such force that the blade broke off at the tip, leaving its needle-like spine embedded in my kneecap. Not in the surrounding tissue, but stuck in the bone. I hobbled back to camp, pulled the spine out with tweezers and wrapped an ace bandage around my throbbing knee.

We took an unnamed canyon off the plateau the next morning, dropping 2,500 vertical feet down a grueling five-mile channel clogged with thousands of boulders and rock slabs the size of studio apartments, a defile Dave came to ruefully christen Long Fucking Canyon. As we exited the backcountry the next day, a newly arriving heat wave boosted daytime temperatures into the high 80s. Running low on water, we got out just in time.

(Left to right) Michael Cooper, Dave Gordon and Ted Greenwald in camp
at the mouth of "Long Fucking Canyon" (DDM 2; February 18, 1995)

-14-

ROUGH SLEDDING

In late September 1994, four months before Desert Death March 2, my brother Mitch and I backpacked up to a glacier-fringed alpine lake on the east side of Broken Top, the eighth-highest peak in the Oregon Cascades. We hiked east from camp the next day along the top of the adjoining Tam McArthur Rim, enjoying spectacular views down either side of the long volcanic ridge into rural Central Oregon. Around twenty miles north of our lunchtime perch on the rim lay the tiny enchanting tourist town of Sisters, closely hemmed in on three sides by deep-green national forest. A bachelor at the time—I had broken up with my girlfriend Linda eighteen months earlier—I could not know as I gazed on the lovely scene that I would move to the town's sylvan outskirts four years later, married to a woman who would before then literally save my life. I would meet her only because of an afterthought.

A few weeks after my backpack with Mitch, I spied an appealing personal ad in Eugene's small artsy newspaper, the Eugene Weekly.[34] Responding to the enchanting pitch, I paid the requisite access fee and left a voice message for my potential paramour. As I was about to hang up, I noticed I still had a minute left to answer another ad without paying more. Loath to pass up a

---

34 In late 1994, the Internet had just very recently been commercialized and online dating was not yet in vogue.

freebie, I quickly scanned the also-rans and replied to one off the cuff. That second ad ended up being my future wife's.

Janet Huerta and I met a few days later at a small cafe. She arrived twenty minutes late—just as I concluded I'd been stood up and was about to leave—wearing a jarringly bright yellow business suit and complaining she'd just been sexually harassed at work. Not a great conversation starter. But she was beautiful, both wholesome and voluptuous, her dark-brown wavy hair framing a healthy complexion and strikingly crystal-clear, almond-shaped eyes. I was impressed she was the Development Director at the Relief Nursery, a local non-profit whose mission was to prevent and assuage the trauma of child abuse. Smart and winsome though she was, her poised bearing and business attire made me concerned she was too cultured and upper-crust to be a good fit with an ex-hippie musician-cum-wilderness explorer like me.

My reservation was moot. Janet had gotten sixty-two responses to her ad and, after our subsequent first date, she ended up choosing another suitor. Perhaps as a parting consolation, she offered to write a personal ad for me from a woman's perspective, a great idea in principle. In preparation, she asked me what I was looking for in a mate. "Health-conscious" was at the top of my list.

The ad she penned for me was dreadful. But thinking she must have better insight into the mysterious female mind than I, I went with it. Her first sentence, intended to attract a health-conscious mate, read, "Do you cherish your body?" The stuff of serial killers. The ad would receive zero responses.

We had a dim affinity and agreed to stay in touch, maybe get together as casual friends for a walk or chat over lunch. I called her phone number on three occasions over the next few weeks, leaving voice mails inviting her on a hike. I never got a reply; unknown to me, her housemates erased each message before she could hear it. Two months after my last unreturned call, I stumbled upon the slip of paper on which I'd scribbled her phone number and threw it away.

A week later, she called me out of the blue. She had broken up with the suitor she'd chosen because he turned out to be a controller, telling her what clothes to wear and so on. But I'd moved on emotionally. I was no longer interested in pursuing a romantic relationship—with any woman. Virtually all my previous love relationships, forged by chemistry, had taken more energy than they'd given and caused disruptive conflict and stress. I was very happy with my life now; my dual careers as a recording studio owner-engineer and pro-audio journalist were going great, and I was making good money and enjoying my freedom climbing and backpacking. Why ruin it? I had decided I would stay single unless and until a woman proved herself over time to be a compatible companion and steadfast ally. It had to be undeniable. I wouldn't reject romance if it came along, but I was done chasing it or even looking.

Still, I liked Janet and enjoyed her carefree company. Over the following six months, we went on many fun day hikes together. After a while I could tell she was falling in love with me, but I wasn't feeling the same. I liked her as a friend. And I was impressed by how adventurous she was. She was impulsive, up for doing anything exciting at a moment's notice. I slowly came to realize we were a lot more alike than I first thought, and not just in our shared love of hiking.

We went tandem skydiving together in July 1995, jumping out of a small prop plane at 10,000 feet with instructors strapped to our backs. When we landed I impulsively kissed her, surprising the both of us. In late August we did a four-day backpack trip in the Three Sisters Wilderness, climbing South Sister and a few smaller peaks (all non-technical "walk-ups") in the bargain. A week later we backpacked off-trail to a beautiful lake in the same wilderness and inadvertently stayed up until 3:30 A.M., talking intimately around a campfire. That night I began to really appreciate who she was, and awaken to who she was to me. I could tell she really understood me, loved me and didn't want to change me. She just wanted to be with me, and not in a clingy way. I really liked how I felt when I was around her, and wanted more. Everything about our relationship checked all the boxes: same likes, goals, humor, diet, politics and worldview. No drama. Easy. I was falling in love with her.

That backpacking trip marked a turning point. We became an item. A few months later, we moved into an old house on a large lot in the north part of Eugene to start our life together.

. . .

DDM 2 in El Niño-battered Anza-Borrego, my escape from the freak snow-storm on French Pete Creek, the wilderness trips and blossoming romance with Janet, a half dozen other backpacks—all that happened in 1995. Ed Lovegren and I also climbed Mount Washington together for the fourth time. Executed with military discipline, that ascent stands in stark contrast to my second attempt on Mount Jefferson a couple months later—the latter climb a case study in how *not* to scale a mountain.

I had arranged to rendezvous with climbing buddy John Englehart in Jefferson Park—a stunning, lake-studded subalpine basin with a clear view of the north side of Mount Jefferson—around dusk on September 19. Extraordinary athlete that he was, John planned to climb "Jeff" earlier that day and then climb it again with me the very next—no easy feat. The mountain, second highest in the Beaver State, is widely regarded as the most challenging and dangerous of the Oregon Cascades' ten highest peaks due to its remote and physically demanding approach, horrendously unstable rock and steeply pitched glaciers.

John arrived at our pre-arranged wilderness base camp with a three-inch-long patch of skin missing from his right forearm, revealing blood-spattered pink meat. While traversing the steep North Milk Creek Glacier on his way down from Jeff's summit earlier that day, the icy snow had given way under his feet. He was able to quickly self-arrest with his ice axe to prevent a fatal slide but left some skin on the mountain in the process.

I was eager to hear all the details about his first successful summit of the infamous mountain, so that I might know what to expect during our climb the following day. Like John, I aspired to summit all of the Oregon Cascades' major peaks.

"How was the climb?" I asked keenly.

"Good to get it out of the way," he replied sullenly. Alluding to the mountain's notoriously rotten rock, he added, "It's nothing but a big pile of shit." I'd never heard him curse before.

Late that night, the wind began to pick up in camp, an inauspicious development. We arose to strong gusts at sunrise but managed to have a relaxed breakfast—way too relaxed. I was infamous for always being the last to break camp, and I was being especially lazy that morning. Famous for his bottomless stomach, John was occupied devouring a never-ending parade of scrambled eggs, stacks of pancakes and sundry other dishes as we all too casually surveyed the mountain and discussed the route up. We wouldn't leave base camp until 9:30 A.M., likely over four hours too late to pull off the climb and return to camp before nightfall. Still we decided to take a stab at it.

We decided a direct assault on the precipitous Jefferson Park Glacier, on the mountain's north side, would be too dangerous due to numerous large open crevasses spanning much of its width and—according to a report I'd heard—frequent rockfall raining down on climbers from the cliffs above the ice. We opted instead to ascend the easier Russell Glacier on the mountain's northwest slope, climb the rocky West Rib eastward to stay above anticipated rockfall on the bordering North Milk Creek Glacier, and then follow Jeff's North Ridge to the summit pinnacle for the final pitch up to the top.

We started out at and maintained a very brisk pace. By the time we made it to the crevasse field on Russell Glacier, the wind was blowing 40 to 50 mph, whipping up clouds of scree on the West Rib 2,000 vertical feet above us. Fortunately, the crevasses on the glacier were easy to hike around. After two hours marching up the ice, we gained the West Rib, a horribly unstable and slanted ridge that successively loosed small rotten rocks down on us as we climbed it higher. The footing was like on ball bearings, climbing the proverbial two steps up and one step back. Traversing around the south side of Prehistoric Monster and Smith Rock, two crumbling gendarmes straddling the arête, we arrived at 3:30 P.M. at the Knife Edge, an aptly named, exceedingly narrow rib of rock.

A 50mph wind was blowing sideways across the exposed rib. We realized we'd each need a belay to protect us from being launched off the sheer rock and into the void, the first bounce 200 vertical feet below. Beyond the Knife Edge, we could expect very high winds on the North Ridge en route to the even more exposed and windblown summit pinnacle. Bolstering ourselves in the gale on the threshold of the Knife Edge, we could all too clearly see Jeff's summit before us, taunting. Although we were only 0.6 mile away from and 450 vertical feet below the summit, it might as well have been on another planet. We estimated it would take us around two hours and thirty minutes to make it to the summit because of the required setup and break-down of serial protective belays. Even if the winds were to miraculously cease, we calculated a trip to the summit would still cost us a descent down the crevasse-laden Russell Glacier in the dark. We were clearly out of time and wisely decided to bag it. "Live to climb another day," the saying goes.

Hurrying down off the mountain, we arrived back in camp around ten minutes after sunset. That night, the winds strengthened to over 60 mph. The lightweight, three-season tent I'd brought along, a recently purchased Sierra Designs Clip Flashlite, was flapping around too much in the wind to expect a peaceful night's sleep inside. I laid out under the stars in my sleeping bag, wearing several layers of clothes and vowing to climb the stern mountain again—eating a much earlier and quicker breakfast next time. Slowly drifting toward sleep, I fantasized about an adventure planned for the coming winter with Ted Greenwald and Dave Gordon: DDM 3, the most ambitious Desert Death March yet.

Scattered light snow, hail and sleet accompanied Ted, Dave and me as we backpacked over stony ground through the desolate foothills of the Eagle Mountains on January 22, 1996. It was our second day backpacking in the low-elevation Colorado Desert section of Joshua Tree National Park, early into a planned eleven-day Desert Death March. The expedition would take us seventy-five miles—around 95 percent of it cross-country—along a huge circular route through two mountain ranges and across the formidable Pinto Basin.

The trip nearly didn't happen. Several weeks before its launch, Ted announced that work and family obligations would force him to bail, a now familiar pattern. Dave and I tried the usually reliable Greenwald Maneuver, telling him we were going to do the trip without him. But this time Ted was unmoved. Determined, Dave and I initiated the crisis Reverse Greenwald Maneuver, telling Ted we were going to cancel the expedition altogether.

Our fallback succeeded. Several weeks later, we all convened in Anaheim on the heels of the winter NAMM Show of 1996, which I attended as *Mix* magazine's new Contributing Editor.

Our wintry second night in the Eagle Mountains proved the coldest of the trip, the temperature dropping to 18°F and forming thick ice in our water bottles. The next morning heralded the start of a mixed-blessing warming trend, only diffuse high clouds blunting the quickly increasing heat of the rising sun. We crossed over a low stony saddle, picked up six gallons of water at a cache off the 4WD Black Eagle Mine Road—one of four water caches we had set along our planned route—and backpacked northwest to the edge of the forebodingly desolate Pinto Basin. We hoped to cross the roughly 200,000-acre basin here, where its fearsome span narrowed between two encroaching mountain ranges and a traverse was more feasible.

It was high noon. Not a single tree—nor any shrub over three feet tall— was in sight across the virtually flat basin for as far as the eye could see in any direction. Stunted creosote bushes sparsely dotted the edges of huge, completely barren patches of sun-scorched earth, the ground looking as if a quarry of black gravel and rocks had been shattered, steamrolled flat and baked at high temperature into hard pavement. Nine miles away to the west, Pinto Mountain, its summit rising 2,400 feet above the desert floor, looked to be only a couple inches tall, a landscape view straight out of a spaghetti western. We hoped to climb the mountain once we got across the basin.

We knew our traverse would be slow and laborious, as carried water boosted each of our packs' weight to over 60 pounds. As we lumbered out onto the shadeless flat, my thermometer read 68°F—this in January. I imagined how backpacking here at any time other than the dead of winter would be absolutely brutal, probably deadly.

"There probably aren't too many days in the year you can cross Pinto Basin," I mused aloud.

"Let's hope this is one of them," Ted retorted, shooting me a poker face. I cracked up, and then wondered if he was joking or truly concerned.

In fact, it took us a day and a half to cross the basin. Arriving at the far side, the desert was much softer, with hummingbirds darting about larger shrubs and even scattered trees in our camp in sandy Pinto Wash, at the foot of Pinto Mountain. We bivouacked under the stars in our sleeping bags that night.

We climbed Pinto Mountain the next day. The summit was very windy, cold and treeless, only dried clumps of grass and shriveled desert shrubs clinging tenuously to life amid large blocks of rock. From our high perch, we thrilled to panoramic "airplane" views across Pinto Basin's vast expanse. In the far distance to the west, we spied some of the high terrain we had explored during DDM 1 two years earlier, neatly knitting the neighborhood together.

Descending to the desert's floor with Pinto Mountain's summit under our belts, we broke camp and backpacked once again across Pinto Basin, this time south to the foot of the Hexie Mountains and the fancifully named Fried Liver Wash—locus of the namesake Curse threatening the expedition. Camped at the mouth of the wash that evening, I surmised the Hexie Mountains must have been misspelled on our map; it was only logical that the Curse of Fried Liver Wash would emanate instead from the Hex-y Mountains. I worried the Curse of Fried Liver Wash had ominous culinary overtones. It would in fact prove to be a warning.

Throughout the trip, we had all taken turns preparing group meals. To reduce cooking times, Ted—a masterful backcountry chef—soaked whole grains and legumes all day in water inside a lightweight closed container, rehydrating them for a later dinner as we hiked. As we set up camp deep in the Hexie Mountains at the end of our seventh day out, Ted pulled a container full of pre-soaked orzo out of his backpack and instantly realized his mistake. The pasta had coalesced into a large slimy clod eerily resembling white snot in woodworking glue. Eat it or go hungry, it would be the worst meal of my life. To rib Ted, Dave and I jokingly compared every meal we had afterwards to his extraordinary counter-masterpiece. The humor escaped Ted.

We backpacked the next day to Monument Mountain and made the quick and easy scramble up to its rocky summit for its sweeping 360-degree views of five mountain ranges plus Pinto and Cottonwood Basins. Our camp in the latter basin twenty-four hours later would be memorable, both for its dazzling beauty and an unexpected nighttime announcement.

First, the scenery: Cottonwood Basin was archetypal desert scrubland lavishly dressed in long dry grasses, Joshua trees and huge junipers. Rimming the gorgeous basin, the Cottonwood Mountains looked like a soft, rumpled blanket in the half-light of that evening's gibbous moon. But against this lovely backdrop, we couldn't escape that we'd been backpacking strenuously out in bone-dry backcountry for nine days without even sponge bathing. (Even when brushing my teeth, I'd allowed myself only one mouthful of water in order to conserve the lifesaving resource.) We were all absolutely filthy and odorous.

As I was drifting off to sleep that night inside the small tent I shared with Ted, I suddenly heard a pained announcement emit close to my left ear. Ted's voice was halting and hushed, tinged with desperation:

"I just . . . want . . . to wash . . . my asshole."

That about summed it up.

Over the following two days, we backpacked west under progressively dark clouds that brought light overnight showers, arriving finally where Dave's 4WD van was parked to end the expedition. As we drove out of the park, the biggest storm of that winter hit with a wallop. We had escaped the Curse of Fried Liver Wash by the skin of our (poorly brushed) teeth.

Returning to Oregon, half the backpacks I did the remainder of that year were with my live-in girlfriend Janet, exploring for three cumulative weeks Eastern Oregon's Blue Mountains, Central Oregon's Newberry National Volcanic Monument, and wilderness areas in the Oregon and Washington Cascades. Being with Janet in the wild had become my top priority, but I still felt the itch to do a couple solo backpack trips that summer; being totally alone in wilderness gave me a calming and anchoring perspective on life. Climbing Mount Washington in July with the Obsidians outdoor club—my fourth summit of that lightning rod—I unexpectedly ran into John Englehart and his new fiancé Kristen on my way down to the rappel point; what a small world the mountaineering community lives in. In September I climbed alone to the top of Lakeview Mountain, a minor summit in the Diamond Peak Wilderness. Every trip went like clockwork. Then, in March the following year, the clock broke.

In the afternoon on March 27, 1997, Janet and I drove up to Santiam Pass in the Oregon Cascades to get in a few hours of cross-country skiing ahead of a fast-approaching snowstorm. I had learned how to ski three years earlier. But although I had skied over 200 miles of backcountry since, I was still a mediocre skier in 1997.

Skiing into the Mount Jefferson Wilderness on the Santiam Lodge Trail that afternoon in March, Janet and I quickly lost track of the trail under deep, hard-packed snow. Following an easily retraceable true-north heading on my compass, we continued farther into the wilderness, alone and making fresh tracks. Around two miles in we decided to head back in the face of increasingly threatening skies.

The imminent storm was forecast to dump six inches of snow in the mountains that evening, but we weren't concerned; we figured we'd be back to our car in about an hour, around sunset and before the storm gathered much force. My thermometer read 32°F. The snow under our skis was terrible quality—not icy, nor powder, but the consistency of wet cement, making turns very difficult for an amateur like me to execute.

As we glided down a short slope, I noted a tree with a deep well dead ahead at the bottom of our run. I tried to turn to avoid it, but the angles of my skis were locked in the cement-like mix. Worse, both skis were pointed slightly outward, resulting in an ever-widening stance I couldn't shift onto one leg to correct. Moments later I crashed into the tree well in nearly a full split and felt something in my left knee snap like a rubber band. Jolted by extremely sharp pain, I immediately knew the damage.

"I've torn my medial meniscus!" I cried out to Janet, referring to the cartilage on the inside of my knee. A later MRI would prove my snap diagnosis correct. What I didn't realize was I'd also suffered a Grade 2, or partial, tear of my medial collateral ligament in the same knee.[35] My knee was shot.

Janet was visibly alarmed but kept a level head. She helped pull me out of the tree well, no easy feat with my six-foot-long skis jammed into the steep, icy sides. Once free, I removed my skis and tried to stand, but doing so caused excruciating pain.

"There's no way I can ski out of here," I grimly told Janet. "You're going

---

35 The medial collateral ligament connects the femur (thigh bone) to the tibia (the largest bone in the shin), helping to stabilize the knee joint.

to have to leave me and go for help. Follow our ski tracks and a south compass heading back to the highway, and get to Hoodoo as fast as you can."

We knew the National Ski Patrol had a tiny office in the Hoodoo Ski Area at Santiam Pass. Enlisting their help was our only hope of getting me out of the wilderness that evening. We both knew I was going to get very cold before then, sitting on snow in subfreezing temperature. Janet gave me one of her layers of clothing and wrapped me in a thin Mylar emergency blanket we had packed in our first-aid kit. As she turned to leave, large snowflakes began to fall. Then she was gone, and I was alone.

I'd been stranded before in a snowstorm in the wild, nearly two years earlier at the head of French Pete Creek, but this situation was far more perilous—I was completely exposed to the elements and crippled. My disabling injury aside, I had no tools with which to dig a cave in the icy snowpack. All I could do was sit on the snow and wait for help. When the sun set an hour later, I was already starting to shiver. By then a hard snowfall was beginning to fill in our ski tracks—the breadcrumbs trail a rescue team would need in order to find me. I figured Janet had probably only then made it to Hoodoo. By the time—or if—she came back with help, our tracks might be completely covered by snow and it might already be dark. I would be a needle in a blind haystack. I began to consider a dreadful option: hiking out.

Another half hour passed while I anxiously deliberated. My hooded head and shoulders were completely draped in fresh snow. I was shivering progressively worse, and twilight was steadily dimming the surrounding forest. Not knowing if Janet had managed to find help, and doubting I could survive the night totally exposed to the storm, I made the grim decision to try to make it to the highway under my own steam; even if I only made it partway, I reasoned, a rescue team would find me that much sooner.

I struggled to stand up on my one good leg. Gripping my skis and poles in both hands, I firmly stabbed their tips into the snow a foot in front of me. These were the crutches I resolved I would use to hop on one leg all the way out of the backcountry.

At this point, I could not know of the drama that had unfolded over the last half hour at Hoodoo. Janet had made it to the National Ski Patrol's office right before sundown, only to find the door locked and a sign stating the office was closed for the night. Panicking, she ran out into the nearly empty, adjacent parking lot shouting at the top of her lungs for help. A couple men heard her cries just as they were about to drive away. Members of the National Ski Patrol, they had closed up shop a couple minutes earlier. They reopened their office and threw together some rescue gear, a process that to Janet's dismay took another thirty minutes.

Back in the wilderness, my and Janet's ski tracks were now rapidly filling in with fresh snow. I set my compass to a south heading, girded myself, and made my first one-legged hop forward with my makeshift crutches. Even landing on my right foot, my torn left knee wobbled on impact, causing me to scream in wretched pain. I waited a few moments to regain my composure and resolve. Replanting my poles and skis, I hopped forward again, screaming on impact. For twenty minutes I repeated the pitiful routine—hop and scream, hop and scream, hop and scream. In all that time I managed to cover only 100 yards.

A short rise around nine or ten feet high now lay before me. I didn't have the will to struggle the long way around it, and decided to go up and over—a grievous mistake. Unknown to me, the rise was a weak snow bridge over a hidden creek. Stabbing my makeshift crutches into the snow, I hopped to the top of the rise on my good leg, screaming on every bound. As I landed on one foot at the very top, the snow suddenly collapsed beneath me. I reflexively threw both my arms out to my sides, catching myself at chest height on the rim of the small hole I had opened in the bridge. To my absolute horror, I saw a creek flowing rapidly downhill several feet directly below me. If I fell into that creek, I'd be soaking wet and trapped inside a hidden snow tunnel—game over.

My heart racing, I slowly inched my arms forward, taking extreme care not to collapse the snow bridge any further. Gingerly, I pulled myself prostrate over the lip of the hole. Still lying face down, I spread my arms and legs to distribute my weight as much as possible and swam on my belly in the snow down the rise. I made it to the bottom shaken and shivering, wet with snow that had gotten pushed down the inside front of my Gore-Tex jacket during my belly-swim. Physically and emotionally done, all I could do now was huddle in the escalating storm.

Another miserable half hour passed. With only a few minutes of faint light remaining before total dark, I resigned myself to a nightlong struggle for survival. Mere seconds later I began hearing voices calling out my name from far off. I recognized one was Janet's. I shouted back frantically, repeatedly, guiding her to my location. To my boundless joy and relief, she appeared a couple minutes later with the two men from the National Ski Patrol, all of them breathless from exertion.

The men quickly assembled a modular sled, gingerly lifted me onto it and strapped me in. Over the next hour-plus, they hauled me like sled dogs out of the wilderness, wearing headlamps to light the dark. It was a jerky and bumpy ride, my torn knee wrenching whenever the sled skidded into a tree trunk, but I truly didn't care. I was going to live, in no small part thanks to Janet.

I would spend the next eighteen days back in Eugene with my left leg immobilized in a splint, waiting impatiently for an opening in the local hospital's backlogged schedule to operate on my torn knee. It would take almost three months after the surgery for me to regain enough strength and range of motion to go backpacking again. But the hard knocks kept coming. That summer, the landlord for my commercial recording studio informed me she would discontinue renting the building—an existential threat to my business. But what at first seemed an unmitigated disaster would ultimately turn out to be a blessing in disguise. One door closes, another opens.

Michael Cooper in Pinto Basin (DDM 3; January 24, 1996)

Michael Cooper and his future wife Janet Huerta, circa February 1997

-15-

JEFF

From the day I got off the operating table for knee surgery in April 1997, I was laser-focused on becoming fit again as quickly as possible so I could resume adventuring. I underwent physical therapy twice a week and did prescribed rehabilitative exercises at home like my life depended on it. As soon as I was off crutches, I began taking regimented neighborhood walks, increasing their duration every other day first by seconds and then minutes, eventually including short hills, until I was once again able to day-hike carrying a light pack on wilderness trails. By early July, I was doing easy two- and three-day backpacks in the Oregon Cascades again with Janet.

At the end of that month, I went climbing with colleague and friend Nick Batzdorf, then the Editor-in-Chief of pro-audio magazine *Recording*. Our bid was an ascent of The Husband, climbing from a base camp still locked in last winter's snowpack two days in from a trailhead. Not a very big mountain, The Husband was nevertheless rock unstable as any I'd ever been on; when I attempted to climb it solo a year earlier, the scree was so steep and loose on the customary route up the mountain's southeast flank that I'd take a step up only to slide instantly back down to the exact same spot. Abandoning the scree slope, I tried climbing instead along the somewhat firmer gendarmes atop the mountain's south ridge, but they ultimately led to a crumbling perpendicular drop-off not forewarned by my map. Dangerously unstable to downclimb, it was a dead end, the climb shot.

Thankfully, when Nick and I climbed The Husband the following summer, much of the fathomless scree burying its southeast slope was itself under an immense snowfield securely stair-stepped with hard-packed sun cups. Easy. But higher up, on the melted slope just below the jumbled crown of summit rock, the mountain was pea gravel on steeply pitched boilerplate slabs, the climbing like wearing skates on marbles, forcing us into cat-like postures for better purchase.

We summited quickly and didn't stay long. An impressively dark thunderstorm ballooning over glacier-clad South Sister—just four miles away—was quickly coming our way, chasing us off the summit. As we bounded down the huge sun-cupped snow slope for the relative safety of short trees below, thunderclaps boomed like howitzers overhead. White snow against black sky—it was, as Ed Lovegren would've said, elegant. Except, there were literally hundreds of ravenous mosquitos waiting to celebrate our return to base camp. Aside from when we were climbing on The Husband, they pestered us every step we took during that five-day trip.

It was a bad year for insects. Five weeks after climbing The Husband, I was backpacking alone off-trail thirteen miles to the south when I stumbled upon a hidden nest of yellow jackets and got stung six times. Hornets stung John Englehart and his new wife Kristen that same day while backpacking in the vicinity. Some equestrians they met reported they'd also been attacked.

The yellow jackets' assaults were bookended by a weeklong backpack with Janet halfway around Oregon's massive Mount Hood and a climb of Diamond Peak with my brother Mitch and the Engleharts. The climb was Mitch's first and followed a new east-side route I had devised, which made it extra-special.

Unfortunately, that was also the summer I received notice I would lose use of the highly specialized building that had housed my commercial recording studio for the past eight years. In a way, I'd become a victim of my own success. The studio was booked with clients five months in advance. The landlord for the building had a son—a musician—who saw how well my business was doing and hoped he could duplicate its success by opening his own recording facility in the space. To get him to put off my eviction until I could wrap up already booked sessions, I paid him double the previously established rent—my initiative—for the next five months. But the clock was already ticking.

I was still looking for a suitable building to relocate my recording studio to when the clock ran out in January. Every available building I had inspected up and down the 308-mile-long Interstate 5 corridor in Oregon was a bust, requiring cost-prohibitive and months-long construction for it to meet a recording facility's highly specialized acoustical and electrical needs. I moved my recording equipment into storage and started looking for freelance work to hold me over until I could figure out my next move.

I began writing recording-related articles for *Keyboard* magazine, my fifth periodical for the music industry. (Although I was a Contributing Editor for *Mix*, that magazine's Editor-in-Chief gave his blessing to my pursuing needed outside writing income.) My recording career was in tatters, but Janet was through it all rock-steady. Months earlier when I first told her I was going to lose the studio, the first words out of her mouth were, "What are we going to do?"

"We," not "you." That's when I realized she was steadfastly committed to our relationship, come rain or shine. On February 14, 1998—Valentine's Day—we married. Having failed to relocate my business in populous Western Oregon, it was time to think outside the box. Janet asked me where I most wanted to live, never mind where I thought would be practical. I told her I'd always wanted to live in Sisters, a tiny tourist town, population 815, lying in the sunset shadows of the Oregon Cascades and on the doorstep of my favorite wilderness areas. Two weeks after we married, she quit her secure job in Eugene and we moved into a small rural development a couple miles west of Sisters. With little foreseeable income, we figured if we lasted there on savings for only a couple years, it would nevertheless be a wonderful adventure. It turned out to be our best move ever.

The day I opened a downsized recording studio in the Sisters area, it was booked seven months in advance with loyal clients from Western Oregon committed to driving over the Cascades to work with me. Janet was offered a high-level position with a non-profit during her first job interview. We rented one of the few available houses we could find outside town, loved it and bought it three months later. Our new home was just a four-minute walk from the Deschutes National Forest and thirty to forty-five minutes by car from multiple trailheads for three wilderness areas on the east slopes of the Cascade Range—much of which I hadn't yet explored. Like a kid in a candy store, I would hike and backpack that first year in Sisters well over 400 miles, mostly with Janet.

I kept close contact with my mountaineering buddies in Eugene and rendezvoused with them in the Cascades for a few climbs that year. The first was almost fatal. On July 18, 1998, I climbed Mount Washington with Ed Lovegren and John and Kristen Englehart to reach the summit for my fifth time. On the way up, two other parties had very near misses with rockfall in the Notch, the cramped couloir between the summit pinnacle and an encroaching gendarme. The first incident is etched permanently into my memory. While climbing the pinnacle, a careless man accidentally loosed a large boulder, sending it plummeting toward his two tweenager kids standing three feet apart directly below him in the Notch. The careening rock shot a diagonal path between the two kids, missing each by mere inches. Had it hit either one, it would have surely propelled their broken body a thousand vertical feet off the mountainside with fatal internal injuries. Ed was totally unnerved by the near miss. Now, after over thirty summits of Mount Washington, he vowed he would never climb the mountain again. Not so much for his own safety. He'd seen enough death on other climbs.

A few weeks later, Janet, Kristen Englehart, Nick Batzdorf and I backpacked to a base camp at the south foot of Middle Sister in support of John Englehart's "Birthday Extravaganza": a couple weeks before his forty-first birthday, John would attempt to solo the Three Sisters volcanoes—North, Middle and South—and the smaller Little Brother in one day, traveling fast and light with worrisomely few supplies and clothing. We first met up with him—we climbing from the south, he from the north—mid-day on the summit of Middle Sister, marking his three mountains down and one to go. As dusk fell later that day, he arrived victorious in his quartet summit quest at our base camp, where we were waiting with a tent and sleeping bag for him.

In early September I climbed South Sister up its less frequented southeast side with my brother Mitch, notching my third time on that beautiful glacier-capped summit. I had long ago summited nine of the ten highest peaks in the Oregon Cascades, five of them multiple times. The only one still eluding me was scary Mount Jefferson, the most dangerous and punishing of them all. A week after climbing with Mitch, I would make my third and final attempt to reach the monster's lofty summit.

Before you even attempt to climb Mount Jefferson via the South Ridge—widely regarded as the easiest route—you've got to backpack through wilderness eight miles and 2,900 feet up in elevation to base camp, hauling not just the usual backpacking supplies but also climbing ropes, webbing, harness, ice axe, crampons, helmet, climbing pack and protective hardware (carabiners, snow pickets and so on) for the summit assault. Then, climbing the mountain from base camp at 6,000 feet altitude, you slog up another 4,000 vertical feet on extremely unstable rock before you even get to the technical bits: angling up the steep Milk Creek Glacier, followed by the final rock climb up the summit pinnacle to the top. John and Kristin Englehart, Ed Lovegren and I planned to do the round-trip backpack and climb's 15,000 feet of combined elevation gain and drop in just fifty hours, including downtime spent sleeping and resting in base camp before and after the climb. We were under no illusion—it was going to be brutal.

My backpack weighed 64 pounds during the grueling backpack in. It would've weighed more but for John taking extra shares of climbing gear from everyone's packs. His extraordinary ability to shoulder monstrous loads, which he did with astonishing ease, had earned him the nickname Human Ox.

In base camp that evening, Ed talked about his coming to terms with what he called "the horrors," the endless grim scenarios that play out repeatedly in the mountaineer's mind the night before a dangerous climb.

"I've learned over the years they don't mean anything," he told me. "They're not omens."

Nevertheless, I tossed and turned in my tent for an hour before drifting off for four meager hours of sleep. Ed took a sleeping pill shortly before retiring—his tried-and-true prescription for the horrors—and fell serenely asleep within minutes. We all awakened at 2:50 A.M. for breakfast in the cold and dark, a grudging concession needed to get an early start on what we hoped would be a fifteen-hour climb (or three hours faster than the typical climbing party on this route).

It was 40°F when we began climbing with headlamps a little after 4:30 A.M. The South Ridge quickly lived up to its infamous reputation, sliding us one frustrating step down for every two steps we took up its steep slope of incredibly loose scree and talus. Bowling ball-size boulders occasionally tumbled toward us from above, prompting evasive maneuvers. After gaining only 2,500 vertical feet from base camp, I was already feeling very fatigued and a little nauseous from the altitude and exertion. Nevertheless, we reached Red Ridge (at roughly 10,000 feet altitude) in just under five hours. The summit was now only a quarter mile away, but we figured to get there would take us two more hours—four hours round-trip—due to the technical nature of the climbing ahead.

The sobering Milk Creek Glacier lay in our way. Situated at the foot of a false summit pinnacle, the route across the glacier is marked in climbing guides as a Death Route, noting a fall here would likely result in a tumbling slide down ice to bone-breaking rocks 1,500 vertical feet below. I spied a boulder-strewn break in the glacier a few hundred feet below us and reckoned it might limit my injuries if I hit it and stopped, a morbid consolation.

We had hoped the late-summer timing for our climb would result in the west-facing glacier being melted out at its top, forming a moat we could safely walk inside along the base of the false summit. The moat had indeed formed, but it was shallow and ragged—breached in many places—and very icy, offering no real protection. We had no practical choice but to climb up and across the face of the precipitous glacier.

Using crampons and an ice axe, we each carefully began front-pointing our way up the snow- and ice-covered slope, off belay except for on one particularly treacherous thirty-foot pitch inclined at roughly a 60-degree angle. My ass hanging over 6,000 vertical feet of mountainside to the valley below, I painstakingly tested each step I kicked into the ice to confirm it would hold my weight before planting my ice axe higher and taking the next. When we finally gained the short west-running ridge of bare red scree at the base of the true summit pinnacle, I breathed a huge sigh of relief.

We removed our crampons and left our ice axes on the ridge for the rock climb ahead of us. The usual route up the summit pinnacle was on its northwest side. John, our climb leader, took us directly up the west side. It was straightforward rock at first, and we free climbed most of it. But forty vertical feet below the summit, the going got tough. John led and then belayed the rest of us on a difficult pitch with around 500 feet of exposure (the vertical drop one would likely fall if the belay failed). The crux of the pitch was a 5.7 move.[36] Difficult for an intermediate-level climber like me, it required hanging onto the lip of an overhang directly above me while swinging my body to the right onto a rock slab suspended at chest height, a move more difficult than anything I'd attempted before. I told John I expected to fall, so he could brace himself and be ready to brake the rope's play, but I succeeded in making the move. Ed followed and, a couple minutes later, we were all on Mount Jefferson's summit.

To say the summit was an unusual place would be a big understatement. Huge light-gray slabs lay at various angles in a jumbled heap, their tops crisscrossed with dark stripes where the rock had been crystallized by white-hot lightning strikes. A crystal-clear blue sky hung over massive distant peaks in stark relief. Over 100 miles to the north in Washington state, we could see Mount Adams's glacier-crowned summit and, fifty miles beyond it, Mount Rainier. The verdant Willamette Valley lay sixty miles to the west and, farther still, Mary's Peak dominated the skyline in Oregon's Coast Range. To the south, Three Fingered Jack, Mount Washington, the Three Sisters and numerous other landmarks of the Oregon Cascades lay strung out like a shiny pearl necklace. Central Oregon's old Ochoco Mountains sprawled far to the east.

The warm, sunny day and intoxicating views—not to mention fatigue—enticed us to linger, but we knew not to do so for long. After a half hour

36 Climbs in the US are rated in terms of their difficulty using the Yosemite Decimal System (YDS), with higher numbers denoting progressively greater difficulty. Classes 5.1 through 5.15 have handholds and footholds but require a belay to protect from a potentially fatal fall.

relaxing and taking photos, we decided to head down off the summit before we got too comfortable and lost our edge. But more important, we knew rising temperatures and a direct afternoon sun would be melting the west-facing Milk Creek Glacier, making the steep ice less solid during our return across and down it. Indeed, when we viewed the glacier after downclimbing the summit pinnacle, it looked like bags of loose crushed ice had been emptied where we had front-pointed up it with crampons a couple hours earlier. Nervous our ice axes and crampons might not hold us, we all traded belays across the ice.

We made it back to Red Ridge at 2:15 P.M. and, using Ed's cell phone, called his wife and Janet in turn to let them know the most dangerous part of the climb was behind us, an assessment that soon afterwards proved overly sunny. We hurriedly secured our helmets, crampons and hardware to the outside of our packs, spurred on by our now worrisome water situation: Ed had only one pint left, and John and Kristen and I were already completely dry. We were still 4,000 vertical feet above base camp.

Dropping down the South Ridge, we immediately got off course when we laxly followed a misguided climber's trail that angled us too far east. We realized our mistake after dropping 200 vertical feet, but now the way directly back over to the South Ridge was blocked by the Waldo Glacier. Too tired and thirsty to countenance climbing back up to where we got off course, we decided to cross a fifty-foot-wide tongue of extremely steep, snow-covered ice near the top of the glacier—unroped and with helmets off—to go directly back to the ridge. A slip during the traverse would likely result in a fatal slide 1,500 to 2,000 vertical feet down the glacier. In that moment, I remembered most climbing accidents happen on the way down precisely because of this sort of incaution and lassitude. But I was too tired to raise an objection.

Thankfully, we made the dicey traverse and regained the South Ridge without incident. We plunge-stepped quickly down the ridge's spine to 8,700 feet altitude. Peering down the west side of the ridge, we spied a pool of precious snowmelt at the bottom of a remnant glacier. John, Kristen and I glissaded with our ice axes down the glacier to the water and joyfully filled our bottles. Perhaps emboldened by our successful but reckless crossing of the top of Waldo Glacier, Ed tried to downclimb the ice using only trekking poles. He slipped but managed to self-arrest using his poles, severely bending them both in the process and shaving generous amounts of skin off his knees and shins before bringing his slide to a halt.

It was Jeff's final affront. We made it back down to base camp a couple hours later, two hours ahead of schedule. The morning after the exhausting thirteen-hour climb, we backpacked the eight miles and 2,900 vertical feet back down to the trailhead. I limped the last pounding mile, both knees throbbing, regurgitating under my breath John's prior assessment of climbing Mount Jeff: "Good to get it out of the way."

John Englehart belays Ed Lovegren (out of sight) forty feet below Mount Jefferson's summit (September 11, 1998).

(Left to right) Michael Cooper, John Englehart and
Ed Lovegren on Mount Jefferson's summit

-16-

BALANCING ACT

The last year of the twentieth century was challenging for backpackers in the Pacific Northwest. Storms in the Oregon Cascades during the winter of 1998-1999 had dumped over twenty feet of snow on Santiam Pass west of Sisters, burying the transecting Highway 20 several times under avalanches. The high country was inaccessible without skis or snowshoes until July. Even then, Janet and Mitch and I had to backpack atop four to six feet of hard-packed snow to get to mid-elevation Midget Lake in the Mount Jefferson Wilderness.

Large snow banks would still block parts of the higher Pacific Crest Trail into September. Late that month, Janet and I rendezvoused with John and Kristen Englehart at a remote camp off the PCT in the Mount Thielsen Wilderness. After we all climbed Mount Thielsen together, Janet and I continued backpacking north on the PCT for another week, bagging Tipsoo Peak and Cowhorn Mountain along the way. The day after we got out of the wilderness, heavy snows shut down the high country to backpackers for the winter.

I would have two dramatic turnabouts the next year. First, to my dismay Janet told me she really wanted for us to have a pet dog. I hated dogs. My father had brought one home when I was a little boy but got rid of it the next day after it bit me. The trauma of the bite and my father's swift expulsion of the mutt made indelible impressions. Twice again when I was an adult, dogs ran up to me and sank their teeth while I was minding my own business, reinforcing my negative perspective. Aggressive dogs running loose near their owners' wilderness camps had also threatened me a few times in the backcountry. The thought of having a pet dog was to me like inviting Satan into our home.

But I didn't want to stand in the way of Janet's bliss. And I realized it was emotionally and spiritually unhealthy for me to keep having negative visceral reactions to every canine encounter. I decided to attempt to make peace with the species. We brought home a female golden retriever puppy. How could I not fall in love? That affectionate and joy-filled creature quickly became our steady backpacking companion and inspired a dramatic one-eighty in my relationship with barking carnivores. But far more dramatic was my second turnabout that year. Except this time, it was not a good one.

In July 2000 I suddenly began having serial episodes of disabling vertigo attacks. The first one was a doozy that landed me in the ER, so extreme it was. Most who get vertigo experience it visually as their surroundings spinning around them on one axis—the horizontal—like on a high-speed merry-go-round. Lying in bed, I saw the room spinning around not one but three axes—vertical, horizontal and diagonal—so rapidly I could not make any sense of my surroundings. Even with my eyes closed, I felt I was tumbling down a bottomless well, head up, then down, then sideways from one split second to the next. Horribly nauseated, I couldn't hold down food. I had to crawl to the bathroom with eyes closed, slowly dragging my forehead along the floor, to keep from immediately vomiting even liquids. After two days with no respite, unable to eat and barely drinking, Janet drove me to a hospital twenty-five miles away; I threw up water—the only thing left in my stomach—before we got out of our driveway.

In the ER, I was given fluids intravenously to stabilize me. The attending physician said I probably had labyrinthitis, an inflammation of the inner ear that would resolve on its own after a few days. It didn't. For weeks after returning home from the ER, I had to hold onto walls while walking in order to avoid falling over. In addition to vertigo, I developed a condition called oscillopsia, a visual disturbance in which everything in my field of vision appeared to jump up and down as I walked.

I consulted a specialist to find an answer to my mysterious, persistent condition. After running a few tests that returned indeterminate results, he told me to see him again in a year if my symptoms didn't resolve. Over the next few months, the oscillopsia petered out and the disabling vertigo spells became far less frequent. Still, a general dizziness persisted 24/7, and there was another bizarre symptom: I felt disconnected from my surroundings, like I was viewing them on a gossamer panoramic movie screen. Discouraged by the failure to receive a conclusive diagnosis, and in light of the fact that my most severe symptoms had abated, I decided I'd try to live with my condition. I wouldn't seek another medical consultation until over six years later. That delay would turn out to be a big mistake.

I couldn't go climbing big mountains with such poor balance, but I wouldn't let it stop me from backpacking. Janet had over the last year become my primary backpacking companion. We started out with an easy overnighter with Mitch in the Mount Jefferson Wilderness in mid-August 2000, barely a month after my trip to the ER and with acute symptoms still not fully allayed. I did okay on that trip, so Janet and I did an off-trail backpack in the Mount Washington Wilderness a week later. By the end of the month, my symptoms had improved enough that we went backpacking for several days in Northern California's Marble Mountain Wilderness with Whitaker, a trip cut short on the fifth day after six inches of snow dumped on our camp beside the Pacific Crest Trail. A couple weeks later, Janet and I climbed two relatively small cinder cones in the Three Sisters Wilderness during a three-day backpack.

Those trips gave me confidence I could handle bigger adventures despite my still constant dizziness. Ted Greenwald and I had talked a couple years earlier, during an autumn backpack in Northern California's Yolla Bolly Wilderness, about wanting to do another Desert Death March. I had since rigorously studied the topo maps for the Coxcomb Mountains, a remote range whose sunset-fired pink and orange crags we'd admired from a distance while crossing Pinto Basin in Joshua Tree National Park in 1996. The terrain shown on the area maps looked really gnarly. I called Ted in late 2000—a few months into my health crisis—and told him I had devised an admittedly iffy route through the most rugged section of the mountains. We met up three months later at the conclusion of the Winter NAMM Show in Anaheim and left for the desert. Desert Death March 4 would be the most hardcore DDM yet.

-17-

SWANSONG

One of the side benefits of having an intimidating Desert Death March looming on my January calendar was it impelled me to stay in great shape during the preceding inclement fall and winter months, when I might've otherwise lazed into couch-potato hibernation—training outdoors in December and January in Central Oregon could be pretty unpleasant. To condition myself both physically and mentally for DDM 4, I briskly hiked three to five miles every other day carrying fifty pounds, often in stormy weather with temperatures nearing 20°F. To harden myself further, I deliberately post-holed with my heavy load through knee-deep snow to the top of a short steep cinder cone in the foothills of the Cascades near my home. Besides making me stronger, the strenuous hiking greatly improved my impaired balance to where I was only mildly dizzy.

It was imperative I got into peak condition. The route I had planned for DDM 4—forty-two miles long, every step of it off-trail—required crossing the shadeless Pinto Basin twice and punching through the rugged Coxcomb Mountains at the east end of Joshua Tree National Park via very steep, remote canyons. Judging by the maps' contour lines and past experience backpacking elsewhere in the park with similar topography, the canyons would likely be jammed with large boulders or stair-stepped with dry waterfalls.

Dave Gordon had bowed out of the expedition, making it even more dangerous for me and Ted, for a serious disabling injury for one of us in the waterless backcountry would force a hard choice by both: send the intact partner for help (thereby abandoning the injured) or stay and tend to the injured while life-sustaining carried water slowly dwindles to zero. The Coxcombs had no cell coverage, and we had no personal locator beacon with which to signal for rescue.

Ted, now living in the Bay Area and working nose-to-the-grindstone as Senior Editor at *Wired* magazine, was so busy at work and home—his wife and he had a small child—that he barely glanced at the topo maps before the trip's launch. He trusted I'd done thorough research and planning, and that my navigation skills would guide us no matter where we were going. But more to the point, he seemed to be up for anything no matter how hardcore. The Desert Death Marches had become more important to him over the years, and he was primed for high adventure. I loved and respected him for that. A physically and mentally sturdy man, Ted was someone with whom I had supreme confidence to tackle the Coxcombs. Which was good, because nobody else we knew wanted to join us. After hearing they'd have to carry a 70-pound backpack (including three gallons of water) cross-country through extreme desert terrain, those who didn't immediately cite scheduling conflicts simply said, "Sounds interesting, but I don't think I'd like to do that."

Maybe that was for the best. You can never tell ahead of time how you're going to get along with someone new once you're relying on each other 24/7 for survival. Just the possibility you could be co-dependently stuck in remote backcountry with someone you don't like is reason to balk at inviting a wild card along, because it's not like you could just up and leave him. Fortunately, Ted and I got along great. And, my balance deficit aside, our athletic abilities were evenly matched, which increased our chances of a successful expedition.

On January 22, 2001, we struck out north across the stone-littered, hard-baked east end of Pinto Basin under sunny skies but thankfully in mild temperatures. The Curse of the Inverted Siphon—emanating from a peculiar eponymous landmark noted on our topo—wasted no time trying to kill the expedition. Ted and I both broke through hidden jackrabbit burrows while crossing the basin, hyperextending our knees under our 70-pound loads. We made camp at sundown within striking distance of the Coxcombs and eagerly unpacked supplies for dinner, only to find the fuel line for our only camp stove was stubbornly clogged; it would barely produce flickering flames for the remainder of the expedition. That night, my inflatable sleeping pad went flat from an invisible puncture that could not be repaired in the field. This was just day one.

The next morning, we climbed east into the mountains up the toughest canyon we'd ever attempted. As I'd anticipated—both with dread and delight—the steep defile was choked fully across its narrow span with hundreds of large boulders, some fifteen to twenty feet high. At each seeming impasse, we dropped our now 60-pound packs—we'd each drunk a gallon of packed water the previous day—to scout around for a climbable crack or knobby holds. Finding a way up, we would free climb to the top and then haul our backpacks up to us with parachute cord. We repeated this scout-and-climb sequence countless times on our way up the clogged canyon. Occasional dead ends forced us to retreat down-canyon a bit, angle around and eventually find another way that would go higher still before stalling. Although the canyon was only 1.0 mile long and gained just 1,200 vertical feet from bottom to top, the going was so tough it took us fully five hours to backpack it, prompting us to name the defile Short Motherfucking Canyon.

The effort was more than worthwhile. We topped out in the mid-afternoon and entered the most beautiful desert basin I'd ever laid eyes on. Inner Basin's flat and sandy floor, sparsely dotted with dusky-green creosote bush, was surrounded on all sides by blond and orange and pink rock pillars, standing apart from sheer cliff walls dissected by long vertical cracks into towering rectangles. The sense of the place was of profound remoteness, undisturbed and quiet and serene, a peaceful refuge. We saw no human footprints—there or, for that matter, anywhere else along our entire trip's route. No footprints for forty-two miles. Wonderful.

In fact, Joshua Tree National Park ranger Jeff Ohlfs would later confirm in a phone conversation "only a dozen rugged individuals make it into Inner Basin each year." Ted and I doubted they did it the way we did. They likely took another canyon—only a third as steep and much wider than Short Motherfucking Canyon—on the less remote northwest side of the mountain range, a way in we'd rejected offhand and called "the Sissy

Route." We wanted to do the Coxcombs the hardest way still deemed possible. See some country maybe no one else ever had.

It would drop close to freezing that night in Inner Basin, adding to the perceived wildness of the area, the feeling it was frozen in time. In the moonless dark, we fell asleep to the *hoo-hoo* of a burrowing owl calling in the distance, breaking the otherwise dead silence that pervaded the place.

The next day we backpacked east out of the Coxcombs down another steep, boulder-choked canyon, this one slightly more than a mile long. Our climb down the jumbled heap took us fully three hours, earning it the name Short Motherfucking Canyon East. To differentiate it for easier reference in lunchtime chitchat, we appended the name of our route *into* Inner Basin with "West" for it to become Short Motherfucking Canyon West.

We camped in an open plain north of the Coxcombs that night, near our only water cache. High clouds came and went the following day as we hiked with fresh stores of water, south over a relatively easy mountain pass that took us back into Pinto Basin. We continued south along the east edge of the 200,000-acre basin, skirting the faceted west base of the Coxcombs and backpacking across the grain over twisted, stony ravines and pebbly washes descending from the mountains. Distant but familiar mountain ranges—ones we'd explored during past DDMs—poked the sky beyond the faraway west end of Pinto Basin as we hiked hard, sometimes a quarter mile apart from one another, enjoying invigorating exercise in pristine air and jaw-dropping scenery. There was no one else in the bleak basin as far as we could see across it for double-digit miles. It's impossible to describe what that feels like to someone who's never been that remote, but it is the most precious of things. Far-removed from the cramped straightjacket of civilization, we camped wild and free that night in a wash stamped with fresh cougar paw prints.

The next morning, just in time for our traverse south across the width of Pinto Basin, clouds and intermittent light rain fortuitously spilled into the area to shade and chill us, prompting us to don extra layers of clothes. We were comfortable now, traveling remarkably cool and fast across the wild, sun-scorched flat and delighting in how the wet, cloudy weather softened the area's vibe to make it feel almost bucolic, a gentle and inviting land. Gaining the impressively broad and deep Pinto Wash in the late afternoon, signs of past flash flooding—remnant muddy patches and uprooted shrubs—reminded us not to camp on its soft, sandy floor with clouds overhead. We backpacked out of the park, both content in our fill of nurturing wilderness and sad to leave. Still, the Curse of the Inverted Siphon had to get in the last word: our rental truck got a flat tire traveling the twelve-mile dirt road back to paved thoroughfares.

Back home in Oregon again, the 2001 economic recession forced me to devote much of my time hustling for work. With Ted as my in, I began writing for *Wired* that summer. Although I ultimately wrote three short product roundups for the magazine—mostly comparing the features and performance of altimeters and GPS devices—I hated it. Ted was not my editor. Serial other editors constantly micro-managed and second-guessed my prose, demanded multiple rewrites, altered my editorial point of view and changed technical wording for the worse, until I could hardly recognize it was I who wrote, or ostensibly wrote, the published thing. I decided to move on. In January 2002 I became a Contributing Editor for *Mix*'s sister publication *Electronic Musician*, which I'd been writing for since 1994.

Janet and I only got off on a dozen backpacks that year and the next, foiled on the back end by an angry Mother Nature: the Oregon Cascades were cloaked in summer 2003 in suffocating wildfire smoke from the 90,769-acre B & B Complex, an inferno that devastated much of the Mount Jefferson Wilderness. The B & B Complex would be the first of many megafires fueled by climate change that would ultimately incinerate virtually every trailhead on the east slopes of the Central Oregon Cascades, a devastating loss to backpackers like Janet and me.

By my fiftieth birthday, in August 2003, I was starting to have intermittent back problems that, in addition to infrequent but unpredictable and disabling vertigo attacks from my as yet undiagnosed medical condition, made me start to doubt the wisdom of my backpacking alone in wilderness. After doing a solo backpack in a remote area of the Three Sisters Wilderness in late September, I decided it should be my last trip alone. But I still felt confident doing hardcore trips using the buddy system. Craving a fifth

Desert Death March, I began planning a weeklong cross-country backpack in Death Valley National Park. Ted was game.

Unfortunately, six weeks before DDM 5's launch I suffered a freak accident that put the expedition in doubt. While taxiing toward an airport terminal on a flight landed at Dallas Fort Worth International Airport, a careless woman ignored the pilot's instruction to remain seated and dropped her poorly stowed laptop from an overhead bin onto my right foot's instep, badly bruising a tendon. (She fled the arrived aircraft moments later to escape responsibility.) Unwilling to let the injury scrap DDM 5, I would limp forty-two miles off-trail through Death Valley National Park using a walking stick I brought for support. The injury would never completely heal.

Ted and I drove into the massive 3.3-million-acre national park on January 25, 2004, eager to begin DDM 5. Optimistic gabbing quickly turned to hushed remarks when we saw through our windshield how incredibly barren the land was; for as far as the eye could see in every direction, only creosote bush, desert holly and other short parched shrubs dotted the stony landscape, providing zero shade. The view was prescient: we would see less than a half dozen trees throughout our entire weeklong trip.

In other deserts, Ted and I could almost always find soft sand in washes to comfortably sleep on after a long and exhausting day's hike. Not here. The washes were unusually hard, with countless rocks of various sizes mixed in concrete-like gray rubble that afforded little padding on which to rest our sore muscles. Death Valley proper was softer but far more foreboding, the epitome of wasteland. We crossed the valley's infamously barren sand and salt flats twice, each of us carrying three and a half gallons of water under frightfully sunny skies, to explore canyons on its opposite sides. During our first crossing, we happened upon a rusted, partially exploded bomb, its nose buried in the sand; we speculated it must've been mistakenly dropped by an off-course pilot training out of China Lake Naval Air Weapons Station,[37] a bombing and gunnery range located just west of the park.

---

37 Covering more than 1,100,100 acres, the massive China Lakes Naval Air Weapons Station comprises, according to Wikipedia, 85% of the US Navy's land "for weapons and armaments research, development, acquisition, testing and evaluation (RDAT&E) use and 38% of the Navy's land holdings worldwide."

Despite my painful foot injury, we managed to backpack the entire route planned for DDM 5 save for one canyon that looked on our map like it might hold dry waterfalls: I didn't want to attempt Granite Canyon unless I was 100-percent fit. And although Ted's small gas stove failed on our second night out—its fuel line hopelessly clogged by microscopic grains of blowing desert sand—I'd brought along a backup stove that kept breakfasts and dinners coming; I had learned to always keep it inside a protective plastic bag when not in use.

It seemed to Ted and me that no matter the obstacle—failed equipment, injury, rough terrain or harsh weather—we could always pull off a Desert Death March roughly as planned. That assumption was blown to bits in the winter of 2005 in Big Bend National Park. All four contingencies would collide to send DDM 6 into a tailspin.

Just getting to West Texas' Big Bend National Park took all day for Ted and I, as it required driving over 300 miles to it from El Paso International Airport, the closest major airport. Once at the park, it took us another two and a half hours to drive just twelve miles along the 4WD road leading to our backpack's starting point, as the unmaintained dirt way was very steeply slanted in places, threatening to tip over our rented SUV on its side, and had ruts up to two feet deep. When we finally arrived at our destination in light rain and cool temperatures, I was ill with a sore throat.

We planned to backpack in the Chihuahuan Desert spanning the park for six days in late January, half our route cutting across mid-elevation ridges and canyons cross-country and the other half taking hiking trails through the Chisos Mountains that towered over the area. But the maps for the cross-country traverse did not reveal a key detail that would prove a fatal flaw in my planning: the park at middle elevations was choked with spiny and thorny vegetation—spear-tipped lechuguilla, Englemann's and Purple-tinged Prickly Pear cacti, Eagle's Claw cactus, cat's claw acacia, sotol and hectia—that immediately slowed our hiking almost to a crawl. The lechuguilla was the worst of the lot, its long, rigid, lance-like basal leaves tipped with stout needles aimed at our lower legs. Even taking great pains to avoid the nasty spears, Ted and I would each have around 100 red puncture wounds in our shins by the end of the first day. So thick was the lechuguilla, it was impossible to walk more than a few paces without having to circle around the next plant, adding at least another third to our previously expected mileage. We made our first dispirited backcountry camp, in rain, far short of our goal for the day. That night, Ted realized he'd forgotten to pack all of our oatmeal breakfasts.

The next morning dawned warm and sunny—nice on the face of it, but always a concern in shadeless desert. My sore throat was thankfully gone, but the arch of my right foot—the foot injured a year earlier from a woman's falling laptop—was aching worrisomely. Based on our insufficient progress the first day, it was obvious to me we would not be able to make it another fifteen linear miles—twenty circuitous, avoiding the lechuguilla and cacti in our way—to our cache in the next two days, by which time we would run out of water. It being January, we simply did not have enough daylight hours to hike it, and traveling through lechuguilla-choked terrain at night was out of the question. I argued, reluctantly, that we needed to abort the route. Ted disagreed; he was confident we could reach our water cache before running dry, and he lobbied earnestly for us to continue on as planned.

After endless debate, we decided—Ted grudgingly—to pull the plug. I hated being the bad guy, the one forcing the route's abort, ruining our dream vacation. The heartbreaking retreat would haunt me, and lead to my making a nearly fatal decision five years later in Utah's Zion National Park.

The summer before the Big Bend fiasco, I had returned to mountaineering. My dizzy spells had become less frequent, and their typically slow onset provided enough warning that I felt I could safely climb again. In late August 2004, I backpacked the Pacific Crest Trail to a base camp at the foot of South Sister with my longtime climbing buddy Ed Lovegren, magazine editor Nick Batzdorf (who I'd climbed with twice before) and Andy Guzie, a fellow musician and experienced outdoorsman from Portland. We would attempt to take the SS-8 climbing route the next day 3,800 vertical feet up the remote northwest side of the mountain to the summit, crossing the Lost

Creek Glacier and ascending a scree ridge above the Eugene Glacier along the way, a route unfamiliar to us all.

We camped at a small lake with a stunning view of the mountain, excited about the adventure that awaited us the next day. I was the first that evening to notice a striking full moon rising above the mountain's spectacular west ridge. Dust in the atmosphere strangely distorted the appearance of the sphere, flattening its top and bulging its sides.

"Look!" I shouted excitedly to my companions. "The moon is coming up over the mountain!"

Ed took one look at the moon's warped shape and declared with mock concern, "It doesn't look right. There's something wrong with it." As if it was sick.

We climbed the next morning up to the foot of Lost Creek Glacier. I had looked down on the glacier, and all of SS-8, from the summit rim of South Sister six years earlier and concluded we would not need ropes and crampons to climb it. Looking up from the base of the glacier now, I realized I had been sorely mistaken.

The ice was hard as a hockey rink, and steep to boot. Lacking the necessary technical gear to climb it, we attempted to bypass it. We dropped down to the almost-level mouth of the glacier, crossed it and climbed up a moraine on its east side. That moraine forms a progressively narrow and steeply ascending ridge between Lost Creek Glacier and the equally dangerous Eugene Glacier. The higher we climbed the moraine, the more unstable and precipitous the rock became, eventually bringing our party to an indecisive halt. As I scouted for a way forward above my buddies, with no rope for protection, each initially promising rock hold came immediately loose in my hands as my ass hung over the Eugene Glacier. There was absolutely nothing solid to grab hold of, and every inch I clawed my way higher made a climb back down increasingly perilous; a fall here would result in a 300-foot tumbling slide down the Eugene Glacier to boulders at its foot and, at the least, grievous injury. Although we were but a quarter mile away from gaining a broader scree ridge that could take us safely to the summit, prudence dictated we abort. Live to climb another day.

Nearly a year later Ed Lovegren and I climbed South Sister again, this time from the southeast along climbing route SS-1. Joining us was my old pal Jon Pope, who I'd lived with two and a half decades earlier at Madre Grande Monastery. (Then known by the sobriquet Jon Cedar, Pope had joined Kim Howell and me during the second half of our twenty-nine-day backpack in the Sierra Nevada in 1980.)

The vibe along SS-1 had changed for the worse in the seven years since I'd last climbed it with my brother Mitch. Where it was once a route only on paper, its exact path improvised by experienced mountaineers and those under their guidance, now there was a fairly obvious trail up the mountain, replete with rock cairns and even orange ribbons marking the way in places. Where the route merged with the far more straightforward and easier SS-9 coming up by worn trail from Moraine Lake, we came upon dozens of people—many woefully unequipped for a potential change in the weather and carrying little to no water—slogging slowly up the mountain. It was to be my fourth and final summit of the grand mountain, undiminished in its physical majesty but ostensibly less wild than it was eighteen years earlier when I first stood on its rocky rim.

Two weeks after summiting South Sister, Ed and I climbed Diamond Peak from its east side, a bespoke route I had surmised from a topo and field reconnaissance nine years earlier and was surprised to learn Ed had never done before. This was climbing like in the old days, unguided and alone, left to our own devices. We saw nobody during the daylong backpack in to base camp, and no one on the mountain the next day. Drought had completely dried up the waterfall below base camp—a harbinger of climate change—requiring us to hike down to get water where a spring bubbled out of the ground just above the Pacific Crest Trail. The usually persistent snowfield above the rock pinnacles on the mountain's east slope was also completely melted, necessitating a very arduous slog up steep scree. I noticed Ed, now seventy-four years old, was atypically lagging behind me. Scrambling around a gendarme on the snow-dusted north ridge that marked the final approach to the summit, he seemed more cautious than usual.

We gained the mountain's scenic summit in the early afternoon, my fourth successful climb to the top, where we took a selfie. That photo would take on extra-special importance to me in later years. Climbing down steep talus on the return to base camp, Ed was visibly shaky. Carefully planting a trekking pole with each step, he was not the boulder-skipping climber I once knew. We made it back to base camp in time for a quiet dinner after sunset.

As the flat light of dusk began to dim and soften our panoramic view of the long, crag-topped mountain, we stood silently gazing at its splendid slopes, dusted lightly with snow like dandruff on a rumpled gray coat. A light wind whistled through the sparse stand of conifers at our backs.

"Elegant," Ed said softly. Then he turned to me, a wistful look on his face, and said, "Y' know, Coop, you don't see that many old climbers. The ones who do make it to old age are the ones who don't try to do the climbs they did when they were younger."

I knew then that was my last climb with Ed. How fitting it was that his last would be on a route new to him, and how special it was to me that I, a far less skilled and experienced mountaineer than he, would be the one to take him up it to stand with him on his last summit. Over the many years, we'd done sixteen wonderful climbs together, Ed joining me on half of my major ascents in the Cascade Range. Ten years after this his last, he would be dead from a brain tumor.

There would be no more watching with amusement him pull up to a trailhead in his classic station wagon with the scratched wood paneling. Kidding him for using a carpenter's level to find the flattest place to pitch his tent in a remote base camp. Watching him survey a mountain on our approach with the poise of an old hand, pointing confidently with his ice axe at the best route up. And most of all, hearing him affectionately call me "Coop" while flashing his magnetically boyish grin.

Little did I know that climb of Diamond Peak with Ed would also be my last major summit. But even then I could tell my own end to wilderness adventuring was not all that far off. I was beginning to slow with age, my endurance beginning to subtly wane. More worrisome, my dizzy spells and general loss of balance—which had begun five years earlier—were growing more pronounced again. I knew instinctively that time was of the essence, that I had none to waste. I had to live my wild bliss while I still could. I pitched an idea for a Desert Death March in Arizona to Ted. Four months later we set out on DDM 7.

Ted Greenwald (bottom right) takes a break during the descent of "Short Motherfucking Canyon East" (DDM 4; January 24, 2001).

Ed Lovegren (left) and Michael Cooper take a selfie on the summit of Diamond Peak, their last climb together (August 27, 2005).

-18-

E R

Desert Death March 7 had an inauspicious start. The airline Ted Greenwald and I flew to Yuma, Arizona, in January 2006 lost our backpacks and supplies during a layover in Las Vegas. Thankfully, everything arrived several hours later, and we were soon afterwards speeding across the moonlit Sonoran Desert for Kofa National Wildlife Refuge, our appointed playground.

Kofa owes its unusual name, a literal contraction, to the defunct King of Arizona gold mine that operated in the area from 1897 to 1910. The 665,400-acre refuge was established later, in 1939, to protect the native population of desert bighorn sheep that roam the area's craggy Kofa and Castle Dome Mountains. Ted and I planned to traverse the latter mountain range during a weeklong forty-mile backpack, all off-trail. We presumed, correctly, we'd be alone in Kofa's little-visited backcountry—a big draw for us. My meteorological research suggested we should backpack the inhospitable area forty miles north of the Mexican border during the historically cool but typically storm-free second week of January—goldilocks conditions.

We had not driven very far out of Yuma on US Route 95 before we came to a border checkpoint, where federal agents stopped us to search our SUV for drugs. An intrigued Ted, wishing to memorialize the operation, asked the agents if he could photograph them and their dope-sniffing dog while they did their once-over. They grimly refused.

We camped that night on a barren desert flat just outside the refuge's west border. A blimp with continuously flashing lights floated far above us, its purpose a mystery; the curious craft would remain visible in the distance throughout much of our backpack, spawning all sorts of fanciful theories. Preparing dinner that first night out, we realized we'd made a huge, careless error in Yuma when buying the twenty-six gallons of water needed for the backpack: the plastic jugs were all fitted with flip-top caps instead of the screw-on type we usually brought on DDMs. For the entire expedition, we would need to be extremely careful not to tilt jugs we'd previously opened—or our backpacks in which we carried them—so the flimsy plastic caps wouldn't flip off and spill our lifeline.

It took until nightfall the following day to set our two water caches, buried many miles apart. We hiked afterwards a mile into the wilderness, against a stiff, cool breeze and wearing headlamps, to make camp. It got down to 19°F overnight. Backpacking across King Valley and into the Castle Dome Mountains the next day, Kofa's many extraordinarily barren flats fascinated us; the hard, sun-scorched grounds looked like steamrolled rock-and-gravel pavement and were totally unyielding under our boots. The sterile flats extended over huge unbroken tracts, some over a mile long, before surrendering to fractured stony areas clothed in scattered creosote bush and other xerophytic forbs. The flats reminded me of the cleared outdoor drive-in movie theaters of my youth—sans speakers on poles—prompting Ted and me to refer to them in shorthand as "drive-ins". We loved and sought out the Kofa drive-ins for their carefree and scenic hiking, for they afforded the fastest travel and wonderful panoramic views of the surrounding mountains. But we camped in Kofa's softer sandy washes, where we were stunned to see many hundreds of birds visiting overhanging branches of mesquite and palo verde trees.

The washes and drive-ins were the only places we were safe from "jumping cholla" cacti, of which Kofa's stone-littered basins and rocky ravines and hillsides had more than any other area we'd previously backpacked—by my estimation, up to 150 plants per acre. The notorious cactus's segmented branches readily detach when lightly brushed against, impaling the incautious hiker with potentially dozens of glass-sharp, barbed needles extremely difficult to remove. Ted got nailed on seven occasions, one needle piercing all the way through one of his fingers and out the other side. (His tendency to become harpooned by the nasty plant, even when seemingly nowhere near it, had already earned him the nickname "Magnet for Cholla," which I'm not sure he appreciated.) So tenacious were the barbed spines, it took all my strength to pull them off my impaled knee with tweezers; I had to pull the hooked skin fully an inch away from the bone before the barbs relinquished their obstinate grip. I wished I'd brought a small magnifying glass to more readily locate the cholla spines that had broken off in my flesh at their buried hooks.

Conversation during DDM 7 often turned to current events. This was the period in which the dignified Ghanaian diplomat Kofi Annan served as Secretary-General of the United Nations, and Ted and I could not ignore the similarity between Annan's first name Kofi and the refuge's name Kofa. We fancied that the Kofa National Wildlife Refuge had been misnamed and was actually the Kofi Annan National *Nightlife* Refuge, a secret and exclusive outdoor discotheque where world dignitaries came to party in the remote desert. The ever-present blimp with the flashing lights became the venue's disco ball. We mused we might even get to meet and party with then Vice President Dick Cheney—infamous architect of the fallaciously conceived Iraq War—in one of our far-flung camps inside the Nightlife Refuge.

But flights of fancy aside, we had fascinating brushes with actual history in Kofa. Navigating through the refuge's middle-of-nowhere Hidden Valley Hills on our third day out, we came across strange, parallel tread marks, wider than any ATV's tires could've produced, imprinting the ground. Kofa biologist Ron Kearns would later tell me the tracks had been made by General George S. Patton's tank brigades, performing military training exercises during World War II—six decades earlier! That's how long tracks can last in the desert.

But even more remarkable was what we saw from the summit of a rocky 350-foot-high hill we climbed on our sixth day in the backcountry. About a mile north of our elevated vantage point, remnant tracks of the Butterfield Overland Mail stagecoach service—which last carried passengers and US Mail in 1861—were clearly visible traversing the base of a small hill. We had evidently crossed an obliterated section of its 145-year-old route, sight unseen, earlier that day.

We were relieved we'd be getting out of the desert the next evening, for the days' highs were now hitting 80°F, making fast hiking across Kofa's sun-baked drive-ins—radiating well over 90°F roasting heat at ground level—a double-edge sword. We camped our last night out under a glorious full moon that lent surreal lighting to eerily anthropoid saguaro cacti and, in the distance, muted silhouettes of the dramatic rock turrets and needle-top spires of the Kofa Mountains. DDM 7 was a wonderfully reassuring success after the previous year's disheartening Big Bend fiasco. But the arch of my right foot—the same foot that had plagued me in Big Bend and Death Valley as a result of previous injury—had bothered me yet again while back-packing Kofa. That foot was quickly becoming the bane of my existence.

Six months after I returned home from Kofa, the 9,400-acre Black Crater Fire raced down from the Oregon Cascades to within a mile and a half of my and Janet's home, forcing our frantic evacuation and temporarily closing local wilderness areas to recreation. Luckily, our home was left unscathed, and a couple weeks after the wildfire was contained we were able to backpack again, cross-country up to a remote, high basin in the Three Sisters Wilderness.

It was late August, a few days after my fifty-third birthday, and a blistering-hot day—95°F in Sisters—made the nearly 2,000-foot climb in elevation up to the basin from the trailhead a tough, sweat-drenched go. Although I drank five quarts of water that day, I had symptoms of heat exhaustion by the time we rolled into our makeshift camp. Eating a hot dinner amplified the danger signs—headache, nausea, fatigue and dizziness—and by 1 A.M. I was seriously ill.

Janet nursed me through the night, spoon-feeding me a sweet and salty raw soup she made of mashed dates (rich in potassium) and salt (for sodium) in water. That improvised electrolyte mix pulled me back from the brink, but I still had to spend all of the next day resting in shade before I fully recovered; even the briefest exposure to sun increased my residual symptoms exponentially within seconds.

I'd had heat exhaustion four times before as a result of hiking strenuously in hot weather. A history of previous heat illness puts one at increased risk of suffering it again. Indeed, barely four months after Janet's Florence Nightingale reprise, I suffered heat exhaustion once more, this time at the start of Desert Death March 8.

DDM 8's itinerary was a weeklong cross-country backpack in Southern California's Turtle Mountains Wilderness, a rugged and exceedingly remote area twenty miles west of the Arizona border. Ted and I flew into Las Vegas on January 5, 2007, and drove south to the wilderness area—into the maw of a ferocious windstorm forecast to deliver 100mph wind gusts. We pitched my three-season tent that night—off an obscure, unsigned dirt road I located in the dark using GPS—in 40mph sustained winds that dropped the temperature to a bone-chilling 27°F with wind chill. Two tent stakes broke while we struggled to set up the nylon tent in the gale, prompting us to lasso guy lines around large rocks to keep our shelter from blowing away. We complained half-jokingly over the gusts that every DDM seemed to feature obligatory bogus gear, and grumblingly accorded our broken tent stakes the dubious 2007 award. But despite the harsh conditions, the apparent lack of jumping cholla in the area impelled me to declare the Turtle Mountains Wilderness as seeming "friendly," a label that immediately drew skeptical response from Ted bent over in the assailing wind.

We set our sole water cache the next morning, burying double the usual number of water jugs for good reason: two days beyond the cache lay a small desert oasis, Mopah Spring, we would rely on for water. If it proved to be dry, we would need to retreat back to the cache (many miles from out) to fully resupply during an abort of the expedition.

But even arriving at the cache for the first time, the water carried in our backpacks would likely be nearly exhausted; because water is so heavy, we never carried any more than we estimated we'd need to hike between caches. While there was exceedingly little chance someone would stumble upon our cache and pilfer it before our dry arrival, the consequence would be deadly. With that in mind, we put a handwritten note, placed inside a waterproof ziplock bag, on top of the water jugs before burying all under rocks. The note read the following in bold black upper-case letters: "PLEASE

DO NOT DISTURB THIS CACHE! WE ARE LONG-DISTANCE BACKPACKERS. OUR LIVES DEPEND ON THIS BEING HERE WHEN WE ARRIVE. THANKS, MICHAEL & TED."

After burying our cache and marking its location on our map and with a GPS waypoint, we drove to and up another dirt access road and assembled our equipment and supplies for the expedition. We had barely enough time afterwards to backpack across a stony desert plain to the foothills of the craggy Mopah Range before dark. That night I got a splitting headache and was nauseous—symptoms of heat exhaustion.

You wouldn't think it could happen, considering the temperature had been in the 40s and 50s all afternoon. But the water-starved desert acts like a vacuum for moisture, sucking it out of you no matter how chilly the weather. I awoke at 2 A.M. feeling much worse and forced myself to down, by flashlight, salt and dates mashed in two quarts of water. The reliable remedy rallied me, and shortly after sunrise we hiked up into the mountains.

Even anchored by heavy backpacks as we were, wind gusts around 60 mph nearly bowled Ted and me over several times as we traversed an inner basin inside the Mopah Range. The scenery was just as wild, with views of spectacular cliffs and nearby rock spires and domes and turrets abounding every step of the way. A series of mountain passes, ravines, dry waterfalls and inner basins took us finally to a stony wash where we guyed our tent again in a strong wind for the night. The temperature dropped into the 20s.

We hadn't seen any footprints during our first two days in the backcountry, and wouldn't along the remainder of our forty-mile route. On the third day we grabbed five and a half gallons of water at our cache—barely enough to sustain us if we subsequently had to retreat back from Mopah Spring two days ahead—and backpacked across a large desert flat thinly clothed in creosote bush. The temperature rose, for once, into the 70s as we made our way on the fourth day up a winding canyon sparsely bordered by green-barked palo verde trees. As we approached Mopah Spring, we heard exotic birdsong and saw a dense cluster of tall and healthy California Fan Palms come into view, promising water. We were fairly confident of the pay-off, as a website for the Bureau of Land Management—which agency governs the wilderness—had described the spring as providing water "sweet and clear." Nothing could've been further from the truth.

Nestled among the shady palm trees was a pool of water all right—four feet across and six inches deep—but the water's edge was fouled with animal feces. The water itself had many dead bees, decomposed flies and wriggling larvae in it. Even after filtering, the water was slightly green from algae bloom and had a lingering odor reminiscent of excrement and a mildly sickening aftertaste, prompting us to call it "doody water." We could barely tolerate drinking it, but the alternative was aborting the expedition's route, the best of which lay ahead of us: on the other side of a low saddle located a half mile farther up-canyon from the spring lay the isolated Vidal Valley, which we were dying—hopefully only figuratively—to explore. We decided to drink filtered doody water for the rest of the day and observe whether either of us felt sick from it the next morning; if not, we'd head deeper into the wilderness with the foul stuff.

We needed eight gallons of water to finish our ambitious itinerary—too much to carry at once along with the remainder of our supplies. The solution was to shuttle smaller loads of water over the pass in stages and establish a base camp in Vidal Valley for exploration. By sundown we'd hauled all the water we needed up to the stony saddle, where we laid our sleeping bags on ground cloths among red and green barrel cacti and stunted palo verde trees. The air was, surprisingly, nearly still. The expansive views falling off to the west into the serene Vidal Valley and to the brown Turtle Mountains dappled by sun and shadow three miles beyond, and to the east down the winding arid canyon we'd just come up, were intoxicating. It was as if the quiet land were frozen in prehistoric time, we the Earth's only inhabitants.

The next morning, we both felt no ill effect from drinking doody water the previous day. We schlepped all our gear and full water jugs in stages the half mile down to Vidal Valley and stashed our reserves on high ground beside the vale's beautiful namesake drainage: Vidal Wash was a wonderfully sandy, flashflood-scoured course lined with innumerable blue-gray smoke trees and fuzzy light-green shrubs. Our supplies secured, we took off north with relatively light provisions on a ten-mile day hike. The jaunt ultimately took us through the most extensive and beautiful ocotillo garden we'd ever seen and to the top of a sheer-sided plateau overlooking Gary Wash, 900 vertical feet below. From our stunning overlook, we thrilled to spectacular views of the northern extension of the craggy Turtle Mountains, desolate Ward Valley far off to the west and peaceful Vidal Valley stretching for miles behind us all the way to an isolated rock monolith named Castle Rock. How wild and beautiful this place was. How lucky we were to be there. I howled ecstatically from the rim of the precipitous overlook, and long-delayed echoes returned in an extended sequence from left to right and then left again, prompting coyotes far below in Gary Wash to yap excitedly in response. This was pure and wild and untouched desert, multiple days' journey from the most tenuous intrusion of civilization, untrammeled and beautiful beyond compare. I nearly wept in gratitude for having been granted safe passage into this most sacred of places. My only regret was we could not linger long.

High clouds and wind cooled our long return to our water stash, where we made camp. That night, revisiting our magnificent day hike over shots of Wild Turkey Bourbon that Ted had packed, I launched spontaneously into the obligatory BBC Evening Report, a make-believe wilderness-wide telecast that competed with Map Talk for airtime. A staple of DDMs for the past eleven years, the fancifully imagined BBC broadcasts commentated on our expeditions' exploits, often with severe embellishment, to our invisible listeners. The faux telecasts had debuted in 1996 in Joshua Tree National Park during our climb of Pinto Mountain, when Ted suddenly began chronicling our ascent as if for a global TV audience. His deliberately cliché-ridden dispatch, delivered with a poorly rendered British accent for added gravitas, quickly became de rigueur on subsequent DDMs. Over the years, I adapted the narrative for it to become ridiculously reminiscent of a Sir David Attenborough wildlife documentary. I always began thus:

"As the men sat around the campfire blithely discussing the expedition's achievements, the circle of beasts began to tighten around the camp. It is a conflict that has repeated again and again and again over eons. Man. Beast . . . [long pause] Man . . . [longer pause] Beast."

The bourbon warmed our bellies, but only for so long before the plummeting temperature sent us into the tent for the night. The following morning over breakfast, it was 24°F. The chilly weather was welcomed, though, for it slowed our water consumption enough to allow drinking mostly what little bottled water we had remaining from our last cache and using the doody water for cooking meals, where its foul smell and taste could be largely disguised.

Vidal Valley, I would conclude that day, was the most beautiful of all desert valleys. Our backpack south down the length of it on our sixth day was remarkable for the number of ghostly smoke trees we saw—easily 10,000—and the incredible assortment of multi-colored rocks and exotic plants, some of which I'd never seen before and still don't know by name.

Cirrus clouds began pouring into the area from the northeast in the mid-afternoon, portending the arrival of cold and stormy weather. Leaving Castle Rock behind, we swung east through foothills at the south end of the Mopah Range. Descending briskly from a saddle down a boulder-strewn ravine, I hopped onto a very large, flat rock that, unknown to me, was tenuously suspended like a seesaw atop a much smaller rock acting as a fulcrum. The large rock immediately tipped forward under my weight, sending me lurching off-balance. In order to avoid doing a face plant into rocks with roughly 56 pounds on my back, I broke my fall with my right hand, bending my wrist and fingers violently back at a right angle in the process while also slamming my left shin into a boulder.

"Fuck-fuck! Goddamn it!" I cried in pain, writhing in a heap on the ground. "I think I may have broken my hand and wrist! Ted, I need the first aid kit!"

We gingerly applied arnica salve to my wounds, and I swallowed some ibuprofen and homeopathic arnica to hold back the quickly accelerating swelling. At the very least I had multiple severe sprains. The leg injury I was not worried about, as it had caused a large lump only on the fleshy portion of my shin and would not prevent me from hiking, if uncomfortably. But we still had a rough, boulder-strewn ravine to hike a mile down to the south end of Vidal Valley, and my right hand was useless for support and extremely vulnerable in case I fell again. The going would be painfully slow.

We managed to backpack without incident for another three and a half miles that afternoon, during which time my right hand and wrist blew up an additional thirty percent in size and began throbbing terribly. Once settled in our valley camp, I swallowed some oxycodone. Ted set up the tent at sunset and wrapped my injured appendage in an ace bandage. I told him this DDM would be my last. I was feeling my fifty-three years, I explained, and Janet had become stressed out over the increasing risks I was taking on desert expeditions.

A gold and blood red sunset swamped the horizon over the stunning Vidal Valley. The scenery was so spectacular, and the solitude so peaceful and quiet and absolute, I wasn't all that bummed about my injury. Besides, our vehicle was now only four miles away over relatively easy terrain. I knew I would make it out the next day, even if the night would be uncomfortable. As the expected cold front moved in, the temperature quickly plummeted into the 20s Fahrenheit and it became bitterly windy. I crawled into the tent and managed to grab a few hours of sleep.

By the time we arrived at our car the next morning, dark clouds were spilling over the Mopah Range and the steely smell of snow was in the air. Flurries were flying as we cleaned up our cache. Hours later, X-rays taken in the emergency room at Desert Springs Hospital in Las Vegas showed no bones had been broken in my wrist and hand. But it would be over four months before they would heal enough for me to resume backpacking. Nevertheless, I considered the Turtle Mountains Wilderness backpack one of my favorite DDMs, the injury a worthwhile price of admission. That expedition had been so fantastic, I was already regretting that I'd told Janet it would be my last. Not that she believed me.

Nine months after DDM 8, I got a phone call from a Portland-area neurologist I'd seen a year earlier about my continuous and worsening dizziness. He asked if I'd received "the MRI results."

"What MRI results?" I asked, confused.

"I ordered a brain MRI a full year ago," he explained, his voice betraying growing concern. "I sent the order to your general practitioner in Sisters. I haven't heard back from her, or you, so I'm following up."

This was all news to me. The MRI order, it turns out, had been mailed without my knowledge to my GP's street address, which couldn't receive mail, and was never returned undeliverable by the post office. Upset over the post office's screwup and the unnecessary, yearlong delay in diagnostic testing, the neurologist ordered the MRI again. A couple weeks later—fully seven and a half years after my vertigo attacks had begun—the devastating diagnosis was finally in: I had a brain tumor.

The tumor, the neurologist told me by phone, was a rare type. Mid-size in medical terms, the good news was it was likely benign (not cancerous). The bad news was it was located deep in the brain, in an area widely considered by neurosurgeons to be the most difficult to access. Worse, it had grown unfettered over the last several years to within a whisker of my brainstem, part of the central nervous system that controls critical functions including breathing and heart rate. Cancerous or not, the tumor would eventually kill me, in a most unpleasant way, if it were allowed to continue to grow. The neurologist urged me to schedule surgery immediately to remove it.

"Uh, okay, thanks for letting me know," I blankly told him, and hung up. The news hadn't fully sunk in. It wasn't until I informed Janet, as she awakened a half hour later from a nap, that it hit me like a ton of bricks and I broke down in tears. I had to speak the words before the diagnosis became real.

But I didn't want emotion to lead to a rash decision. Before I agreed to allow sharp objects inside my head, I wanted to educate myself, explore every alternative. Over the next six weeks, I did 200 hours of research online about my condition and consulted with six neurosurgeons. Because of the expected collateral damage to my brain that would result from surgically removing the tumor, every one of the surgeons I met with recommended I receive radiation treatments to kill the tumor rather than excise it. Better to have a dead, scarred lump in my brain than further neurological damage from surgery to remove it.

I searched far and wide for the doctor having the most experience with CyberKnife radiosurgery—the type of fractionated radiation therapy I decided on getting—ultimately choosing neurosurgeon Dr. Steven D. Chang to treat me at Stanford Medical Hospital in Palo Alto, California. Chang, widely regarded the world's leading brain surgeon at the time and one who other neurosurgeons from around the world regularly traveled to for CyberKnife training, was eminently brilliant and practiced: he had already performed several hundred operations on patients with the same type of brain tumor I had, recently averaging two or three radiosurgery treatments or surgical resections per week. And it was Stanford that had invented the CyberKnife medical robot and treatment protocol sixteen years earlier. When asked by family members and close friends why I didn't consider getting treatment from a neurosurgeon closer to home—for the sake of convenience and to avoid extra travel expense—my response was blunt: "You know the saying 'this isn't brain surgery'? Well, this *is* brain surgery." I wanted the best shot at a successful outcome.

Still, I wasn't totally convinced I should let someone beam radiation into my brain. CyberKnife would deliver to the tumor a higher cumulative Gray (Gy)—the absorbed dose of ionizing radiation measured using the International System of Units—than that received by people at ground zero during the atomic bombing of Hiroshima.[38] Hoping for a possible reprieve, I told Dr. Chang I wanted to hold off on treatment until a second MRI confirmed the tumor was still growing. Because the type of tumor I had typically grew very slowly, Dr. Chang allowed I could afford to wait six months for follow-up imaging before taking interventional action.

In the meantime, I decided I'd try various natural treatments my research suggested might shrink the tumor: taking anti-angiogenesis supplements to starve the tumor of new blood supply, anti-inflammatory proteolytic enzymes to digest the tumor's fibrin, adaptogenic herbs to strengthen my immune system, and so on. I wanted to exhaust every natural option before resorting to Western medicine.

There was one other major consideration that impelled me to delay treatment for six months: I knew if and when my brain received radiation, it would knock me out of commission for backpacking for quite some time. I was determined to delay the debilitating treatments until after I returned from a hardcore Desert Death March I had planned for the coming spring. To Janet's dismay, DDM 9 would be the most daring and dangerous

---

38 CyberKnife delivers radiation, typically in three automated treatments spaced out over as many days, from collimators on a mobile robotic arm aimed at the tumor from up to 140 different directions, their beams converging on the aberrant growth. This approach results in healthy brain tissue the radiation passes through receiving no more than one percent of the total dosage, largely sparing it from collateral damage.

expedition yet, attempting to pioneer a new route across the core of Utah's Capitol Reef National Park, an area likely devoid of water.

Nobody had ever traversed the remote, trail-less area I was looking to cross, a formidable labyrinthine maze of sheer-walled canyons, perpendicular rock palisades and dry waterfalls. In fact, no one had even tried. The park's superintendent and rangers told me no backcountry permit had ever been issued for the area in the park's seventy-one-year history, and they warned me the rugged terrain could easily prove impassable. The problem, they explained, was that because of widespread severe erosion in the sandstone geology of the area, vertical obstacles likely lay unmarked between the topo maps' contour lines, blocking ways forward that looked good only on paper. If my route came to a dead end somewhere well past the halfway point, I'd run out of carried water before I could fully retrace my steps back to safety.

I had studied the area's topographic maps, derived from aerial photography, for weeks on end and thought I'd discovered a possible way through. The only way to tell for sure was to backpack it and see if it worked. In mid-April 2008, Ted Greenwald and I would roll the dice.

Ted Greenwald backpacks a "drive-in" in Arizona's Kofa
National Wildlife Refuge (DDM 7; January 2006).

-19-

FIRST TRAVERSE

In the weeks leading up to the launch of DDM 9, I began to question whether my ambitious plan to traverse the trail-less, high-elevation core of Capitol Reef National Park was bucket-list initiative or a blueprint for disaster. But the allure of going somewhere nobody else in recorded history had gone, and the challenging navigation needed to pull it off, was a siren call. I loved that the physically demanding terrain, navigational complexity and remoteness of the area along my conceived route virtually guaranteed Ted Greenwald and I would have complete solitude, a certainty the park's superintendent Al Hendricks echoed during an investigatory phone call I made to him. I called Ted immediately afterwards to report Hendricks's assessment and psych Ted up for the expedition.

"Hendricks told me once we're out there we, quote, 'won't see another living thing,'" I rhapsodized over the phone.

Ted exhaled like a leaky balloon, and responded with characteristically hilarious understatement, "I wonder if there's a good reason for that."

Maybe it wasn't that funny. Ed Lovegren had taught me to ignore what he called "the horrors," the scary what-ifs that haunt the alpinist's night-time thoughts before a risky mountain climb. But my worries about DDM 9 were not so easily dismissed, because of one outside factor: water, or specifically the likely absence of it along my envisioned route. Ted and I could each carry no more than three gallons of water—enough to last us three days—without our packs becoming too heavy to hike the rugged terrain, and my route (assuming it was doable) would take at least that long to execute. There was very little room for navigation error, and failure held potentially mortal consequence.

Even if we did pull off our bid, it would constitute only the first half of the expedition. I had planned for the weeklong backpack to take us, in a roughly thirty-two-mile cross-country loop, not once but twice through the formidable Waterpocket Fold, a geological uplift that together with heavy erosion over a span of fifty to seventy million years had formed Capitol Reef's tightly packed mishmash of sheer-walled canyons, impassable palisades, dry waterfalls, spires and rock domes. Our first way through the Waterpocket Fold would be along my unproven route traversing the western section of the park's high-elevation core, after a short approach across lower, open desert. The second way would arc through the eastern part of the core along a high route Al Hendricks and a buddy had pulled off a few years earlier.

At the mid-point for the loop, where my route ended and Hendricks's began, Ted and I would be running low on water and need to backpack a so-called "lollipop stick"[39] route down from the high country and out to our sole water cache buried off Utah State Highway 24—the two-lane blacktop that crosses the park from east to west—and then back, adding another ten miles. There was just one problem: the crux of the lollipop stick required a dangerously steep descent of 900 vertical feet—the last 500 feet dropping in just 0.1 mile—down a hidden break in a sheer cliff that would take us into Spring Canyon, a route that looked impossible on the map but which Hendricks had affirmed and described to me over the phone. (He could not provide GPS coordinates.) That break was the only known way down from the top of a long line of spectacularly sheer cliffs, hundreds of feet high, which ran continuously for fifteen miles— blocking our high-elevation loop route above the cliffs from life-saving

---

39 In route planning, a lollipop stick is an out-and-back route that connects to a loop trip. In the analogy, the loop is the circumference of the candy and the hike out from the loop and back again forms the stick.

water below. Finding and climbing down that solitary break, with heavy backpacks and at a point when Ted and I would likely be running almost or completely dry, would be essential to our survival.

Even if we pulled off my risky route, and the subsequent climb down to water and back up, the second, or eastern, half of our loop—what Ted and I came to refer to in shorthand as "the Al Hendricks Route"—was not cut and dried. It had been Hendricks's anonymous buddy who had devised and led that route. Describing it to me as best he could over the phone, Hendricks could not precisely remember the route in three areas as they related to the corresponding topo maps. Nevertheless, I felt he'd given me sufficient descriptions of the topography to go on, and Ted and I would navigate and groundtruth the sketchy bits. At least we knew for certain there was a way through that eastern part of the Waterpocket Fold, because Hendricks had done it before. I couldn't say that about my new route. Nobody could.

I had one other concern, this one not germane to our prior eight Desert Death Marches. Hendricks had mentioned Ted and I might find water flowing at the bottom of the cliffs in Spring Canyon. If there was, I wasn't sure I'd want to drink it, as long as I could wait until we reached our water cache four miles beyond to quench my thirst. Capitol Reef National Park, and all of Southern Utah for that matter, lay directly downwind from where over 200 atomic bombs had been detonated above ground at the Nevada Test Site throughout the 1950s and into the early 1960s. Cesium-137—a radioactive isotope with a half-life of thirty years—had been released in those detonations, and it can travel very long distances in the air and is highly soluble in water. Strontium-90, another highly toxic radionuclide produced by the bombs, has a marginally shorter half-life of 28.8 years. The water-soluble plutonium-238 is much more stable, having a half-life of 87.7 years. By my calculations, roughly 25 percent of the highly toxic cesium-137 and strontium-90 deposited across Southern Utah by the Nevada Test Site's atmospheric detonations would still remain in 2008, when Ted and I would be backpacking Capitol Reef National Park. Plutonium-238 would have decayed far less. If Spring Canyon had water flowing in it, I worried drinking it could cause deleterious, long-term health effects from lingering radioactivity.[40] I already had one tumor and didn't want another.

Surprisingly, no officials I talked with by phone, including an expert in nuclear fallout, urged caution about drinking from streams in Southern Utah, although they failed to explain or justify their insouciance. I decided to put those concerns in the back of my mind in favor of the grand expedition. Foremost were fears of running out of water or getting injured somewhere far along our cross-country loop route, for we would be climbing in and out of multiple canyons before and after Spring Canyon and my sense of balance had deteriorated markedly due to my unchecked brain tumor. If I were to become incapacitated by a fall, it was highly doubtful Ted had the navigation skills needed to find his way out of Capitol Reef's severely convoluted backcountry to get help, except possibly by retracing our steps from memory.[41] As the expedition's launch date drew closer, I began losing sleep worrying that I was sending us both to our doom. Two days before I was scheduled to fly to Salt Lake City to meet Ted for the expedition's launch, I ordered a personal locator beacon online with overnight delivery service.[42]

---

40 In "Cancer Incidence in an Area of Radioactive Fallout Downwind From the Nevada Test Site," published in 1984 in the Journal of the American Medical Association, author Carl Johnson reported an increase in multiple types of cancers in St. George, Utah—a city roughly 150 miles west of Capitol Reef National Park—starting in the mid-1950s.

41 Although I would bring a GPS receiver on the expedition, the waypoints I created beforehand marked unproven breaks in the Waterpocket Fold—presumed after examining maps—and were not to be relied on. A straight-line hike between waypoints was virtually not possible due to cliffs, dry waterfalls or peaks blocking the way, and navigating the complex terrain required expert map and compass skills beyond Ted's relatively unpracticed means. (Although he'd learned the fundamentals of navigation, a Desert Death March was often the only opportunity Ted would get to refresh those skills in any given year due to work and family obligations.) Furthermore, my GPS receiver was very crude by today's standards, typically only able to locate four or five satellites while hiking in flat and open terrain and so interminably slow in downloading data that we could afford no time in our tight schedule to edit waypoints to mark forced detours along my route for the purpose of backtracking.

42 Working in conjunction with satellites, a personal locator beacon is used to send a distress signal to Search and Rescue (SAR) in the event of a life-threatening emergency.

I could tell Janet was more worried about this expedition than the others I'd done previously. Looking at my route traced in fluorescent high-lighter across multiple topo maps for the area, she said it looked "scary," a word I'd never heard her use before when scrutinizing—reluctantly—my off-trail schemes. But she never once asked me not to go, or even questioned it aloud. She knew I had to, that the pull, like gravity, could not be denied.

The die was cast. On April 19, 2008, Ted and I buried our water cache a couple hundred yards off Highway 24 and nervously drove our rented SUV, in defiance of our rental contract's restrictions, across the unbridged Fremont River (only twelve inches deep and fifteen feet wide on that day). We drove another fifteen miles north along Capitol Reef's dirt Cathedral Valley Road, through strikingly colored bentonite hills white and pink and brown and gray, to Lower South Desert Overlook (which name we jokingly shortened to "LSD Overlook"), arriving in the afternoon.

Looking west from the overlook's elevated dirt parking area, a mag-nificent panoramic view of the Waterpocket Fold greeted us. Bulging the high horizon were the Fold's imposing white domes of Navajo Sandstone that early Utahan settlers had likened to the Capitol building in Washington, DC, lending the national park the first part of its name. ("Reef," the second part, was a metaphor for the Waterpocket Fold's for-midable barrier to travel.) Two hundred vertical feet immediately below LSD Overlook lay the austere South Desert we had to first cross to get to the Waterpocket Fold. The desert's barren sands, pigmented salmon and white and gray, looked nearly devoid of vegetation. Jailhouse Rock—an isolated, sheer-sided, triangular monolith 500 feet high, composed of alternating gray and red sedimentary strata—rose incongruously from the desert floor's moonscape close to the overlook, as if to mark no man's land beyond the tower's station.

Stimulated by the scenic view, we decided impromptu to backpack that afternoon into South Desert to make camp in the outback a day earlier than originally planned. But the store-bought sliced carrots I'd eaten that morn-ing were, it soon became apparent, contaminated, and escalating symptoms of food poisoning stopped me in my tracks just several hundred yards from the overlook. We retreated regretfully back to the SUV, where I brewed a bespoke blend of antiseptic and carminative herbs to quell my intense abdominal cramps. By evening I had thankfully recovered.

The next morning, I wrapped my already aching right foot—the one that had bothered me on the previous four DDMs—with athletic tape for support. To mitigate my handicap, Ted charitably agreed to carry three of the five gallons of water we packed. The total amount was a gallon less than we'd normally carry to hike a three-day route easier than what now lay ahead. But Al Hendricks had told me we had an 80 percent chance of finding water in Deep Creek Canyon on the far side of South Desert. To cut down on our pack weights at the start, we gambled we could begin the trip with less water and supplement later with water from the canyon.

We quickly hiked a short abandoned and disintegrating dirt road from LSD Overlook down through a gallery of eroded sedimentary hoodoos and pinnacles to the desert floor, where the road abruptly ended. As we strode out onto the open desert, we were assaulted by winds gusting to 60 mph whipping up a biting and blinding sandstorm. Like a constant barrage of little insect stings on our skin, the sandblasting prompted us to don full-coverage clothing and sunglasses, with bandanas wrapped over our noses and mouths. It wasn't enough—the storm left a microscopic grain of sand, one I could not find to remove, in one of Ted's eyes. We were not off to a good start. Nevertheless, a couple hours later we had crossed South Desert and left the sandstorm behind. We dropped our packs and set out up Deep Creek Canyon in search of water. The canyon proved to be bone-dry.

Our gambit had failed. We now found ourselves faced with a difficult decision. If we hiked back to the SUV for more water, we'd fall too far behind in our tight schedule to do our fantastic loop route. (To accommodate Ted's paltry vacation allowance at *Wired* magazine, we never planned more days for our DDMs than what we thought were absolutely necessary.) If on the other hand we hiked onward, we risked exhausting our relatively light water supplies before making it to Spring Canyon—also possibly dry—or our cache four miles beyond. The siren's call was strong. After a brief debate, we decided to throw caution to the wind and hike on.

Deep Creek Canyon's magnificently fluted and terraced palisades—kaleidoscopic red, pink and gray in discrete horizontal layers—towered a thousand feet at our backs as we climbed up the more moderate south wall of the canyon. Gaining 600 vertical feet from the canyon floor, Ted's left hip was paining him as we stumbled onto the deeply eroded remnants of an old dirt road.

I'd previously heard the partially collapsed road had been constructed decades earlier, prior to the park's protective designation, in a failed bid to explore for gas in an area called Little Sand Flat, immediately beyond which my unproven route through the Waterpocket Fold would begin. We took the deeply rutted way one mile into the flat, where it quickly shrank to an obscure and narrow footpath before becoming completely lost to the ravages of time.

Little Sand Flat was thoroughly enchanting. The sagebrush basin, serenely dotted with scattered green juniper and piñon pine trees across its lovely span, was exquisitely rimmed with striated orange and white sandstone domes, flat-topped turrets and pointy spires, strange rock sculptures even my imagination could not conjure. We camped joyously on the edge of a small stand of pines in the basin and lazily prepared dinner while gazing across the flat at Mother Nature's artistic flair.

It was a brisk 19°F when we awoke the next morning for a quick breakfast. Ted's painful hip, his sandblasted eye and my aching right foot had improved overnight. Brimming with excitement and armed with our maps, compasses, GPS receiver and a wristwatch altimeter, we headed off into the park's unexplored interior. We dropped down off Little Sand Flat via a west-trending ridge that led us into a pink-rock ravine, headed south over a high U-shaped mountain pass and then hiked across an enormous sandstone slab at the base of a drastically weathered peak. Avoiding the need to downclimb sheer cliffs blocking a straight-line attack—impossible—we skirted along a narrow lip at the top of a box canyon's sheer headwall. Crossing over a second high pass took us into rolling terrain bordered by fantastic dark-red rock amphitheaters and arches. We cut across two more ravines in quick succession, hiked over a narrow gap between two rock buttresses and crossed a rocky gulley before coming to a sudden stop at the top of a long, cliff-rimmed red and white canyon that, at first glance, seemed to staunchly block our way forward. This was all in just three miles since leaving Little Sand Flat.

"This is fucking ridiculous!" exclaimed the usually unexcitable Ted upon seeing the sheer canyon walls before us. "This isn't DDM 9, it's DDM X. X for Extreme."

It wasn't exasperation on his part, but wonderment for how incredibly challenging and complex the terrain was. We both loved the challenge. Navigating the area was like solving the world's best jigsaw puzzle.

We scouted along the canyon's rim and found a spot where the cliff face had crumbled into huge blocks of rock lying in a steeply descending pile. Carefully stair-stepping our way down the heap, we attained the canyon's soft red bottom, crossed it and climbed the opposite wall via a hidden breach that demanded every ounce of my strength to win. Continuing south, we passed more red amphitheaters and rock terraces at the head of yet another canyon, hiked over a short ridge and across another rocky ravine, and tramped over a pass at 6,980 feet. That's where things began to look really dicey.

We were now a little more than halfway to Spring Canyon from LSD Overlook—the farthest we could go and still retrace our steps back to our SUV without running out of water. We had come to the head of a slot canyon jammed between a steep-sided ridge and the highest peak in the park's core, the peak marked simply "Capital"—a misspelling, I thought—on my USGS 7.5-minute series topo.[43] The slot had a perpendicular drop-off of a few feet immediately at its head, forewarning snowballing erosive forces farther down-canyon might have created impassable dry waterfalls. We opted to try an alternative go-around—atop and then down off the canyon's west rim—that I had planned for just such an eventuality. But the route ultimately failed, arresting us above sheer cliffs.

We backtracked to the head of the slot canyon, down it now our only

---

43 The primary series of USGS topographic maps for the United States are organized such that each covers a 7.5-minute grid, or an area spanning seven and a half sixtieths of one degree of the Earth's arc. The 7.5-minute topos typically offer the best available resolution, or smallest interval between contour lines, and thus are important tools for cross-country navigation.

possible way forward. Somewhere along our retreat Ted lost the partially filled canteen he'd hung on the outside of his backpack, a relatively minor yet ill-afforded reduction in our precious water supply. Thankfully, our luck turned next for the better: heading down the slot, we found it was far easier than we'd expected. Half a mile down its strangled course, it started to become progressively wider, promising it was a go. A little farther along, we exited up its steep east slope to make camp, thoroughly exhausted, on a pretty saddle clothed in short pine trees situated at just over 7,000 feet altitude.

From our high camp, we had a sweeping view northwest across the park's interior and, beyond, to a snow-capped escarpment in the Fishlake National Forest outside the reserve. Aside from the whisper of our camp stove cooking dinner, it was dead quiet. With just a little imagination, I could briefly convince myself cities and roads and airports and even other people no longer existed beyond my contemplative view of the wild and empty land.

We broke camp at sunrise the next morning, urged on by our dwindling water reserves and a vivid, cloudless sky. A hike across a dissected red basin and thence over an easy saddle took us to the head of a beautiful slot canyon hewn with multiple short dry waterfalls we easily bypassed or downclimbed in turn. We were irrevocably committed to completing the route now, as we'd gone too far to retrace our steps without running out of water. Traversing the boulder-strewn west side of Peak 6981, we got our first humbling views of Spring Canyon—or rather the top portion of its soaring perpendicular cliffs, for the canyon's bottom was hidden deep below.

We each had only one quart of water remaining, in sunny short-sleeve weather. As we backpacked down off Peak 6981's west shoulder, views of Spring Canyon's bottom opened up. From our vertiginous vantage, we spied a thin ribbon of darker soil 900 vertical feet below us in the canyon. Was it just mud, or water flowing? It gave us hope.

Now was our make-or-break moment. We made our best guess as to where the hidden crack in the sheer cliffs was that Al Hendricks had told me would take us down into Spring Canyon. Descending down massive rock slabs a few hundred vertical feet, we came to the lip of a perfectly perpendicular cliff hundreds of feet high. No go.

"Absolutely fucking ridiculous!" Ted exclaimed once again, as we turned to climb back up to where we figured we'd gone off course. Only this time he sounded slightly concerned.

After reviewing the map again, we tried another way down, angling toward a side canyon. Dropping 400 vertical feet down off sequential rock terraces, the slope became progressively and exponentially steeper. Slowly, a boulder-choked, nearly vertical couloir came into view below us, partly hidden behind a massive rock fin. From the top of the couloir, we could see a partial view of the side canyon's floor far below. To our utter relief we could tell this was the break in the cliffs we'd been looking for, formidable but, from what we could see, doable. My altimeter indicated we had 500 more vertical feet to drop to get down—in the length of one and a half football fields. From our high vantage, scattered trees on the floor below looked like short shrubs.

We started the sketchy descent with our unwieldy backpacks on, climbing down from one huge boulder to the next, an exercise all the more difficult and dangerous for me due to my tumor-caused disequilibrium. Ted, whose balance was like a mountain goat's, did each pitch first. At the top of one particularly gnarly sixty-foot pitch, I shouted down to Ted that I didn't think my balance was good enough that I could safely downclimb it with my cumbersome backpack on. Without hesitation, he climbed back up to me and carried my pack down the pitch so I could climb without it. When I rejoined him mid-way down the couloir, I patted him on the back.

"I couldn't do this route without you, man," I said gratefully.

"I couldn't do it without you, either," he replied in a nod to my navigation chops. Ours was now more than ever a symbiotic partnership.

Fully an hour and forty minutes after we began our knotty 0.9-mile descent, we finally arrived at the bottom of the side canyon in the mid-afternoon, gleeful in the realization we had just pulled off putting in a new route across the core of Capitol Reef National Park. A short hike took us into the main branch of stunning Spring Canyon. At the base of its towering perpendicular red cliffs, the canyon's soft bed of pink sand was lined with cottonwood trees just beginning to leaf out in a gentle breeze. Hawks and swallows glided overhead in an updraft toward azure sky. From an elevated flat in a bend in the canyon, we could see the unmistakable sign of water flowing a short distance up-canyon. Ted took off for the water, filter and empty plastic jugs in hand, while I set up our tent.

Minutes later I approached Ted where he sat beside the dribbling stream, only an inch deep and a couple feet wide. He handed me a full liter of freshly filtered water.

"How's it taste?" I asked, the memory of Mopah Spring's doody water still etched in my mind.

"A bit heavy in minerals," Ted replied, "but not bad."

I took a tenuous sip.

"It tastes pretty good!" I exclaimed in surprise, and then enthusiastically added, "And it's probably got some things in it we can't get in our water back home—like cesium-137, strontium-90 . . ."

We both laughed. We pumped another four gallons of water and carried them leisurely back to camp. We were completely relaxed, partly from sheer fatigue but also from knowing we'd completed our iffy route through the Waterpocket Fold and were safe—for now, at least. That evening, as had happened on every one of the last few DDMs, Ted's brand new stove died, the victim of blowing desert sands. The zipper for my tent's front door followed suit, irreparably skipping its ground-down track.

We hiked with light packs the next day four straightforward miles down the flat-bottomed Spring Canyon and Chimney Rock Canyon to our water cache, where we also had more food and a spare camp stove stashed. A mile and a half before reaching the cache, we joined a short park trail where we ran into three men day-hiking with small packs. One of the hikers noticed I was looking at my map.

"Are you lost?" he asked, apparently eager to demonstrate his knowledge of the area.

"Uh, no," I replied. I didn't bother telling him where we'd been the previous three days.

We made it back to our camp in the late afternoon. At eight o'clock the following morning, we began the brutal climb out of Spring Canyon, each of us now loaded down with twenty pounds of water to sustain us along the Al Hendricks Route through the eastern section of the Waterpocket Fold. We started slowly up the boulder-choked couloir we'd descended two days earlier. Or so we thought. The couloir formed an obscure fork with another at its very bottom—easily overlooked, not shown on our maps—and we took the wrong fork going back up. It became increasingly, dangerously steep the higher we went.

I realized our mistake when we came to the base of a perpendicular dead end 500 vertical feet above the canyon floor. Accommodating my poor balance, Ted shuttled our 65-pound backpacks in turn across a steep rock rib to the correct couloir. I followed, unweighted but nevertheless unsteady. All told, it took us three full hours to make the arduous climb out of Spring Canyon, a distance of less than one mile. My right Achilles tendon barked at me in protest the entire way.

We regained Peak 6981's west shoulder and headed east into new terrain. Hendricks's route took us over a high saddle and then up a crumbled crack in an otherwise unbroken palisade to a higher ridge, the only way possible, we concluded, to head east out of the immediate area. Beyond the ridge, we backpacked north atop a canyon rim in high winds before striking out northeast across a jigsaw puzzle of high, broken land. Here, fractured rounded loaves of white and salmon rock, each hump just tens of yards across, had pitifully stunted pine trees clinging to life in the cracks between them. The buffeting wind was very cold. In the far distance, Jailhouse Rock loomed like a mirage out in South Desert a thousand vertical feet below us.

We soon came to a pivotal nexus of several knife-edge ridge tops that spread before us like fingers on a hand. The ridges looked virtually identical: the same height, very closely spaced together and almost parallel to one another. I couldn't tell which one to take from our vantage and based on the poorly resolved contour lines on our map, which lumped the lot into one broad virtual ridge. I took my best guess, which ultimately proved wrong.

After a couple minutes hiking the ridge, I realized my mistake when it began slowly veering toward the wrong compass heading. We backtracked. Taking the correct ridge now, we plunged down its steeply descending line from the high country, hiked the rim of a deep sheer-walled canyon, and then dropped steeply again into a narrow wash, where we made camp just after 5 P.M. It had taken us nine hours to backpack just four punishing miles. We were both utterly exhausted.

The going would be just as tough the next day, when we would once again make it only four miles cross-country. To bypass dry waterfalls in a slot canyon we spied from above, we hiked up and over an adjacent plateau. What looked on our map to be the best way down off the far side of the plateau ultimately led us to the top of a cliff. No go. With our packs off, we scouted around and found an alternate way down. We hiked the next few miles down a spectacularly painted bentonite canyon, its perpendicular textured walls of absorbent sedimentary rock broadly striped horizontally in red and pink and white layers. An attempted climb out of the canyon, up interconnecting, loose bentonite ridges colored pastel green and red, took us to a vertical dead end. We retreated back down to the canyon floor. The next ridge we tried proved a go, taking us up out of the canyon and onto bizarre rolling terrain replete with thirty-foot-high bentonite mounds white and red and rust-colored. Crossing the phantasmagoric hills, we came finally to an expansive overlook several hundred vertical feet above the red and orange South Desert. Jailhouse Rock stood like a reassuring beacon in the distance. Exhausted, we decided to bivouac on the overlook, laying out our sleeping bags in the open. Just before dark, we scouted our planned route down to the desert floor and discovered it had an impassable drop-off not shown on the map.

We found another way down to the desert floor at six o'clock the following morning. A cold and very windy hike six miles north across the multi-colored sands of South Desert took us ultimately back to our SUV, where we arrived shortly after noon. Our grand expedition was over.

Backpacking twice through the Waterpocket Fold had taken every ounce of my stamina, not to mention every jot of my navigational skills. That's what I'd hoped for, what made the adventure so deeply satisfying. That it was risky was the cherry on top. But as we packed up our SUV, I told Ted that for safety's sake—acknowledging my deteriorating balance, unresolved foot injury and generally declining athletic ability with age (fifty-four years old, I was six years Ted's senior)—Capitol Reef should probably be my last DDM.

I should've heeded my own counsel.

Michael Cooper in front of Jailhouse Rock, at the start of
DDM 9 in Capitol Reef National Park (April 20, 2008)

Ted Greenwald at an overlook of the Waterpocket Fold, during the
pioneering traverse of Capitol Reef National Park (April 21, 2008)

Michael Cooper starts the descent into Spring
Canyon, after blazing a new route across the core of
Capitol Reef National Park (April 22, 2008).

Ted Greenwald rests during the climb out of Spring
Canyon (DDM 9; April 24, 2008).

-20-

DRIVEN TO DRINK

Returning to Oregon on the heels of Desert Death March 9 in late April 2008, I was brimming with optimism. Navigating a previously unexplored section of Capitol Reef National Park had instilled in me confidence I could meet any challenge back within the tame confines of civilization. Months earlier, I had put off treatment for my brain tumor until after the expedition in hopes that a follow-up MRI would show the lump had stopped growing and radiation was not necessary. Now I was all but certain the next MRI's results would be favorable and affirm my postponement.

But in the six months since the first MRI had been taken, the tumor had in fact continued to grow—alarmingly, at five times the usual rate. Worse, the growth was now pressing on and indenting my brainstem, controller of critical bodily functions including breathing and heart rate. I could no longer delay treatment.

Two months later, a robot beamed radiation into my head while I lay on a surgical table at Stanford University Medical Center, the first of three treatments scheduled for as many days. The attending nurses told me I should expect to feel fatigued for two weeks afterwards. That turned out to be the understatement of the year.

For a full month after the treatments, I was so utterly exhausted that I couldn't even sit upright in a chair, needing to rest my forehead on a table in front of me. I was constantly short of breath, the top and back of my skull felt numb, and I felt queasy and strangely disconnected from my body and surroundings. My doctor, world-renowned neurosurgeon Steven D. Chang, told me my severe reaction was a good sign indicating the tumor was responding strongly to the radiation. I just had to tough it out.

But I couldn't wait forever to get well. I had ambitious plans pursuant to my incipient songwriting career. Over the past four years, I'd traveled every six to twelve months to Nashville to record demos of country songs I'd written and arranged for my music publishing company, Michael Cooper Music. (Country music at the time was virtually the last remaining market open to outside songwriters; acts for rock and pop, the only other music genres I was well versed in, now almost exclusively recorded self-penned songs.) Not expecting such a severe and prolonged reaction to radiation, I had scheduled my next work trip to Music City to occur just six weeks after my treatments.

Why record in Nashville, when I had my own recording studio in Oregon? If I wanted my country songs to gain the cachet necessary to find a home, their demo recordings would need the iconic Nashville sound that was splattered across heartland and Southern airwaves, and the only way to get that sound was to use musicians suckled in the idiom. To that end, the varying lineup of musicians I hired for each recording session—playing drums, bass, electric and acoustic guitars, pedal steel, piano and fiddle—included many of the virtuosos who regularly performed on hit country records.

I loved producing music in Nashville, but the high-pressure recording sessions required I bring my A game, and radiation treatments had left me severely weakened. As my next trip to Nashville fast approached, I called one of Dr. Chang's assistants to ask whether they thought I should delay undertaking such a demanding project 2,000 miles from home until I was stronger.

"These recording sessions feed my soul," I explained, "but I'm afraid they'll be too much for me to handle in my condition. I can't walk more than twenty paces without having to sit down and rest to catch my breath."

"I can't tell you what to do," the nurse replied. "I can only tell you that the patients who have been the happiest after radiation are the ones who haven't let it stop them, who've just gone on living their lives."

It was great advice. By the time I got off the plane in Nashville, my excited anticipation for the recording sessions had me already feeling stronger.

Working with some of the world's best musicians, and hearing my penned songs come to vibrant life beyond my expectations, proved to be the best medicine. Two and a half weeks after I returned home from Nashville—just two months after my last radiation treatment—Janet and I went backpacking off-trail again in the Three Sisters Wilderness. Two more wonderful backpacks followed in the fall. My life was once again on an upswing.

But not for long. A follow-up MRI of my brain, taken five months after treatment, showed the radiation had caused my tumor to swell a third again in volume. Somewhat anticipated and likely only a temporary setback, that ruction wasn't the bombshell. What riveted the radiologist's attention was something totally unexpected: I had a second brain tumor, growing in a different location. A type affecting only one in every ten million people, this second tumor was even rarer than the first. And the odds of having two different rare brain tumors, well, that was off the charts. I'd won the shit lottery.

"I've seen this only twice before," Dr. Chang told me. "Nobody knows why this occurs. Some people's brains just like to grow these things."

Dr. Chang re-examined my very first brain MRI, which had been taken thirteen months earlier on a relatively imprecise machine in Oregon. Lo and behold, one tiny fuzzy image among dozens—easily overlooked—showed the second tumor had already taken root back then. Luckily, it had not grown in size in the interim and was very small, about the size of a pea. It was also growing in a very resilient area of the brain and was, so far, asymptomatic. As long as it did not grow any larger and I didn't start to exhibit a new neurological deficit, Dr. Chang said I could afford to leave it untreated. Best to avoid unnecessary radiation.

The discovery of the second tumor was my nadir, and my luck would soon improve in a roller-coaster upswing. Eleven months after receiving radiation, imaging revealed my treated tumor had shrunk around 60 percent in volume—a result seen in only one in four patients, and then usually only after five years following treatments. My balance had also improved a little as the tumor shrank, and for the first time in several years I felt sensorily connected to my physical surroundings, exiting the movie screen and joining the audience.

My health resuscitated, Janet and I did several fun backpacks in the summer and fall of 2009. It should've been enough for me, but it wasn't. I began fantasizing about doing another Desert Death March, one even more hardcore than Capitol Reef. I wanted to see how far I could push it.

This time I would push it too far.

In the southwest corner of Southern Utah's Zion National Park is a trail-less area, encompassing roughly thirty-five square miles, where relatively few people dare to tread. Sheer cliffs, some extending for miles in an unbroken wall well over 1,000 feet high, guard remote high-elevation desert backcountry replete with unimaginably beautiful white and orange sandstone domes, weirdly wind-sculpted hoodoos and claustrophobic slot canyons vertically stair-stepped with sequential waterfalls. A few slots in the area have been traveled top to bottom by canyoneers schooled in technical climbing techniques and equipment, rappelling off the waterfalls and swimming across cold pools of water below in a one-way day trip exiting at the canyon's mouth; some ill-prepared have gotten stranded—with insufficient rope length to rappel down an unexpectedly high pour-off and no way to retreat—and died of exposure or by drowning in a flash flood in the slot. Elite mountaineers have also climbed the area's remote domes and peaks. But before 2010, nobody had backpacked fully across the area from one end to the other. That's what Ted Greenwald and I would attempt in May that year.

The nine-day cross-country route I had cooked up would require carrying climbing gear—rope, harnesses, belay device, webbing and carabiners—in addition to our usual desert backpacking equipment and supplies, resulting in extraordinarily heavy and unwieldy packs arguably not suitable for such precipitous terrain. My plan was to backpack the first day down a steep climber's route into a section of dark slot canyon called the Subway and then climb a short wall, hauling our packs up behind us with rope, to exit the opposite side of the slot. On our second day, we would climb a sandstone peak called South Guardian Angel to enjoy the airplane views from its summit. The plan for the next day would up the ante: we would attempt to climb up to and backpack across remote highlands south of Greatheart Mesa, an exceedingly rugged area reportedly never traversed by anyone before. If we made it across that, a reported break in a 20-foot-high band of cliffs would lead us down to the Right Fork of North Creek, a remote canyon known only to expert canyoneers. On day four we would try to traverse a bench on the east side of the Right Fork—reportedly impassable due to streams deeply cutting the canyon's rock. If we found a way through, we would then endeavor to climb over two passes—the first also possibly impassable going one direction—to get into the very core of the area, sky-high terrain called Terry Wash. After climbing surrounding domes and peaks on a layover in Terry Wash, we hoped to retrace the previous day's steps north along the Right Fork and exit the area via Wildcat Canyon.

In my investigative correspondence with members of the Zion National Park Hiking forum, a Yahoo-sponsored online group frequented by knowledgeable canyoneers and climbers, I was warned that my route was way too precipitous and technical to pull off while carrying a large and heavy backpack and likely impassable in a number of places. A couple people declared Ted and I were "insane" to attempt it. But countering the alarm bells, storied climber Courtney Purcell, author of *Zion National Park: Summit Routes* and other outdoor guidebooks, called my route "inspired." After Ted's and my success pioneering a new route across the core of Capitol Reef National Park two years earlier, I was cautiously optimistic we could run my Zion gauntlet. If it were impassable, I reasoned, we could always retreat the way we came, as long as we were careful not to rappel down anything we couldn't climb back up. Why not give it a try?

It wasn't just thrills driving me to roll the dice again. I was addicted to that singular brew of pristine beauty, mute stillness and complete solitude only very remote backcountry holds; the more remote, the more magnified that sublime alchemy. Every fiber of my being was pushing me to feel the rapture again. A high like no other, I felt I couldn't live without it.

But a perfect storm—a constellation of freak circumstances, trust in wrong information and serial critical thinking errors—would doom the Zion expedition almost from the start. And if I'm being honest, our prior success in Capitol Reef probably made Ted and me a little too self-assured and heedless of the snowballing warning signs. Whatever, our dream expedition through Zion's core would quickly devolve into a fight for survival.

The first mistake was mine, as the trip planner: considering how precipitous the terrain was, I should've broken up the continuous route into three separate out-and-back trips that would've availed carrying much lighter backpacks. (I was attached to making a pioneering traverse across the area and having an unbroken week-plus in the boondocks.) Carrying climbing gear and food for all nine days would boost each pack's starting weight to around 70 pounds—much too heavy. We eventually realized we needed to lighten our loads. That need, along with erroneous information given us by two Zion National Park Hiking forum members and a park ranger, would lead us to make a grievous miscalculation at the start of the backpack.

But there was a confluence of events beyond our calculation and control that doomed the expedition hours before it even began. En route to Zion from the airport in Las Vegas on the evening of May 3, we car-camped in the narrow Virgin River Gorge in Arizona for the night. As we approached the on-ramp for Interstate 15 before sunrise the next morning, we discovered a line of vehicles backed up for miles in a standstill on the highway. An 18-wheeler had crashed and caught fire, blocking the interstate. No emergency personnel were yet on the scene. We surmised it might take hours for the wreckage to be cleared, a delay we could ill afford.

We drove back to Littlefield, a small town we'd passed the night before on I-15. One of the locals there told us we could get to Saint George—gateway to Zion—driving a winding two-lane blacktop byway through the surrounding mountainous countryside. We drove the back road, but the detour nevertheless put us behind schedule. Hours later, as we approached Zion National Park's south entrance near Springdale, our hearts sank when we saw road construction had backed up traffic once again, a second delay compounding the first.

Once through the traffic jam, I ran to the park's "backcountry desk" to secure our backpacking permits. There, a long queue would delay us yet again. When I finally reached the front of the line, I showed the ranger at the desk where Ted and I wanted to backpack, tracing my finger over an area map. The ranger seemed confused and called his manager over. After conferring with his subordinate, the manager said he had no idea how to record our route in the standardized permit system.

"Nobody ever goes there," he said of the area we planned to explore.

After a frustratingly long debate, the manager shoehorned our route onto the required form. Handing me my get-out-of-jail-free backcountry permit, the subordinate ranger informed me as a matter of protocol, "There's lots of water in the area where you're going. You shouldn't have any problem finding water." It was an odd assertion, I briefly thought, considering "nobody ever goes there" who could've reported this.

But the ranger's assurance accorded with what a couple people on the Zion hikers' forum had previously told me, that there would be water "everywhere" and Ted and I could each get by carrying just two quarts of it along our cross-country route—advice that would turn out to be perilously wrong.

By the time I got through the permitting bottleneck and Ted and I drove to the Wildcat Canyon Trailhead—road construction delay again—it was 12:30 P.M. on our arrival. Sorting and packing all of our equipment and provisions, which had been less-than-optimally divided up before flying to Vegas in order to minimize airline baggage fees, took us until 1:30 P.M. I had previously figured we needed to start backpacking no later than midmorning in order to make it to the Subway, where we expected there'd be water, before dark. We now chose to ignore that we were hours behind schedule. This, after packing heavy for a continuous nine-day route, was mistake number two.

As we were about to leave the trailhead, I told Ted I thought we should each carry three liters of water, one more each than we reportedly needed and a margin for error. Trusting the assurances we'd consistently received that there would be plenty of water along our route, Ted pushed for us to carry only two liters each so we could hike faster with packs two pounds lighter and make up for lost time. His reasoning made sense, so I agreed— mistake number three. We each drank a bunch of water before leaving the vehicle so we would be hydrated from the start. Then we were finally off.

We first had to hike two miles on easy trails to a dead end, where our cross-country route through the core of the park would begin. Heading east under sunny skies from the trailhead at 7,000 feet altitude, the Wildcat Canyon Trail took us through a somewhat sparse pine forest laced with a few latent snow banks and numerous ephemeral streams. The actively flowing brooks reinforced our now firm belief there would be plenty of water all along our route.

As we turned south onto the Northgate Peaks Trail half an hour later, Ted mentioned he had a steadily worsening headache. Surmising he hadn't drunk enough water over the past twenty-four hours, we stopped long enough for him to drink, eat a snack and down a couple ibuprofen tablets. By the time we arrived at the dead end for the Northgate Peaks Trail, he was feeling significantly better.

Leaving groomed trails behind now, we took off cross-country through an area informally known as Brushy Bowl, where we passed highly unappealing potholes filled with manky water darkly stained reddish brown by tannin. Confident we'd find more palatable water farther along our route, we decided not to top off our bottles with the yucky stuff but push onwards—mistake number four. After bushwhacking through fairly dense shrubs and contouring around an unnamed peak, we came to the first open view of our route down the steep north slope of Left Fork North Creek Canyon—a 1,100-foot plunge in altitude.

The land immediately before us dropped sharply down bare red slickrock, below which sprawled a chaotic maze of steeply descending and bone-dry corrugated ridges sparsely dotted with stunted pine trees and, lower still, jumbles of crumbling hoodoos sided by sheer cliffs—virtually none of which was delineated on our map. (I had only been able to find maps with 80-foot contour intervals—bereft of critically necessary detail—for the area.) From where we stood, I saw no sign or promise of water.

The rugged terrain now slowed our progress to a crawl. Due to my poor balance, I found the extremely steep descent down the slickrock slope very difficult to execute while shouldering my unwieldy backpack, and Ted had to carry my kit down one particularly sharp twenty-five-yard stretch. The day was very warm and we were hiking into the sun. Checking my altimeter wristwatch and gauging my diminishing water supply against our progress, I realized for the first time we would not make it to the Subway before nightfall halted our descent and we ran dry. I told Ted we must backtrack to the potholes in Brushy Bowl to top off our water bottles. Reluctant to retreat, he insisted earnestly that we could make it to water in the Subway before dark and refill there. I reluctantly deferred to his judgment—mistake number five.

In the sharply dissected and twisted terrain below the slickrock slabs, navigation became increasingly time-consuming and more reliant on seat-of-the-pants groundtruthing. We spied and followed a few small cairns, very widely spaced apart, that ostensibly marked the climbers' route down, but they soon petered out. The day was getting late. I was running low on water. Genuinely worried now, I urged Ted we must abort the route and climb back up to the potholes in Brushy Bowl for water. He asserted again we could make it to water in the Subway before dark, and lobbied strongly we should continue onward.

Now I had a difficult decision to make. I could unilaterally force our retreat back up to Brushy Bowl, but doing so would kill our planned nine-day itinerary; Ted's paltry vacation allowance at work precluded extending our expedition, and we would not be able to make up the lost day in our regimented schedule if we retreated. If instead I agreed to continue onward, it was, in my judgment, highly likely we would run completely out of water well before nightfall and reaching the Subway, and navigating the complex, steep terrain ahead in the dark was neither feasible nor safe.

History and ego would handicap my critical decision. I had been the one who had forced an abort in Big Bend National Park five years earlier for fear we would run out of water before reaching our cache. In the years since, Ted had steadfastly maintained the abort had been unnecessary and we could've made it to water before running dry. His was a dispassionate opinion; he hadn't assigned blame for the failed venture. But I did not want to be the spoiler again, the guy aborting yet another dream expedition. There was still a chance, however razor-thin, Ted was now right and we could make it to the Subway by dark and save the grand expedition. After all, we'd both thrown caution to the wind while traversing Capitol Reef National Park—hiking onward with likely insufficient water after Deep Creek Canyon proved dry—and we'd won that gamble. I decided now to ignore prudence and my escalating unease, and agreed to continue onward—mistake number six. We began rationing our water.

A couple hard hours later, we came to a nexus where two steep-sided, brush-choked ridges diverged before plunging crazily into the Subway, out of sight very far below. I'd previously heard only one ridge in the area led to a break in the high cliffs lining the Subway's north wall, and our poorly detailed map was of no use telling which of the two now before us was the go. It had taken us a little over five hours to descend 900 vertical feet, and we had another 600 feet to drop to get into the Subway; with only an hour and a half of light remaining, there was no way we'd make it there before dark. And no guarantee we wouldn't pick the wrong ridge and have to retreat back up. But the choice was moot—I now had only one ounce of water left and was feeling very ill.

I had a headache, nausea, muscle cramps and, even at rest, a racing pulse. Extremely weak, I was beginning to stumble. Adding to these classic symptoms of heat exhaustion, I was finding it difficult to think clearly—a troubling development, as I was our only able navigator. Hitting a figurative wall, my tottering gait came to a sudden halt.

"I'm virtually out of water," I announced. "We won't make it to the Subway before dark. I'm suffering heat exhaustion . . . headache, nausea. We must abort," I now insisted.

For the first time, I saw the gravity of the situation written across Ted's face.

"I'm really sorry," he said, contrite. It would be the only time—until again thirteen years later—that he would acknowledge, implicitly, his urging us onward had been a mistake.

"We need to save our urine, pee in our empty water bottles," I said grimly. "We might have to drink it at some point to make it out of here, up to Brushy Bowl for water."

"The Subway is closer," Ted reasoned.

"Yes, but we don't know which ridge to take down," I argued. "If we take the wrong one and come to a dead-end at the top of the cliffs, we'll have to retreat all the way back up to here to access the other ridge. I don't have the strength to do that. And even if we choose the right ridge," I continued, "there's no guarantee we'll find water in the Subway. The assurances we were given that there'd be water all along our route have turned out to be dead wrong. We need to head back to the one place we know for certain there is water."

Ted reluctantly agreed. Girding myself for the arduous climb out of the canyon, I drank my last ounce of water, but it barely moistened my dry mouth. Ted said he had a pint and a half left in his bottle. We climbed only a short distance, making it to the top of a steep-sided rib of rock fifteen feet wide, before I fell completely apart, out of gas and feeling too ill to go on. We dropped our packs. Seeing what bad condition I was in, Ted gave me his remaining water to drink, an incredibly selfless and noble sacrifice. Drinking it—all at once—took the edge off my symptoms, but I still felt too ill to climb any further.

I was gripped now by a growing sense of dread, knowing all too well what would likely come next. I'd had heat exhaustion at least six times before (medically predisposing me to getting it again). The worst time was on a cross-country backpack in the Oregon Cascades with Janet four years earlier. During that episode, my condition had quickly deteriorated to the point of complete helplessness and Janet had to nurse me through the night; I only recovered after drinking six quarts of water mixed with bespoke electrolytes over a thirty-six-hour period while resting continuously in shade. Now the situation was far worse. There was zero shade. We were completely out of water, in moisture-sucking high desert. Even at sundown, it was still alarmingly warm. I began to feel panicky and worried aloud whether I would make it through the night without slipping into deadly heatstroke.[44]

Seeing how weak I was, Ted suggested he hike alone down to the Subway in search of water. I argued there was no way he could make it there, let alone back to our bivouac again, by dark—we now had only about forty-five minutes of daylight remaining—and I worried he might get lost or injured

---

44 According to Mayo Clinic (https://www.mayoclinic.org/diseases-conditions/heat-stroke/symptoms-causes/syc-20353581), "Without prompt treatment, heat exhaustion can lead to heatstroke, a life-threatening condition . . . Untreated heatstroke can quickly damage your brain, heart, kidneys and muscles. The damage worsens the longer treatment is delayed, increasing your risk of serious complications or death." The clinic further advises a person suffering heat exhaustion should stop all activity and rest, move to a cooler place and drink cool water or sports drinks (https://www.mayoclinic.org/diseases-conditions/heat-exhaustion/symptoms-causes/syc-20373250).

in the attempt. Especially considering my serious condition and the lack of suitable alternatives, I should've agreed for him to go. In our entropy, it occurred to neither of us that he could've made a GPS breadcrumb trail for his return and followed it by flashlight. I wasn't thinking clearly, and I was single-mindedly consumed with concern for his safety. In his private journal (shared with me a decade later), Ted wrote he grappled with the decision:

> The best course of action seemed to be going down to the Subway with water bottles. But when I thought about the possibility of losing my way, that choice scared me. There was also the very real possibility that I might fall and injure myself—no more real than usual when we were backpacking, but with a much higher cost, endangering the lives of us both. Going up [to Brushy Bowl for water] was much safer.

In the waning light, I told Ted I thought the safest thing we could do is activate our personal locator beacon—alerting Zion National Park Search and Rescue that we were in trouble—and stay together; splitting up would only complicate rescue efforts. Ted balked. He debated whether we really needed to send a distress signal, considering water was only around three hours away (albeit up very challenging terrain), and he suggested we reassess our situation the following morning. I don't think he realized how sick I was already and how much worse I could get (or the danger he too was in). I was afraid we might wait too long to signal for help, when it would be too late for me.

My panic was mixed with cold calculation of the odds: if we didn't activate the beacon, my survival would totally depend on Ted—who'd only drunk five cups of water since leaving the trailhead—making the over six hours round trip to water and back (allowing time to filter) the next morning. Assuming he'd have the strength to climb out of the canyon and could find me on his return—neither a given—he likely wouldn't make it back until noon at the very earliest, roughly seventeen hours from now. If I survived that long, exposed to direct morning sun for several hours, water without added electrolytes and time recovering in shade (not available) might not restore me enough to climb out of the canyon. And if Ted got lost or injured or ran out of gas in his quest for water, I'd be done for. Considering the mortal risk at play, I didn't want to put all my eggs in one basket. Calling for help would significantly increase the odds I would get out of the canyon alive.

After some debate I convinced Ted we should activate our locator beacon, but the decision was virtually wholly mine. I pressed the button. As darkness fell, we laid out our sleeping bags on the ground, although I resolved I would barely cover myself in order to stay cool and prevent escalating my heat illness. The rib of rock we were bivouacked on fell off sharply six feet to either side of us, dropping perhaps a couple hundred feet. Dehydration had worsened my inherently bad balance. To (hopefully) protect myself in the event I stumbled dizzily off the edge of the ridge in the dark, I donned my climbing harness and clipped myself into a rope I tied to the base of a short, bendy pine sapling.

The evening was very warm. An hour or so after I'd drunk the last of Ted's water, its benefit had already faded. My headache and nausea were now quickly escalating again. Opening the plastic water bottle I had peed into a couple hours earlier, I steeled myself and took a sip of the urine inside. As long as I didn't breathe through my nose while drinking, it wasn't nearly as disgusting as I'd feared; I'd had the good sense to start saving the fluid waste while it was still coming out relatively clear. I forced myself to drink over a cup of urine. I was encouraged and relieved to note it eased my headache and nausea considerably.

I tried to sleep, but I was too frightened over our predicament and feeling too sick to relax enough to drift off. Also, my body's ability to regulate its core temperature had gone haywire: I couldn't cover myself with my sleeping bag without instantly overheating, but pulling the cover off made me descend into shivering within seconds. Unable to get comfortable, I lay there fidgeting.

I obsessively replayed in my mind how we'd gotten ourselves into such terrible trouble. I was secretly upset with Ted for recklessly pushing us to continue down into the canyon despite our diminishing water supply and dwindling daylight. On past expeditions he'd always been quietly gung-ho—self-confident but not cocky—and had a habit of plunging head-long into risky situations without fully considering the serious consequences of failure. I was more methodical and risk averse—yet the very architect of our increasingly dangerous expeditions. Sooner or later, that mix—success-ful 99 percent of the time—was going to lead to trouble. And now here we were.

But lying there in the dark, I resolved that I would not play the blame game. I loved Ted and didn't want to risk damaging our friendship, or the potential for doing more expeditions together, by re-litigating the past. Besides, there was enough blame, enough critical thinking errors, to go around. While he had pushed for us to hike on, I had ultimately agreed. And it was I who had planned our arguably foolhardy expedition in the first place. We had both ignored our dangerously late start at the trailhead and, most critically, failed to pack enough water—only half what we usually car-ried—for strenuous backpacking in desert terrain. We were both to blame for the situation we now found ourselves in. Now it was critical we put all that aside and remain a united team, focused on getting out of there alive.

I didn't sleep a wink that night. Ted—also thirsty, queasy and anxious—slept for only around twenty minutes.[45] Every time I felt my headache and nausea worsening, I drank more urine until my symptoms eased, but each respite lasted only an hour or two before I had to drink more. As the night wore on, it also became increasingly obvious I was approaching the point of diminishing return: drinking urine was making me pee more often and in progressively greater volume, as my body sought to eliminate the increas-ingly concentrated waste in my bloodstream.

At around 4 A.M., I sat up to gaze at the moon rising over Greatheart Mesa, looming on the other side of the Subway. Despite our desperate situ-ation, I could somewhat appreciate how beautiful the mesa on the dark

---

45   In his private journal, Ted would attribute his nausea overnight not to illness but to worry, partly because he gradually began to realize how sick I was. In one entry, he would write, "At one point he [Michael] lay still, and then I realized I would rather hear him stirring. I thought about how I would handle things if he slipped into uncon-sciousness. The burden I faced set in, and I realized how little responsibility for our safety I had taken. He had always been more concerned about it than I."

horizon, and the rim of the jagged canyon below us, looked limned in moonlight. And checking my watch, I was grateful it now seemed likely I would survive the night.

By daybreak I had drunk over a liter of urine. It had not been so disgusting at first. But now, as the hidden sun began brightening the sky, my third catch was darker yellow, slightly foamy and foul smelling. Ted had resisted drinking any of his urine throughout the night, but now he was too thirsty to hold off any longer. Unscrewing the lid on his bottle, he took a tentative sip of piss. Swallowing slowly, he shot me a poker face.

"Hmm," he murmured, sounding surprised, and then gave his assessment: "Hints of English leather and orange blossoms." Like he was judging a wine-tasting contest.

I was amazed at how relatively well he was evidently faring: just very thirsty, exhausted and queasy. He had peed a pint throughout the night, pitifully little of the stuff to drink now. As the sun rose over the horizon, it felt alarmingly warm, and there was no way to shelter from it in our bivouac on a virtually bare, south-facing slope. We would not last long just sitting there in the sun. But the daunting prospect of trying to climb out of the canyon in our miserably dehydrated and weakened state convinced us it was safer to stay put and wait for rescue. To be honest, we hoped a helicopter would haul us out of there.

Two hours after sunrise, we had not yet seen any sign of a rescue party and were beginning to fear it might arrive too late, especially for me. Or perhaps our personal locator beacon had failed to put out a distress signal and we were senselessly waiting for help that would never come. I couldn't stomach drinking any more of my urine; it had become too concentrated and foul, and drinking it was no longer giving me much benefit. We could already tell it was going to be a very hot day. The clock was quickly counting down toward disaster. Reading the situation, Ted now took the initiative.

"I think I can carry my pack to Brushy Bowl," he said, sounding more determined than optimistic. "Do you think you can make it up to there?"

"I dunno," I mumbled. In my brain fog, I couldn't tell what was riskier, resting in direct sun for an indeterminable time or attempting the steep climb, also in direct sun, up to water and shade. Merely walking around our relatively level bivouac site—with my backpack off—immediately escalated my heat illness, leaving me breathless and stooped, my headache pounding like a jackhammer. If I were to have any chance of climbing out of the canyon without crashing into full-blown heat stroke, I would need to jettison weight from my backpack.

I dumped ten pounds of food onto the ground. I hated leaving trash in this beautiful wilderness; it went totally against my environmental ethic. But it was either that, or stay and slowly roast. Hoisting our backpacks, Ted and I agreed that if we proved too weak to carry them up to Brushy Bowl, we'd discard them along with all of our supplies, in a naked drive for survival.

The climb was a dizzying blur, slow and incredibly arduous, and I consistently lagged behind Ted. We didn't try to follow exactly the same route we'd taken on the way down; I didn't have the cognitive capacity to do so. An hour or two into the ordeal—I couldn't tell how long—we stumbled into an unfamiliar ravine. I was extremely encouraged to see a small patch of mud. At my suggestion, we dropped our packs and dug two shallow holes in the wet dirt where a tiny trickle of water—no more than half an inch wide—was still dribbling. The holes slowly filled an inch deep with muddy, slightly scummy and foul-smelling water. It was then that I knew we were going to make it out of the canyon alive.

We eagerly dipped our Sierra cups in the light brown water and drank freely; we were so incredibly thirsty, we didn't bother to filter it first. After drinking urine for the past thirteen hours, the muddy water tasted absolutely wonderful to me, like feather-light ambrosia.

Over the next half hour or so, we allayed our thirst and filled two liter-size bottles with the unfiltered water. Revived and climbing again, we came before long to the steep slickrock boilerplate below Brushy Bowl. Looking across a sheer-walled defile immediately west of us—off-route—I spied a seep dripping down the far side. We worked our way around the head of the cut to the top of the spring, which was choked with algae but flowing with water. Dropping our packs, we filtered a cup or two at a time and guzzled until we had each downed a liter, our first drink of clean water in over fifteen hours. As I drank, I could feel my energy and mental acuity quickly rebounding, like awakening from a dream with a shot of adrenaline.

Suddenly we heard a whistle, coming from somewhere above us, break the silence. We hailed back. Four men appeared. It quickly became apparent they were members of the Zion National Park Search and Rescue (SAR) Team. Our beacon had worked after all. I now ruefully wished it hadn't. Having made it to water shortly before the team's arrival, just before noon, Ted and I both felt very embarrassed for having activated the beacon—with hindsight, unnecessarily—the day before. Ted apologized first for the both of us for having put the SAR team through the trouble of and inherent risk in finding us.

"No problem!" the team leader exclaimed. "Better embarrassed than dead. We're always relieved when we don't find dead bodies. It doesn't always turn out that way."

The SAR team was eminently attentive. They immediately offered us electrolyte drinks and energy bars. I gulped down three bottles of electrolyte drink in roughly as many minutes and ate a bar. The leader of the SAR team, a man who looked a little older than I, was an accomplished and locally well-known canyoneer named Bo Beck. He told me his team had not been exactly sure where to search for us, as our beacon kept alternately transmitting a different location, first on one ridge and then on another relatively far off to the east. He also told me that sending a distress signal is often not a quick solution for an emergency in Zion; because of the rough terrain, he explained, it often takes forty-eight hours to rescue people in remote parts of the park.

Against Ted's and my objections, the rescue team insisted they carry most of our supplies to lighten our packs for the hike out to the trailhead. Even so, Ted and I struggled to match their deliberately moderate pace, we were still that exhausted. The SAR team members, taking care to observe if Ted or I were about to crash from the exertion, repeatedly asked how we were feeling as we hiked.

Arriving back at our vehicle parked at the trailhead, Beck asked us to follow the team to SAR headquarters inside the park. During the drive we called our wives, who had been notified earlier by SAR that a distress signal had been received, to let them know we were okay; Ted and I fretted over the worry we'd put them through.

Ted was so knackered, he barely made the drive to SAR headquarters without falling asleep at the wheel. Inside HQ, a ranger and his supervisor interviewed Ted and I, first separately and then together, to determine if we'd had good cause to activate our beacon.

"No judgment," the ranger said to Ted first off, before beginning his questioning. After finishing, he said there had been four deaths and one close call in the park in the last week alone, and he was glad we were both alive and well. His supervisor, a dour desk jockey named Dan (not his real name), was far less charitable.

Dan argued I hadn't become dehydrated but had probably developed instead a condition called hypernatremia (a dangerous increase of sodium in extracellular fluid that, in fact, is caused in part by dehydration).[46] He went on to incorrectly theorize my supposed hypernatremia was likely caused by not eating enough food. (Low caloric intake does not cause or contribute to hypernatremia.) But Dan's dismissive armchair diagnosis was irrelevant besides, as both hypernatremia and heat stroke—the next stage of untreated heat exhaustion—can damage vital organs and be fatal if not quickly corrected by increasing water intake.

In Dan's defense, it was his job to make sure Ted and I had activated our locator beacon for good reason. But his truculent interrogation left me feeling traumatized all over again. After grilling Ted and me for around twenty minutes to assess our actions over the prior twenty-four hours, his stern demeanor suddenly and inexplicably did an about-face, his squared shoulders relaxing as he leaned back in his chair.

"Okay, I'm going to come down off my high horse now," he said. "I'm

---

46 In a paper published by the National Institutes of Health and updated online on August 1, 2021, at https://www.ncbi.nlm.nih.gov/books/NBK44196k0/, authors Bhavin Sonani, Srividya Naganathan and Mohammed A. Al-Dhahir write that "The basic mechanisms of hypernatremia are water deficit and excess solute [chiefly urea and/or electrolyte] . . . Most patients present with symptoms suggestive of fluid loss and clinical signs of dehydration." The authors go on to state "it is important to remember that rapid correction of hypernatremia can lead to cerebral edema" and "the estimated free water deficit should be corrected over 48 to 72 hours." My rapid rehydration—over the course of roughly one hour—without ill consequence suggests I did not have hypernatremia but heat exhaustion.

satisfied you believed you were in mortal danger when you activated your beacon." He ended his edict by tersely lecturing, "Next time, plan a trip that's more realistic."

The interrogation was over, and Ted and I were free to go. But while Dan was done with us, I was not so ready to let myself off the hook. The entire backcountry episode—the many amateur mistakes Ted and I had made, my lapse in being self-sufficient in wilderness and activating the beacon, the ruined expedition—sent me into a tailspin of inconsolable self-reproach.

Ted and I left SAR headquarters feeling totally wasted, contrite and demoralized. But we were determined not to have our trip be a complete write-off, the imbroglio its endnote. We decided we would regroup and attempt to pull off part of our aborted itinerary the next day via a different approach.

I'd always considered the Terry Wash area the crown jewel of my originally planned itinerary through Zion's core, and I was loath to forego seeing it. After Ted and I left SAR headquarters and resupplied our food in the nearby town of Springdale, we decided we would try to backpack into Terry from an alternative direction, starting in a trail-less canyon named, oddly, Trail Canyon. This time we would leave all of our climbing gear behind to lighten our loads—ostensibly a wise decision, but it turns out a mistake.

Hiking on our second day up an unnamed side canyon, we came to a dry waterfall blocking our way directly forward. Below the pour-off was water, above it apparently none, so we filtered four gallons to carry; it was a hot day, and we had learned the hard way not to overestimate water availability in Zion. With our packs each now weighing over 65 pounds with water stowed, we clawed our way 200 vertical feet up the canyon's west wall in an attempt to bypass the dry pour-off. A widespread fire had incinerated the area three years earlier, leaving the steep slope—a 60-degree incline in places—devoid of all but spindly shrubs to grab onto and footing treacherously loose underfoot. Because of my poor balance, I had to ask Ted to carry my pack up the last 100 feet, which he ungrudgingly obliged.

Clearing the pour-off, our view of the way forward looked formidable, requiring a long traverse across the face of a very steep slope in the fire scar to get around another dry waterfall perhaps four times higher than the first. Ted probably could've executed the traverse without falling, but I doubted I could while carrying 65 pounds. (Ironically, had we this time brought our climbing gear along, we both could've made it.) The last thing we wanted to do was risk a disabling injury that would necessitate activating our locator beacon again (assuming its battery wasn't drained by the previous activation). We decided to play it safe and dispiritedly aborted the route.

I'd heard, vaguely, of a third way to get to Terry's high country via a long approach from the south across low, open desert, but the next day's weather forecast called for a daytime high in the mid-80s Fahrenheit—too hot, we decided (especially for me, still vulnerable to heat exhaustion), for hauling heavy packs in shadeless terrain. We reluctantly gave up on Terry. As a consolation, we opted to do an ostensibly easy backpack in higher and cooler country: to Wildcat Canyon by trail and thence cross-country down the canyon to the Right Fork North Creek, where we hoped to do some easy, non-technical climbing on surrounding peaks.

But when we arrived at Wildcat Canyon the following day, our hearts sank. The expectably slight Wildcat Creek was flowing swiftly in the canyon from bank to bank and up to twenty feet wide in places, leaving no streamside margin to hike along. We tried fighting our way—again carrying 65-pound packs—along the broken west slope just above the flooded channel, but it was choked with nightmarish thickets of brush and jack-straw blowdown—numerous downed trees lying interlaced at knee- and chest-height—across the grade. After making only a quarter of a mile progress in an hour, we became discouraged and decided, crestfallen, to abort once again.

We'd had our butts kicked on all three routes we'd attempted over the past five days. Soured on backpacking the core of Zion and desperate to salvage what little remained of our shattered vacation, we drove the next day to the southeast corner of the park, which reportedly afforded much easier cross-country backpacking through thinly forested sandstone country.

Carrying three gallons of water each, we backpacked up to and over a narrow pass a mile west of Checkerboard Mesa to establish a base camp atop a dry ridge. High winds were gusting to around 45 mph and we had no tent stakes—I'd left them at home to save weight—so we guyed out my three-season Marmot tent with parachute cord secured in loops around large rocks.

The next day, we finally had our just reward for having persevered through serial deflating washouts. A leisurely seven-mile day hike cross-country from camp, in picture-postcard-perfect weather, took us along the south edge of a chain of exquisitely beautiful white and orange sandstone domes and pyramidal peaks sparsely garnished with green pine trees. We climbed to the summit of two small peaks in turn for breathtaking 360-degree views of the park and had an absolutely wonderful time.

As we returned to camp late that afternoon, the sky started rapidly filling with cirrus clouds. Grabbing Ted's attention, I pointed out four lenticular clouds—two huge and forebodingly dark—to the west. I'd never before seen more than one such cloud at a time.

"Lenticular clouds always spell trouble," I said. "We're going to have a powerful, cold storm tonight."

Winds gusted to around 45 mph again that evening. Shortly before drifting off to sleep, I heard the pitter-patter of rain on our tent's flapping fly. When I crawled outside the tent at 2 A.M. to take a leak, the wind was icy-cold but the sky reassuringly crystal-clear. Not for long. When I next awoke at seven and poked my head outside the tent, there were two inches of snow on the ground and it was snowing hard. Every forty-five minutes thereafter, Ted and I crawled out of the lightweight nylon tent to clear its roof and walls of snow so it wouldn't collapse. By the time it stopped storming at 10 A.M., there were four inches of snow on the ground. Like a child thrilling to his first white Christmas, I rushed outside to revel in the spectacle.

The scenery surrounding our camp was breathtaking: the green pines, yucca and beavertail cactus dressing the ridge we were on were heavily laden with snow, and the towering red domes and cliffs surrounding us—too sheer to hold much cover—were artistically streaked in white as if by fine paintbrush strokes. It had snowed enough to grandly decorate the area for us, but not quite enough (as yet) to really endanger us. The privilege of safely witnessing a winter-like storm in such a gorgeously primeval setting left me ecstatic, grinning silently from ear to ear while turning in circles to take it all in. My only regret was the snow had killed our plan to hike that day down to the bottom of Parunuweap Canyon, for the steep sandstone boilerplate en route would surely have been too slick for safe travel.

Dark clouds and high winds continued to threaten more weather well past noon, but winter's sylphs held off storming our camp. By 2 P.M. the snowpack had amazingly all but melted, draining into the parched and porous red soil like in a time-lapse video on fast-forward. But the cold air, super-charged with oxygen, still had that smell of clean steel and a dry crispness that portends snowfall.

"This storm isn't over," I told Ted. "I think we should pack up and leave. If we don't, we might have to post-hole out of here tomorrow and could miss our flights home."

Two minutes later it began to snow again. We quickly packed up, hiked over the pass and scrambled downhill to our rented car. An hour later, I looked back up to the Checkerboard area in our car's rearview mirror to see it completely engulfed in ominously dark clouds. Surely all hell was breaking loose up there.

Our Zion expedition had concluded in spectacular fashion but on the whole had been an epic fail. As we drove out of the park, my joyful recollections of the last three days quickly evaporated, and I was left feeling sorely disappointed, beaten and spooked. The core of Zion National Park loomed in my mind like a stern headmaster, intimidating and reproaching. Its rugged and inviolable backcountry had shaken my self-confidence and shattered my self-identity as a skilled and self-reliant outdoorsman. The only way to reconcile the unnerving experience and regain my power was to return and confront the monster again.

-21-

THE CURSE OF THE
ALTAR OF SACRIFICE

Two months after returning home from the disastrous DDM 10 in Zion, I found myself in a most unlikely place: inside an actor's trailer for a movie shoot in Bend, Oregon. Auditioning on a lark three weeks earlier, I had won a small speaking role in *The Wait*, an indie film starring Hollywood actors Jena Malone, Luke Grimes and Chloë Sevigny. Now I was hanging with Malone, Grimes and a hair-and-makeup stylist in a trailer parked outside the movie set while the director prepared our upcoming scene with the film crew.

I'd worked with celebrity several years earlier, but on the other side of the microphone as a recording engineer. In March 2005, Dow Jones & Company hired me to record Barry Serafin, former weekend anchor of ABC World News, in a voice-over segment for the *Journal Editorial Report* that subsequently aired on PBS member television station Thirteen/WNET. A year later, Simon & Schuster Audio hired me to record Academy Award-winning actor William Hurt reading Ernest Hemingway's *The Sun Also Rises* for release on CD; a producer flew from New York City to my recording studio in Central Oregon to direct the weeklong slate of recording sessions for the venerated—yet, off-screen, manifestly unassuming—actor, whose scores of film credits already included *Kiss of the Spider Woman*, *Broadcast News*, *Children of a Lesser God* and *A History of Violence*.

Unfortunately, my part in *The Wait* would end up on the cutting-room floor, preempting my fifteen minutes of fame. It was a minor disappointment compared to the physical setback I would suffer a month after the shoot. My longtime backpacking buddy Whitaker—who I'd met off-trail twenty-five years earlier in the middle of Olympic National Park's remote Bailey Range—had driven from Santa Cruz to Sisters with his two teenage daughters and a girlfriend (he'd recently gotten divorced) to join Janet and me on a summer backpack in the Mount Jefferson Wilderness. On the last day of our trek, my right foot's old injury flared up again during a pounding ten-mile slog entailing 3,000 feet of elevation change, most of it tromping downhill. I would be hobbled and benched for the remainder of the season.

The reinjury, and aging fifty-something bodies, was the impetus for Janet and me to lighten our backcountry loads by purchasing state-of-the-art ultralight backpacking equipment; replacing our traditional backpacks, tent, sleeping bags and much of our clothing with lighter substitutes made each of our loads over ten pounds lighter.

Outfitted with my slick new gear, I attempted climbing Middle Sister with my brother Mitch and his twenty-year-old son Evan in August 2011, my first time on that particular mountain in thirteen years. Unfortunately, I as leader managed preparations for the climb poorly: we left base camp too late in the morning, not fully hydrated and with insufficient water packed for what turned out to be a hot day on our route up the sunny south-facing side of the volcano. Mitch ran out of gas 850 vertical feet below the summit, but we weren't going to make it there with enough water for the return trip anyway. We had to abort. I was disappointed we hadn't summited.

Janet and I backpacked that summer in beautiful wilderness timeless on its face, mercifully unaware it would be rendered unrecognizable by climate change in less than a decade. In the Northern Oregon Cascades in late August, we explored the gorgeously lake-studded Olallie Scenic Area, de facto wilderness that would be incinerated nine years later by the 204,469-acre Lionshead Fire. In mid-September, we backpacked through verdant coniferous forests on the east side of the Three Sisters Wilderness; we could not know then that, just a year later, it would be razed by the unusually fast-spreading 26,795-acre Pole Creek Fire, a blaze ultimately smaller in reach than the massive Lionshead but equally destructive within its infernal confines. And a couple days before the 2011 fall equinox, we backpacked Southern Oregon's little-visited Gearheart Mountain Wilderness, which would be virtually wiped off the map in 2021 by the monster 413,765-acre Bootleg Fire, the third largest in Oregon's history at the time. Devastating crown fires fueled by accelerating climate change would leave us only precious memories and photos of these and other primeval mountain forests, unchanged for millennia and then gone in a week.

My beloved mother turned a frail eighty-eight years old as 2011 drew to a close. After she suffered a couple bad falls and received a dementia diagnosis, she reluctantly agreed to Mitch and me moving her from her cherished condo in sunny Florida to an assisted-living facility in Oregon, where we could keep closer tabs on her. As my fifty-ninth birthday approached the following summer, I could tell I too would soon have to abide Father Time. My stamina was in slow but inexorable decline, and my right foot—injured and reinjured multiple times over the past eight years—was now frequently refusing to tolerate my wilderness adventures. I knew I would soon have to give up mountaineering, and I began planning my last hurrah.

In late August, my nephew Evan and I backpacked to Camp Lake at the foot of Middle Sister, determined to finish what we had unsuccessfully attempted to do, with Mitch, the prior summer—reach the mountain's 10,052-foot summit. I had scheduled the summit assault to occur the day before my fifty-ninth birthday as a celebration and life marker. But while meticulously packing our rucksacks in base camp the evening before the climb, I discovered Evan had failed, due to inexperience, to bring a warm hat and gloves on the trip, and he had only one relatively thin insulating layer for his core. I lectured him about how dangerous his oversight was, how he would struggle to survive overnight if he had a disabling injury high on the mountain in bad weather—mountains, I explained, can attract dense clouds, freezing rain and snow even when the sun is shining below. After long deliberation, I decided I would let him climb only if my altimeter's barometer held steady overnight and the sky was completely clear of clouds the next morning. And even if so, I would keep an eagle eye out during the climb and abort at the first sign of clouds gathering on the horizon.

Fortunately, the next morning, August 23, 2012, dawned pin clear and my barometer signaled we were good to go. Unlike a year ago, this time we packed plenty of water—nearly a gallon each—and got an early start, leaving base camp at 6:30 A.M. But after climbing only 600 vertical feet, my argumentative right foot suddenly developed disabling, stabbing pain. Using skeletal-realignment techniques taught years ago to me by Rich Phaigh—the esoteric massage therapist who had healed my horribly injured left knee in 1992—I mobilized my foot's metatarsals on the spot and stuck an aspirin patch on them. Within minutes, the pain completely disappeared and Evan and I were climbing again.

Evan was inexperienced but strong, and I had a hard time matching his energetic pace as we clawed our way up Middle Sister's unstable talus- and scree-plagued South Ridge. Typical for men his age (twenty-one), he was overly confident and heedless of risk; I sometimes had to yell up to him as he climbed ahead of me, instructing him to veer left or right to avoid exposure or potential rockfall. But because of his boldness and both his and my stamina that day, I became increasingly convinced our summit quest would be fulfilled.

By mid-morning we had reached a place, 550 vertical feet below the summit, where the South Ridge narrows and views of the impressive crevasses on the Diller Glacier, below us on the mountain's sprawling east slope, open up. Here the South Ridge also joins with and traces the rim of the mountain's steep and barren west slope. For an experienced mountaineer, this is considered a safe place—assuming good weather—with no nearby exposure and solid footing. I'd been here before in 1998 and was completely comfortable, in fact downright ecstatic for having made my return.

Not so, Evan. The totally alien place—Diller Glacier's open-grave crevasses, the mountain's lifeless west slope plunging down to remote wilderness far below, and the safety of base camp out of reach 2,500 vertical feet below us—was too much for him, and he descended into a quickly accelerating panic attack. Knowing how important attaining the summit was to me, he bravely sucked up his angst until we reached the steep jumble of large rocks about 350 vertical feet below it. Above that last obstacle, I knew from past experience, an easy walk would lead us up to the wind-blown apex. But it might as well have been a thousand miles away.

"I have to head down," Evan said, shaking in terror.

"I can make it to the summit and back in forty to fifty minutes," I replied, nearly pleading. "Are you okay sitting here until I return?"

He wasn't, and not just because he feared I might get injured on my round trip to the summit and back—a possibility, though slight—leaving him to make the perilous climb back down to base camp alone. Like an anguished astronaut stranded on the moon, he was done with the mountain and would not wait another minute to get off its terrible rock. As if an invisible hand pushed him, he spun around and started down, not even looking to see if I would follow.

I looked longingly back up at the summit, so close I could almost touch it. I ached to stand on its majestic perch once more before surrendering that sacred privilege forever. But I could not in good conscience abandon Evan. He might not climb down safely in his mental state and, lacking navigation skills, could easily get lost; if he took an errant straight-line descent off the mountain, he would end up disoriented in the remote Chambers Lakes area on the west (wrong) side of the Pacific Crest. Evan's safety was my first priority, not just as climb leader but, most important, as his uncle who loved him. The summit push was over.

After descending 400 vertical feet to familiar ground, Evan regained his composure. The remaining climb down to base camp was uneventful and free of significant injury. Once safely back in camp, Evan regretfully confronted his forcing the summit abort.

"I feel bad we didn't summit," he said quietly. "This was your last climb."

"It's okay," I consoled him. "You pushed yourself to your very limit. That's the best anyone could ask for."

I shared with him my embarrassing washout in Zion two years earlier.

"Nobody bats a thousand in wilderness; everyone comes up short at some point, if they're out here long enough," I said. "The climb was still fantastic, and reaching the summit was comparatively trivial—I've stood on it twice before." I placed my hand on his shoulder. "The important thing is we got to spend quality time together on an awesome adventure, and we both made it safely up and down the mountain."

Truthfully, the abort had not ruined the trip for me. I had climbed well—strongly and confidently—and rejoiced in reliving my wild youth, now in its sunset years. And the abort was somehow fitting, for I realized it meant my last big-mountain summit was with my beloved longtime climbing buddy Ed Lovegren—now in his eighties and too frail for mountaineering—on Diamond Peak in 2005.

I squeaked in one more backpack that summer, with Janet, before the explosive Pole Creek Fire shut down wilderness access in the Central Oregon Cascades on September 8. That climate change-fueled wildfire would produce in the Sisters area unimaginable smoke pollution—continuously for a full week, over three times the concentration deemed downright hazardous by federal government agencies—propelling me to my doctor with chest pains and a deep cough. During a town hall meeting, a visiting DEQ official declared it was the worst smoke pollution he'd witnessed on-site from conflagrations in the US over his decades-long career.

I recovered from the local wildfire but still felt in thrall to a place a thousand miles away. Despite my philosophical retelling of my Zion washout to Evan, DDM 10's epic fail was in truth still gnawing at me two years on. Even after all that time, just thinking about the fiasco tied my stomach in knots. Try as I might, I could not reconcile it—and knew I would not unless and until I stood triumphant in Zion's redoubtable core. In phone conversations with Ted, I broached a few times our making a second attempt to reach Zion's vertical interior—specifically an expedition into the far-flung Terry Wash area—but was always met with lukewarm response.

"I'm not sure I want to attempt something like that again," Ted told me. "It's not fair to my wife and kids—not just because of the risk involved but also because of time off from family obligations—and the required arrangements take a ton of work." He paused and then added quietly, "I know I say that before every DDM."

I had gotten more "beta" (informal explorer-speak for detailed first-hand information) on a southern approach to the Terry Wash high country from an acquaintance I'd made online. Deborah Davis, an experienced backpacker living in Salt Lake City, fleshed out for me a route I'd previously heard vague mention of, one that Ted and I had not yet attempted. Most every year for the past several, Davis and a few adventurous friends of hers had backpacked to Terry Wash following the route taught to her by an old friend who had since died of ALS.

With her companions' blessings, Davis graciously invited me to join her group for a backpack to Terry in 2013. But I was reticent to accept because of my susceptibility to heat exhaustion; her group wanted to do the trip in the middle of May, by which time, my historical meteorological research for the area informed, daytime high temperatures could potentially be dangerously hot. And there were other considerations: I didn't need to explain away my tumor-caused balance issues with Ted while tackling a hardcore route—he was one of only a few people who knew of my condition—and he always lent his assistance on the most precipitous pitches without making me feel less than. I also balked at casually following others' predetermined footsteps into the backcountry; I wanted to do the fun off-trail navigation myself. But most of all, there was no one I would rather be on expedition with than Ted. DDM 10's train wreck aside, we were a competent team that complemented each other's skills, and I greatly enjoyed his company besides. I just had to convince him Terry was worth a second shot.

Nearly three years of serially emailing Google Earth satellite images, Davis's backcountry photos of Terry, additional beta from experienced Zion mountaineer Courtney Purcell, and my topo maps with the route overlaid gradually wore down Ted's resistance until he became sold on the expedition. In mid-April 2013, we took the leap. But the expedition would have an alarmingly rocky start.

The low-profile, desertic southwest corner of Zion National Park lies in stark contrast to the park's sky-piercing nucleus. At just below 3,700 feet altitude, the relatively level sagebrush- and juniper-lined Coalpits Wash leaves Utah State Route 9 opposite the ghost town of Grafton to gradually climb between low hills and increasingly higher mesas toward the reserve's remarkably perpendicular core. Starting around five miles north of the highway, the low desert becomes progressively pinched in an inverted-U shape by an encroaching, ragged semicircle of spectacular cliffs: the 800-feet-high perpendicular face of Cougar Mountain to the west, unnamed 2,000-foot serrated cliffs directly north, and the astounding 3,000-feet-high walls comprising the Towers of the Virgin to the east—formidable ramparts barricading the park's remote interior and forcing an ostensible dead-end retreat. On my topo maps, one fancifully named sky-high turret in the Towers of the Virgin caught my attention: The Altar of Sacrifice. Its evocative and menacing title led to its peremptory designation as the Curse for DDM 11.

The Curse of the Altar of Sacrifice proved its overlordship from the get-go. Driving south toward Zion from Salt Lake City International Airport on April 16, snow flurries quickly accelerated into near-blizzard conditions, the white stuff accumulating a few inches deep by the time we acquired our backcountry permits at the park's westside Kolob Visitor Center around four o'clock in the afternoon. In an offensive replay of the ignominious start of DDM 9 five years earlier, I contracted food poisoning from eating contaminated store-bought sliced carrots during the drive and ended up doubled over with terrible intestinal cramps later that afternoon in a car-camp off a dirt road outside the park. When the snowstorm mercifully abated at sundown, I brewed up carminative caraway-seed tea outside our tent while involuntarily vomiting. The tea barely helped, and I tossed and turned all night in the cold nylon tent, worrying that DDM 11 would prove to be yet another epic fail.

My gut was still in acute spasms the next morning when I stumbled bleary-eyed out of the tent. Pilfering some remnant charcoal from some-body's disused fire pit beside our camp, I ground the black lumps into a powder, mixed it with water and quickly drank the gritty slurry down before the sediment could settle. A couple hours later, the foolproof remedy had killed the bacteria in my gut and quelled my cramps, and I was ready—barely so—to start hiking.

A trail led Ted and me up the lower reach of Coalpits Wash. The blustery morning's wintry temperatures slowly warmed to a comfortable 50°F as we hiked beside the sandy channel, flowing with ample water, under partly sunny skies. Lost in casual catch-up conversation during our ostensibly straightforward approach to the high country, we unintentionally deviated into a wide side canyon about a mile and a half from the highway. I quickly realized our mistake and we corrected our course to regain Coalpits Wash, chastened and refocused.

A mile farther up the wash, off-trail now, we came upon four fit but dour backpackers—two couples—hauling ass in the opposite direction. Unwilling to chat for long, they tersely reported they had spent the previous night up in Terry's high country "in survival mode," caught in a vigorous storm that had dumped three to four inches of snow on their camp. Ted and I thanked them for the beta and moved on. We would not see another soul for the next five days.

A mile farther along, we left the main drainage to head cross-country up Jennings Creek, auspiciously flowing with water. We slept that night in a make-do camp shoehorned onto a bank verdantly clothed in pine and cottonwood and service berry trees at the confluence of Jennings and Terry Creeks, surrounded on three sides by sheer cliffs towering over 1,500 feet above us. The profound wildness and isolation of the place heightened our anticipation of backpacking into the core of Zion the following day.

We broke camp around nine o'clock the next morning. Leaving Terry Creek behind, we backpacked cross-country up a dissected ravine clogged with car-size boulders, landslide-downed juniper trees and scratchy thickets of oak brush. We soon exited the ravine to climb a ridge and cross a plateau below Cougar Mountain's sheer 800-foot cliffs. We knew we had to get to the top of these seemingly unbroken cliffs to get eventually to Terry Wash inside Zion's core. The cliffs looked impassable, both on the map and from our vantage point on the plateau below, but Deborah Davis had assured me there was a narrow break in the wall. Indeed, an obscure elk trail led Ted and me, along a very steep traverse of the mountainside below the cliffs, up to the hidden crack. Standing in the notch, we peered 1,000 vertical feet down the mountain's opposite side to where dry waterfalls in an unnamed canyon had urged our abort while carrying much heavier backpacks during DDM 10 three years earlier. To be much higher now supercharged my confidence we would this time reach Terry.

Climbing still higher, we threaded our way through a steep labyrinth of exquisite orange and salmon sandstone hoodoos to gain an expansive, high plateau choked with scratchy oak brush. Following game trails wherever possible across the plateau minimized our need to bushwhack and ultimately led us to an open and incredibly beautiful sandstone bowl, lightly populated with pine trees in an almost bonsai tableau. Here, the recent snowstorm's beneficent side revealed itself: while its wintry white blanket had completely melted away over the past couple days, seeps in the bowl were still lightly flowing with water and small potholes in the hard sandstone floor offered relatively fresh ephemeral pools to drink from. After DDM 10's "piss-drinking party"—my sardonic reference to our survival test in Zion three years earlier—the water-filled potholes were a reassuring sight. But we still had to make our way down intimidating Goblin Gulch.

A steeply descending and progressively narrow slot canyon hemmed by contorted orange and red sandstone hoodoos, Goblin Gulch's claustrophobic channel was stair-stepped with multiple dry waterfalls that looked at first impassable; the way down or around them only became apparent when we came to stand atop their flashflood-polished lips. A short distance beyond the last navigable pour-off, the haunted gulch dead-ended on the lip of a perfectly perpendicular 600-foot cliff, at the base of which an extremely steep escarpment continued plunging another 700 vertical feet down to Terry Creek, the stream there still a couple hundred feet above our morning camp.

The only way out of the sun-starved confines of the slot, besides retreating, was to climb up a rock wall around fifteen feet high. Accommodating my compromised balance, Ted carried up the wall my 40-pound backpack—outfitted with ultralight gear, it weighed much less than during past expeditions—and I easily followed unencumbered. Rounding the base of weathered sandstone cliffs at the top of the wall, a short walk took us finally to the spectacular view long imagined in my previously unfulfilled dreams: the fabled fairyland of Terry Wash. The breathtaking beauty of the place stopped us dead in our tracks as if paralyzed. For the next couple minutes, we stood speechlessly gaping at the remote basin's indescribably beautiful white sandstone domes, decapitated rock turrets and improbably sheer orange cliffs.

We had made it into the core of Zion National Park. The moment we set foot in Terry, I felt a nagging burden I'd carried for three years lift off my shoulders. My eyes watered as my heart soared with unbridled joy. Call it redemption or requited obsession or whatever. But fuck the unfinished business—we'd finished it. And the bucket-list place was even more beautiful than I'd imagined.

We followed a game trail north into the basin, but it petered out in half a mile. Bushwhacking another mile brought us to the bottom of a beautiful waterfall, gently cascading down a steep orange sandstone escarpment. A flat area at the top of the falls, my map informed, would offer a grand overlook of the basin back in the direction whence we came. It was there I hoped to camp, but we were both already beat to shit from a long day of hardcore cross-country travel.

"I don't think I want to haul my pack up there," Ted said, evidently exhausted. Having not yet made the transition to ultralight gear, his pack was considerably heavier than mine and had taken its toll.

I convinced him to make the one last push, and minutes later we were atop the cascade and setting up our tent in a sandy area dressed sparsely with short pine trees and stamped with innumerable cougar tracks. The low afternoon sun kissed the white-rock horizon as I walked a short distance off to cook our dinner on a supremely inviting salmon sandstone shelf; broad and virtually level, it was perched on the lip of the waterfall.

Half an hour later, dinner ready, I turned off our small camp stove. But I didn't want to eat just yet; the distraction would have spoiled the moment. I gazed lazily from my high perch on the waterfall's lip, down to and across the elegant, unspoiled basin. My eyes relaxed out of focus, and I felt myself slowly melt into the soft view, into the land, and become one with it. Aside from the sound of the gently lilting stream several feet to my left, all was dead quiet. The slightest silent breeze kissed my cheek. I just knew we were alone in the basin. Once again, I had that priceless feeling one gets only in very remote wilderness: a deep and abiding calm, primitively simple and absent of thought, unshackled from all obligation and carefree. Left only to be. I was in my true home again.

The next morning, my thermometer read a frigid 20°F as Ted and I loaded up our daypacks for serial out-and-back hikes from our remote camp. My right foot had started to pain me the day before while downclimbing Goblin Gulch, so I now swallowed a couple pills of anti-inflammatory naproxen sodium for prophylactic measure—a big mistake, it would soon turn out.

We hiked to the north side of the basin and climbed to the top of peak 6474, a rocky prominence on the north rim of Right Fork North Creek, for its jaw-dropping 360-degree views of Zion's wild interior. Looking down into the creek's deep canyon—1,700 vertical feet below us, almost as if viewed from an airplane—and across the gorge to the far horizon, the South and North Guardian Angels poked the sky above Kolob Plateau, familiar landmarks in the area where we had run out of water three years ago. From our vantage point now, I could see we would not likely have made it over to Greatheart Mesa during that earlier trip even with sufficient water, for our roughly 68-pound packs would've been too heavy to climb what from here appeared to be technical terrain. I was strangely relieved to discover that trip was doomed to fail even had we not royally screwed it up.

We returned briefly to camp around noon to refill our water bottles, filtering yellow water from stagnant pools at the top of the waterfall, and then took off on a hike to the opposite side of the basin. Even though our topo maps promised there would be a spectacular clifftop view there, nothing could have prepared us for the wonderfully terrifying abyss that confronted us. From our windblown stance on a frightfully downward-slanting ledge, the world veritably collapsed before us in a sheer drop-off 1,800 feet by air down to Coalpits Wash. On the other side of the yawning chasm, the impossibly perpendicular cliffs of the Towers of the Virgin and The Altar of Sacrifice soared fully 3,000 feet above the desert floor, exceeding even the wildest animator's imagination. In all my thousands of miles of wilderness travel, never had I been so awestruck.

On our way back to camp, we detoured to climb a steep red sandstone slope up into The Bishopric, a highly unusual basin only 400 feet wide. The confined tract, a bewitching place graced by diffuse stands of stately Ponderosa pines through which meandered an evidently ephemeral stream, was hemmed in on three sides by eroded albino domes rising abruptly up to 800 feet. We wished we could linger under this pristine sanctuary's quiet spell, but the sinking sun urged our return to base camp.

No sooner had we arrived back at our tent than I began having intense abdominal cramps and stabbing pains in my gut. Attempting to make light of the worrisome situation, I blamed my illness on the Curse of The Altar of Sacrifice. But the true cause was gastritis from taking a double dose of naproxen sodium that morning (perhaps too soon after suffering stomach-churning food poisoning a couple days earlier). For the rest of the expedition, I wouldn't be able to tolerate eating anything more than a few dates, mashed in water to form a demulcent purée, every couple hours.

Determined not to let my ailing gut derail our long-planned itinerary, I toughed out a day hike the next morning with Ted. We made it almost to the north end of Terry's basin before intense stomach cramps pulled me to the ground, where I lay curled in a fetal position a mile from camp. After fifteen minutes lying in the dirt, I forced myself to my feet and, stooped like a centenarian, sluggishly retreated back to camp with Ted.

We packed up for our two-day trek out of the wilderness and struck out for Goblin Gulch a little after noon under a blue sky. Just shy of the gulch, we detoured briefly over to the lip of the Terry Wash pour-off, where the namesake creek, here barely more than a seep, plunged 600 vertical feet down a perpendicular cliff face before tumbling a further 900 vertical feet down a steep channel to the desert floor below. The view was so utterly spectacular, I hardly cared I was sick.

Familiar now with its challenges, the route through Goblin Gulch was less intimidating on our return. But it nevertheless commanded our respect, for a disabling injury here would be a very serious turn; a rescue in the remote slot canyon would be a long time coming, exceedingly complicated and far from assured. That peril was foremost on my mind as, on a climb around the steepest series of dry falls in the gulch, a large slab came loose when I put my weight on it and nearly peeled me off the slope into the hard rock channel.

And there was a new danger now: many of the potholes that were filled with fresh snowmelt on our way in to Terry had since had their life-sustaining cache evaporate with the return of warm, sunny weather. Fortunately, we found three small potholes in the shaded Goblin Gulch that still held manky water with dead bugs floating in it—palatable enough after filtering.

Escaping the gulch with palpable relief, we headed off toward another viewpoint on our must-see agenda, taking gallons of filtered water with us. A half hour later we found ourselves standing slack-jawed on the lip of a long, unbroken line of sheer cliffs, plummeting 700 feet at a perfect right angle before sloping sharply down to Coalpits Wash and the lower desert fully 2,000 vertical feet below us. From our top-of-the-world vantage, Ted pointed out what might've been our rental car glinting in the late-afternoon sun eleven miles away on the park's southern border. Looking the opposite direction, the grand white domes of The Bishopric soared in stately array above Terry, two very rugged miles away from our position. We made camp atop our primitive high-rise, watching the sinking sun set the sandstone peaks in Terry's basin ablaze in neon orange light, and then hours later observing the same stupendous scene bathed in the mysterious silver glow of a nearly full moon.

Rough passage down the sharply eroded slopes of Cougar Mountain awaited us the next day, but for now I was savoring this very special place to which I would likely never return. Not for want, but for physical ability. Four months shy of sixty years old, I realized I should give up doing DDMs before I got hurt or worse. Still, in my heart I knew I would not—could not—stop until forced to, until I could not go on. That day was always going to come too soon. But I wasn't going to worry about it now. I was already planning Desert Death March 12.

Ted Greenwald stands on the lip of an 1,800-foot
chasm plunging into Coalpits wash in Zion National
Park's interior (DDM 11; April 19, 2013).

Michael Cooper at the sheer drop-off into Coalpits wash

Michael Cooper in camp, across from the canyon Ted
Greenwald and he navigated into Terry Basin

Ted Greenwald descends from a break in cliffs blockading Zion
National Park's interior, during DDM 11; the white domes
of The Bishopric loom on the horizon (photo center).

-22-

THE MAZE

Backpacker magazine ranked it the most dangerous hike in America, for multiple reasons. The Maze, a sunken labyrinth of dozens of interconnected canyons in Utah's Canyonlands National Park, is so remote, even satellite-phone service is unreliable. There are virtually no trails in the canyons. If you get injured or sick, you're largely on your own; it can take rescuers up to three days to get to you, assuming they can find you—even national park rangers have gotten lost inside The Maze. Temperatures can reach 110°F in summer, and what little water there is, it's often out of reach in potholes at the bottom of cliff-walled slots.

All this made The Maze irresistibly appealing to Ted and me. But just getting there was going to be a challenge, for it's one of the most inaccessible places in the United States. With a high-clearance 4WD vehicle, you can drive a series of primitive dirt roads to The Maze, but even jeeps aren't guaranteed to make it through some sections in one piece. Reports of ripped tires and sheared-off skid plates are not uncommon where an ostensible road drops steeply down the face of exposed rock along a notorious stretch named Teapot Canyon. Along other narrow one-lane routes traversing steep mountainsides—with no guardrails—rainy weather can turn the bentonite roadbed into a slick mud bath, trapping vehicles for days in the most precarious of positions.

Ted and I decided it would be too risky financially to drive our rented

4WD Jeep Grand Cherokee through Teapot Canyon, as the vehicle's rental contract forbade—and voided all insurance coverage for—driving on unimproved roads. We opted instead to take reportedly less perilous (yet still primitive) routes to the high-elevation Golden Stairs trailhead several miles away from The Maze and backpack down to the canyon complex from there.

From its trailhead at over 6,000 feet altitude, the Golden Stairs Trail leads east across a white sandstone land bridge called China Neck—as little as fifteen feet wide—to arrive within minutes at an unnamed mesa. The mesa, which Ted and I christened "China Plateau" for easy reference, continues north but the trail doesn't follow it, making instead a U-turn and dropping 700 vertical feet off the mesa's south end to the technical 4WD Land of Standing Rocks Road. Hiking the road several miles north could've brought Ted and me relatively quickly to the vicinity of The Maze's south rim, but we couldn't stomach the idea of backpacking for a few hours along a bulldozed route, with jeeps occasionally driving by. After studying the area maps and satellite images for several days, I proposed a daring alternative.

Instead of dropping down to the road, we would backpack cross-country north along the top of China Plateau for three miles, to where the mesa terminates in a sharp drop-off down to a steep-sided saddle, named The Gap on our map. We would attempt to downclimb 200 vertical feet to The Gap and then descend the saddle's precipitous east slope—dropping another 500 vertical feet in only a quarter mile and negotiating serial palisades en route—to the desert floor below. On the map, it looked doable. Maybe. Satellite imaging looked less promising.

If we made it down from The Gap, the rest of my proposed route would only be more hairy. Backpacking a little less than a mile east across rolling desert would lead us to the ragged west rim of The Maze, where we would try to find a way down the sheer walls of an unnamed canyon that fed into the heart of the labyrinth. Inside the canyon was a formidable dry waterfall we would need to scramble around in order to get below it. I called that last pitch The Crux, for it looked even iffier than negotiating The Gap and would be a pivotal maneuver to take us down to water in The Maze—we'd likely be almost dry by the time we reached the top of the pour-off.

In fact, it would take us over a year after my route was set in stone just to get to the Golden Stairs trailhead. Our weeklong trip had originally been planned for spring 2014. But in January that year, a deep-massage "therapist" injured me, rupturing blood vessels and spraining a tendon in my groin. I couldn't walk without crutches for weeks and, when I still hadn't recovered a few months later, ultimately had to cancel DDM 12 for 2014. My weakened core subsequently led to a disc bulge in my lower back in June, setting me back another couple months. I was barely able to do several easy backpacks before summer was over.

As the launch date for DDM 12 approached the following spring, it was still not clear I'd recovered sufficiently from my groin injury to pull off another Desert Death March. But it had been two years since the last DDM, and I was desperate to go on another hardcore adventure. On May 2, 2015, I stuck my neck out and flew to Salt Lake City to meet Ted.

From the very start, DDM 12 would be tested by the Curse of the Chocolate Drops, four prominent monoliths in the core of The Maze whose scrumptious name belied their threat. The dirt roads to the Golden Stairs trailhead were in such terrible condition, it took Ted and me over six hours to drive their forty-one miles, with the last—worst—nine miles slowing us to a 3.5mph crawl, sometimes stopping to inspect on foot the best way around or over sharp tire-eating and axle-crushing rocks.

Arriving finally at the trailhead at 1 P.M. on May 3, Ted volunteered to carry an extra half-gallon of water beyond what we'd initially planned to take, as a failsafe. That decision would turn out to be a lifesaver.

It was very warm and sunny as we started out across China Neck. Leaving the Golden Stairs Trail on the far side of the land bridge, a short scramble up rimrock gained us the sandy top of China Plateau. A light breeze fanned us as we backpacked cross-country north through serial groves of juniper along the top of the mesa, enjoying the magnificent airplane views down to the sunbaked desert floor below. But inauspiciously, my right Achilles tendon had already begun to ache. And our balmy weather was about to take a sudden turn for the worse.

Hiking strongly, Ted was the first to reach the north end of China Plateau at around 4 P.M. Storm clouds were fast obliterating the sun as I approached him standing at the mesa's terminus. The look on his face was dour as he surveyed the land falling off to The Gap below.

"You're not going to be happy when you see this," he said ominously.

Contrary to what our topo map implied, the mesa plummeted down a perpendicular eighty-foot cliff—impassable—before sloping steeply another 120 feet in altitude down to The Gap. What I could see of our route down off The Gap also looked intimidating, with multiple tiers of sheer cliffs festooning the scarp all the way down its sharp 2,000-feet-per-mile grade to the austere desert floor below.

I had planned for this contingency, determining beforehand in my map and satellite-imaging studies that, if a direct north assault on The Gap were to prove unworkable, it might be possible to climb partway down the west side of China Plateau and then traverse the mesa's steep skirt northward to reach The Gap. In fact, reconnaissance without packs brought us in just a couple hundred yards to a cairn some Good Samaritan had placed to mark a jumbled break in the cliffs exactly where I expected to find one.

We retrieved our packs. Returning to the break, we easily pulled off the short downclimb, but the following steep traverse required we lose more altitude than we'd hoped would be necessary. The forfeit subsequently forced us to make an arduous climb up The Gap's steep west slope to eventually attain the top of the rocky saddle. It began to rain.

We donned our foul-weather clothing and traversed a rocky rise in the middle of The Gap to reach the north end of the saddle. There we got our first up-close look down the saddle's vertiginous east slope. My planned route had aimed to take us partway down the scarp before angling left to a rocky couloir that led less precipitously to the desert floor below. But the way over to the couloir now looked way less obvious—and exponentially more dangerous—than the map and satellite imaging had suggested. We could now see that, with rare exception, the tiers of sheer cliffs we'd spied earlier from afar straddled the full span of the scarp, blockading our descent. A narrow terrace ran along the top of each line of cliffs. Our only recourse was to hike along each terrace in search of a break or viable crack in a cliff we could climb down to the next lower terrace. We would repeat this process over and over, first reconnoitering and then climbing down from one line of cliffs to the next in the rain.

Our mood was tense, and not just because of the bad weather. I had to repeatedly deter Ted from taking us down highly precarious cracks—ones he later conceded were dangerous—before exhausting our search for safer alternatives; his penchant for risk was a quality I both admired and felt I needed to keep in check. But there weren't always obviously safe alternatives to choose from, and we sometimes had to roll the dice. To avoid a very steep and unstable slope with deadly exposure—we had not brought rope—we decided to climb down a partly obscured break in a cliff we feared might leave us "rimrocked" below, with no way to climb farther down or retreat back up. Our gamble thankfully paid off, leading us finally over to the boulder-strewn couloir that was our escape. We carefully descended the steep gully to reach the desert floor at 7 P.M. It had taken us fully three hours to backpack down from the north terminus of China Plateau—a distance of just 0.7 mile as the crow flies.

Now we were racing over the juniper- and sagebrush-clad desert against nightfall. By the time we reached the rim of The Maze, there was only an hour of daylight left. We didn't want to take on the route's most dangerous stretch in the dark—with rainy weather also threatening flash floods in the narrow canyons below us—so we decided to make camp on high ground well short of our planned destination. We were both thoroughly exhausted.

Despite my deep fatigue and an aching Achilles tendon, I was ecstatic. The descent from The Gap was the adventure I'd longed for over the past two years, and we still had The Crux to look forward to the next day. Our camp, perched on the lip of a juniper-costumed orange canyon, was thoroughly enchanting. The place was dead quiet and held no footprints save for our own. The sky cleared, and the setting sun lit ablaze pink and gold rock pillars in the distance atop black shadows lengthening across The Maze. We were alone in the middle of the most remote area in the continental United States. Night fell, and a rising full moon kindled The Maze and The Gap in soft silver light. Ted lumbered off to sleep, but I forced myself to stay awake a while longer to revel in the mystical scenery.

The break in the weather didn't last long. A hard rain drummed on our tent overnight, and the next morning dawned cloudy—a temperate blessing actually, considering we were now running quite low on water. Breaking camp quickly, we backpacked in returning light rain down serial slickrock domes, en route to a terminal slope my map indicated was likely the easiest way down into the canyon that was the gateway to The Crux.

Just 100 vertical feet from the canyon's floor, we came abruptly to the lip of sheer cliffs, extending in an unbroken line as far as we could see off to our left and right. Below us tantalizingly lay the The Crux's host canyon, its hard white and orange walls sharply contrasting with the soft red sand along its bottom, scoured smooth by past flash floods and elegantly lined with green juniper and piñon pine trees. We stood silently on the cliff's edge, all that beauty just barely out of reach below us.

"Suicide route," I muttered, crestfallen.

We spent the next twenty minutes scouting potential ways down the cliff face, but each was a bust. Had we a lot more time—like a full day—to reconnoiter the wider area, we might've found a way into the canyon. But we now each had only one liter of water remaining (exactly the supplemental amount Ted had prudently packed at the trailhead the day before as a failsafe). The sky was beginning to clear again, the sun threatening to break out and bake us. Prudence dictated we now abort the route as a matter of survival.

We initiated a second contingency plan I'd made in case The Crux route failed, hightailing it cross-country two miles south across open desert to the head of South Fork Horse Canyon, where hearsay had it there was a way down to water in The Maze. Hiking briskly in the lead, I reached the canyon's head before Ted. Several closely spaced ravines there—none showing discretely on our maps—dropped steeply together toward the canyon at first before quickly diverging to head out of sight to who knows where. Taking special care to solve the critical puzzle on the first attempt, I took several compass bearings and gauged each ravine's attitude in relation to a nearby forty-foot-high knoll shown on our map to narrow the selection down to the correct one. Then we headed down.

Within a minute, we came to a cairn that seemingly confirmed we were in the right ravine. Dropping further into the steadily narrowing sandstone channel, the slot became booby-trapped with impassable perpendicular pour-offs, blocking our direct descent. We spied a second cairn off to our left, on a rock ledge that led away from the canyon. We decided to follow it, hoping it would lead us, if not to the canyon's bottom, then at least to water. It had better, for we had too little left now to make it back to our vehicle, and figuring out a way into the canyon by trial and error could possibly take us a day or more—the terrain was that complex, often vertical, and our maps useless here. I thought back to DDM 10 in Zion and hoped we wouldn't have to resort to drinking our urine again to survive.

Arriving at the second cairn, we spied and followed two more that led us along a ledge on a terraced sandstone wall. The ledge led us into another slot canyon stair-stepped with impassable pour-offs. More cairns steered us back to the canyon wall, where they flagged cracks in short cliffs we down-climbed to lower ledges. The cairns then doubled us all the way back to the first canyon, making us anxious we were on a fool's errand. Continuing back and forth along the zigzagging course, we slowly worked our way from one ledge down to the next until one last pitch—the most difficult of all—dropped us down to a shaded pothole holding a pool of skanky water about five feet wide and several inches deep. Water at last!

Twenty yards away, we discovered a cleaner and much larger pool of water at the bottom of a dry waterfall, where we refilled our water bottles. It began to rain again. Hoisting our backpacks, we hiked along successive rock ledges into yet another side canyon. There, a lightly forested, sandy slope took us steeply down to the main canyon's floor. We had made it into The Maze.

A particularly convoluted section of The Maze less often visited, South Fork Horse Canyon was supremely quiet and positively resplendent. Backpacking easily down its winding course, we passed huge red alcoves, contorted orange pillars and wind-sculpted beige porticos artfully staging the canyon's walls. Leafy green cottonwoods and gnarled juniper trees provided shade beside ephemeral pools of water cupped in smooth rock pockets. We saw no one, and no footprints. It was heavenly.

A couple miles down the South Fork, we came to a junction with the side canyon that held The Crux. Looking up the side canyon from its mouth, we poignantly determined that had we made it down the 100-foot cliffs that stopped us that morning, we would've been home free, with only a pitched traverse, rock ledge and talus slope to negotiate in succession around the dry waterfall to get down to where we now stood. If only.

We hiked a mile farther down the South Fork to camp near a large pool of water thickly surrounded by lush willows, long green grasses and other sweet-smelling vegetation, where we refilled our bottles. It began to rain again as I cooked dinner. I would've been perfectly happy cooking in the rain had it not been for the fact my right Achilles tendon was now very painful when just standing. That night it began to throb despite my taking anti-inflammatory medication. Adding to my escalating disability, I also started getting a sore throat, token of a virus I'd evidently picked up during my flight to Salt Lake City two days earlier. I got very sick that night and was impelled to dash out of the tent three times, limping, for urgent bowel movements in the rain.

The next morning my sinuses were oozing quicksand and my Achilles throbbing worse than ever. Resting the tendon overnight and mobilizing my foot's metatarsals in the morning had not helped at all. I feared the last couple days of hardcore backpacking had finally pushed my chronically injured right foot past the point of no return. (In fact, it would never completely recover.)

Backpacking farther into The Maze while sick and injured seemed highly risky and irresponsible. After long and painful deliberation, I told Ted I felt I needed to abort. That is, if I could: my Achilles was hurting so badly, I figured I had no more than a 30-percent chance of making it out of the wilderness on my own steam, and then only if we took the easiest route possible. Whatever backpacking I did that day would likely be my last for quite a while.

We retraced our route out of the South Fork and hiked the sorry Land of Standing Rocks Road and steep Golden Stairs Trail back to our vehicle, a distance of over nine miles. I limped every step of the way, my Achilles protesting with stabbing knives. Adding insult to injury, it rained heavily that night on our camp at the trailhead. At least the place was deserted. I was in no mood to be around a bunch of happy people.

The next day, we carefully drove the horrible 4WD roads out of Canyonlands' Maze District and into the adjacent Glen Canyon National Recreation Area, where we car-camped in a narrow gap between a towering butte and a massive plateau sided by orange cliffs 800 feet high. It looked pretty enough and we had the place to ourselves, but I was severely depressed. It had taken months of planning and Herculean efforts to get to The Maze, and we'd only seen less than a fifth of what I'd planned for us to see of it. I felt defeated, a sixty-one-year-old write-off whose adventuring days were now behind him. It was painfully obvious my thrashed right foot was from then on going to hold me back from doing what I loved most.

"That was my last DDM," I told Ted in camp, fighting back tears.

"It seems like you're done," he replied quietly. He tried to console me. "But there are other things you can still do, wilderness backpacks that aren't so hardcore."

"It's not the same," I said, crying. "It's not the same."

Truly, the dozen desert expeditions I'd done with Ted were not the same as my other adventures. Just the fact that we had to hike long distances to get to water, or die of thirst failing, gave the Desert Death Marches a background edge other adventures didn't have, and the striving to cover ground and accomplish the essential goal was quietly thrilling. Carrying gallons of water off-trail for days also required I be in peak physical condition, and it felt great to be that strong walking the wild land. But even while I felt comfortable in my literal bones, my limbic brain would constantly remind me that I shouldn't be so far from water in the remote places I got to. Beautiful places. Places so quiet, you can hear the background hiss generated by your inner ears' electrical circuits. Places so far away from the bloated leisure of civilization, so difficult to get to, you've got it all to yourself when you arrive and for as long as you want after. And there's the stillness, the unhurried tranquility of the desert. Navigating cross-country was an exercise in ecstasy, with uncluttered views that would sometimes stretch for tens of miles. Free as a bird, carefree as the coyote. But all that was over for me now.

It was always going to end this way. I was never going to stop doing the big hairy adventures until my worn-out body insisted. Funny how bittersweet it is at the end, I reflected: the good thing is I'll have memories of incredible trips I've done. The bad thing is I'll have memories of incredible trips I can no longer do. Remembering them was almost worse than if I'd never done them.

On the long drive back to Salt Lake City International Airport, we took a lonely dirt road thirty miles southeast of Price up into the foothills of the Book Cliffs to camp for the night. The temperature dropped into the 30s Fahrenheit, and it rained yet again. We awoke the next morning to a dusting of snow 500 feet above us on the cliffs. It was springtime but felt like winter, in more ways than one. My thoughts turned to home. I hoped backpack trips in my beloved Oregon Cascades would be enough to satisfy my need for the wild. But even that was about to change.

Michael Cooper points out the distant slope he and Ted Greenwald would descend from The Gap, en route to The Maze (DDM 12; May 3, 2015).

Michael Cooper, after the descent from The Gap

Michael Cooper points out the ledges he and Ted Greenwald
would negotiate to get into the The Maze on May 4, 2015.

-23-

WILD HOME

It was unusual for my old climbing buddy Ed Lovegren to call me; usually it was vice versa. Retired from mountaineering, the both of us, our last climb together had been ten years earlier, in 2005. Ed sounded strangely wistful on the other end of the line. I thought he was feeling nostalgic. But fresh from the desert wilds of Utah after aborting DDM 12, I was too slammed with deferred work for *Mix* and *Electronic Musician* magazines to reminisce with him about old times right then. I told him I would call him back in a few days, after I met looming deadlines. Diving back into my all-consuming work, I promptly forgot he'd called me.

My right foot, reinjured in The Maze, took four months to recover enough to return to backpacking, but it would never again be 100 percent. In late September, I backpacked with Whitaker for four days in Central Oregon's Three Sisters Wilderness. Visiting some of my favorite high basins off-trail was a healing balm for the shattering realization my DDM days were behind me. A snowstorm had blanketed the surrounding peaks a few days earlier. Taking in the exquisite scenery, I was elated again, and I began to feel like maybe rambling in my old stomping grounds would be enough to satisfy my wild heart.

That winter, I finally remembered to call Ed back. His adult daughter answered the phone.

"Hi, can I please talk with Ed?" I asked cheerily, happy to be reconnecting with my old mountaineering pal. My greeting was met briefly with uncomfortable silence before she replied.

"Ed died several months ago," she said quietly.

"No, no, no, no!" I wailed, as if repeating the word enough times might alter the horrible news. "But he . . . he called me. I thought there was more time."

Ed had died of a brain tumor on August 25, 2015, one day after my sixty-second birthday. I hadn't even known he was sick. Over the prior year, we had talked about doing an easy day hike his frail eighty-four-year-old frame could manage, but we never got around to it. Now it was too late.

"I loved Ed," I told his daughter through tears. "I have stood on more mountain summits with him than with anyone else."

"He talked about you all the time," she replied thoughtfully, trying to console me. "He adored you."

She told me Ed had forbidden family members to tell any of his friends he was terminally ill; he didn't want his climbing buddies to visit and see him in such horrible decline. And yet there was his last phone call to me. Reaching out just a few months before his passing, was it his attempt at saying goodbye? If only I hadn't rushed him off the phone. There would be no way for me now to shed that forever regret.

Ed was gone, but he'd left behind more than precious memories of him. He had taught me a valuable lesson, one I carried through more than the many climbs of major peaks we'd done together, informing also all my Desert Death Marches.

"Ignore the horrors," he had advised me, referring to the dreadful worries that torment mountaineers the night before a difficult and hazardous climb. "I've learned they don't portend disaster." Hearing this from such an experienced climber had brought me great comfort on the eve of all my most dangerous adventures. A calmer, more confident adventuring me—that was Ed's parting gift.

As heartbreaking as it was, learning of Ed's passing was just a preamble to a devastating 2016. That spring, norovirus swept through the assisted-living facility where my ninety-two-year-old mother lived, forcing a long quarantine that barred entry even to family members. Before the visitor ban was lifted, she died in her sleep. Once again I was robbed of the chance to say goodbye to someone I dearly loved. Mitch and I surmised it was only our frequent visits that had kept her alive in her last fragile months, and alone in her apartment for two weeks under quarantine, she'd had nothing to look forward to that could keep her in this world.

I had told her several years earlier, as her days of independent living in Florida were undeniably drawing to a close, of my growing dread of her inevitable passing. She listened quietly before responding with characteristic equanimity.

"Death is a part of life," she said, thoughtfully but not sad.

"But I'll miss you terribly when you're gone," I said, needing to say the uncomfortable words to her if only once, while I still had the chance.

"Life is for the living," she replied softly but resolutely. I could tell she empathized with me but had long ago come to a place of total acceptance of her inevitable end. She'd always been so deeply spiritual, if not in the way that's generally expected or that she herself even identified as such. She was an accidental saint, accepting all people and events in her life with laissez-faire. She had no enemies. Everyone who knew her loved her and would mourn her passing. But losing her struck me the deepest blow.

Because of her, the insecure little boy I once was had become a wilderness adventurer. Because of her, I had followed my heart to become a successful entrepreneur, recording-industry journalist and audio engineer—not the typical predestined path for a buttoned-down high school valedictorian from suburban Long Island. "You're Michael Cooper," she often told me during my childhood, placing exaggerated emphasis on my name as if it held universal sway. "You can do anything."

Her support had continued undiminished throughout my adult years. She would predictably say "I'm very proud of you, sweetheart" upon hearing of even my minor accomplishments (and would also frequently confer the acknowledgment on Mitch and her grandchildren). For the longest time—decades—I couldn't understand why she felt proud of me, only that it was genuine. Years later, after her death, I would come to a deeper understanding while sorting through family memorabilia. In a long-forgotten letter she'd written to me when I was in my mid-twenties and living in the jungle in Mexico, she'd written, "You are very special to me. You have a real feeling for life." She knew my DNA. Nobody had loved me like her. Her death left me crushed for months on end.

My only solace was found in wilderness. There my perspective always returned to a healthy balance, the broad arc of life making perfect sense and bringing acceptance of the things I could not change. That's where I would turn to on the two-month anniversary of her death, during the first week of July. My twenty-five-year-old nephew Evan and I backpacked off-trail up to a high basin on the north side of the glacier-encrusted North Sister. We made our second camp early in the afternoon just below snowline. Evan napped in the tent while I hiked alone up to the head of the basin. There I came upon a beautiful half-circle of fifteen-foot-high conifers, growing tenaciously in the fractional summer of the High Cascades by a whispering brook and just a few hundred yards from the hard, perpendicular face of North Sister. I made a mark on my map so I could return at a later date with Janet to camp there. Had I known then that it was the last time I would ever stand on that spot, I would've lingered far longer.

It would be my last substantial backpack. After returning home, my right hip began to ache horribly. Anti-inflammatory drugs and, later, physical therapy did not help. Janet and I managed a couple more backpacks that summer, but I couldn't go more than a couple miles without suffering throbbing pain. My hip's condition deteriorated so badly that by the next year, 2017, I couldn't walk more than a half-mile on level ground without limping, even carrying no weight. An MRI taken in the fall finally revealed the problem: bone on bone. Carrying a heavy pack through 8,000 miles of wild country over the past four decades had ground the cartilage in my hip down to zilch, and now the joint was badly inflamed.

I searched far and wide for a remedy. In the spring of 2018, a brilliant doctor named Rahul Desai, an expert in regenerative medicine, injected stem cells and platelet-rich plasma into my bum hip to heal the inflamed tissues. The injections helped so much that, on his recommendation, I had him inject my chronically injured right foot with plasma lysate. By November I was hiking six miles again in my beloved Three Sisters Wilderness, carrying a light daypack.

It was a tremendous improvement and emotional lifeline, but the treatments hadn't grown new cartilage in my hip. Lacking nature's shock absorbers, I still couldn't carry more than ten pounds without arresting pain. The only way I was going to backpack again was with help. Over the next couple years, Janet and Mitch were my wild angels, getting me out on a couple easy overnighters by each taking on an extra five pounds from my backpack, lessening my load. Still, backpacking a few miles into wilderness was all I could manage without excessive pain and long subsequent setbacks. Extended backpack trips were out of the question; after two consecutive days of hiking, I needed rest to allow resurgent inflammation to subside. I felt incredibly frustrated.

I considered getting my hip replaced but was told by a few surgeons I was not a candidate, as the bone in my ball and socket was still in excellent shape; cutting through hip flexors and chopping off the head of my femur—requisites of the operation—would cause unacceptable tradeoffs in muscle strength, balance and flexibility, they said. Still I considered having the operation if I could find a doctor willing to perform it and it could get me back into remote wilderness. I asked one surgeon if I could do mountaineering and hardcore desert backpacking again if I got my hip replaced.

"You could," he said, " but the question is, should you." If I fell in a remote area and dislocated the artificial joint, he explained, I'd be royally screwed. Another surgeon advised me a hip replacement was a great solution for someone who suffers disabling pain while simply walking around their home, but athletes who opted for the operation were, in her experience, generally not satisfied with the prosthesis for "high-performance use" such as I intended. The friction from strenuous use would also cause microscopic bits of plastic and metal to shed into surrounding soft tissues, risking metallosis (blood poisoning). Considering the tradeoffs and limited benefits, did I really want to have my femur amputated? After all, I had little or no pain at home and while doing easy hikes.

There was also the question of how many backpack trips I could do after an operation, to make it worthwhile. The opportunities had diminished. Climate change-fueled mega wildfires were incinerating larger tracts of Western national forests with each passing year, enshrouding wilderness areas in thick, toxic smoke for most or all of summer, prime backpacking season. In 2017, wildfires burned more than 400,000 acres in Oregon alone. In 2018, well over 500,000 acres went up in smoke in The Beaver State. In 2020, more than 740,000 acres burned. Not a promising trend.

But the choking wildfire smoke was no longer just local, or even regional, in origin or extent. Even before wildfires exploded in Oregon in the summer of 2020, smoke from massive conflagrations in California— the state saw a staggering 4.3 million acres cremated that year—spilled north into Central Oregon, enveloping the Sisters area in an unrelenting hazardous blanket for months. Janet and I had to evacuate our home that summer not because it was threatened by flames but because the air—both outside and inside the house—was so toxic we were finding it difficult to breathe. How much backpacking was I going to be able to do after hip replacement in a post-climate-change world smothered by wildfire smoke?

Despite my bleak prospects, for years I held onto a shred of hope I could someday backpack The Maze again. Stand on Middle Sister's lofty summit. Explore for a week off-trail above timberline in the High Sierra once more. Even now, I have all the relevant topo maps, with routes overlaid, mileages and elevation changes tabulated, historical meteorological data compiled to time the trips perfectly. I can't bring myself to throw the maps and spreadsheets away, but I've stopped poring over them. My brother Mitch and erstwhile climbing buddy John Englehart have counseled me to try to be happy with what I can still do in the outdoors. It's taken me years, but I'm beginning to come around to their point of view.

At dinner parties and wedding receptions, friends and family members occasionally rope me into telling stories about my past adventures, particularly relishing hearing me recount the close calls. Surviving the scorpion sting in Mexico. Swimming the Owyhee River's Class IV Montgomery Rapid without a wetsuit during a winter storm. Drinking my urine to survive in Zion's backcountry.

"*Why* are you still alive, Uncle Michael?" Evan exclaimed in wonderment after my retelling of the Owyhee story. That was four years ago. He literally begged me to write it down, put it in an autobiography with all the other stories he'd heard while growing up.

In fact, Janet had been after me for years before Evan to commit my memories to prose. Daunted by the work it would demand and the nebulous reward, I resisted undertaking the multi-year project. But in my sixty-sixth year, I realized I was beginning to forget salient details. I knew then I must start writing or forever surrender my past to the mists of time. I started pulling old handwritten journals and Kodak slide projector trays out of poorly annotated cardboard boxes stored in dark closets, traveling back in time.

Looking at the old photographs now as I write this in my seventieth year, I hardly recognize the young athlete I was, staring back at me from inside the frame. The photos I love the most are the ones that show me grinning with my adventure buddies miles from the nearest trail. Those places are now beyond my physical reach, but I finally feel okay about it.

If I close my eyes in a quiet place and slow my breathing, I'm there again. I close my eyes, and I am sitting once again with Ted at the top of the waterfall in Terry Wash, looking out over the elegant wild basin as the setting sun ignites majestic sandstone domes aflame in pink and orange light. I close my eyes, and once again I am with Ed in base camp above Mountain Creek, watching lengthening shadows creep slowly across the snow-dusted slopes of Diamond Peak. I close my eyes, and I am off-trail again in the High Cascades with my sweetheart Janet, sitting beside an alpine stream lined with hundreds of pink monkey flowers waving softly in a gentle breeze. I close my eyes, and I am in my wild home again.

Author's Acknowledgments

I am forever indebted to those who saved my life on numerous occasions: Janet Huerta, the Santiam Pass National Ski Patrol, Rick Stuman, Richard Watson, and the river guides and other companions—whose names are virtually all long since forgotten—on the March 1985 Owyhee River white-water run chronicled herein. I am equally grateful for the world-renowned expertise and care of Dr. Steven D. Chang, without whom I wouldn't be alive today. My heartfelt thanks also go to Bo Beck and the other members of the Zion National Park Search and Rescue Team for their assistance. And I will always remember with gratitude the late Santiago (surname unknown) for aiding in my recovery from a mortal wound in Yelapa, Mexico.

This book is so much the better for important contributions made by several people. First and foremost, my wife Janet Huerta tirelessly lent invaluable insight, feedback, suggestions and encouragement. Ted Greenwald's editorial assistance and Mitch Cooper's perceptive suggestions likewise contributed to a better read. Especially helpful, Ted Greenwald graciously provided access to his private journals and photographs chronicling our many expeditions throughout the Desert Southwest, filling in critically important details and providing a valuable alternative perspective. John Englehart and Bruce Schumm (aka Whitaker) also helped reconstruct, through supplied photographs and telephone conversations, significant aspects of wilderness adventures we shared. Special thanks go to Owyhee River trip member Allan Siegel for forwarding to me photographs documenting my nearly fatal incident on that river.

Al Hendricks generously shared invaluable information that helped make my expedition in Capitol Reef National Park a success, and Deborah Davis and Courtney Purcell likewise contributed indispensable beta supporting my treks to the redoubtable core of Zion National Park—high points in my life for which I will be forever grateful. Joshua Tree National Park Ranger Jeff Ohlfs, Kofa National Wildlife Refuge Biologist Ron Kearns, and Anza-Borrego State Park Interpreter Sally Theriault each provided helpful background information about the natural areas in which they served.

Many of my adventures would not have happened but for the unsurpassed skills and dedication of massage therapist extraordinaire Rich Phaigh, whose scores of therapeutic sessions repaired my many injuries and otherwise maintained my fitness at the required level. Dr. Rahul Desai's exceptional expertise in regenerative medicine was key to getting me back out into wilderness in my post-expedition years.

I've had the great honor to collaborate in recording studios with Grammy Award-winning singer-songwriter Ashley Cleveland, Academy Award-winning actor William Hurt (since departed), and former weekend anchor of ABC World News Barry Serafin; learn from the late healer William LeSassier and visionary Viktoras Kulvinskas; and work alongside esteemed actors Jenna Malone and Luke Grimes on a movie set.

My career in the recording industry would likely not have flourished to the extent it did without Matt Morgan, Jason Lynn, and Tom and Paul Hemphill—collectively the band Red Over White—tipping me off in 1989 about an empty recording studio on the outskirts of Eugene, Oregon, which became my business's location for the following eight years.

Last but not least, I want to genuinely thank Brian Knave, former Senior Associate Editor of *Electronic Musician* magazine, for holding my feet to the fire to more rigorously structure my journalistic prose during the late 1990s. His criticisms—unsparing in both the positive and negative sense—impelled me to become a better writer.

About the Author

Michael Cooper

Michael Cooper's journalism career spans four decades and over five hundred articles written for seven pro-audio magazines and *Wired*. A noted authority on music production and sound for film, he has served as recording engineer on projects featuring Academy Award-winning actor William Hurt and former weekend anchor of ABC World News Barry Serafin, and worked with Grammy-winning singer-songwriter Ashley Cleveland. A contributing editor for *Mix* magazine (and formerly for *Electronic Musician*), his spare time has been devoted to backpacking, climbing, hiking, skiing and rafting eight thousand miles in the wilds of North America. He lives with his wife in Central Oregon.

For more photographs and video of Michael's adventures,
visit his website: https://michaelcooperadventurer.com.

www.ingramcontent.com/pod-product-compliance
Lightning Source LLC
Chambersburg PA
CBHW021612120626
46545CB00001B/185